Presented to the

Portage
Public Library

in memory of

Jack Dudley

by

Mr. & Mrs. Neal Stager

DISCARDED

THE MARRIAGE THAT DID SUCCEED for MARY QUEEN of SCOTS

by James Walter Deppa

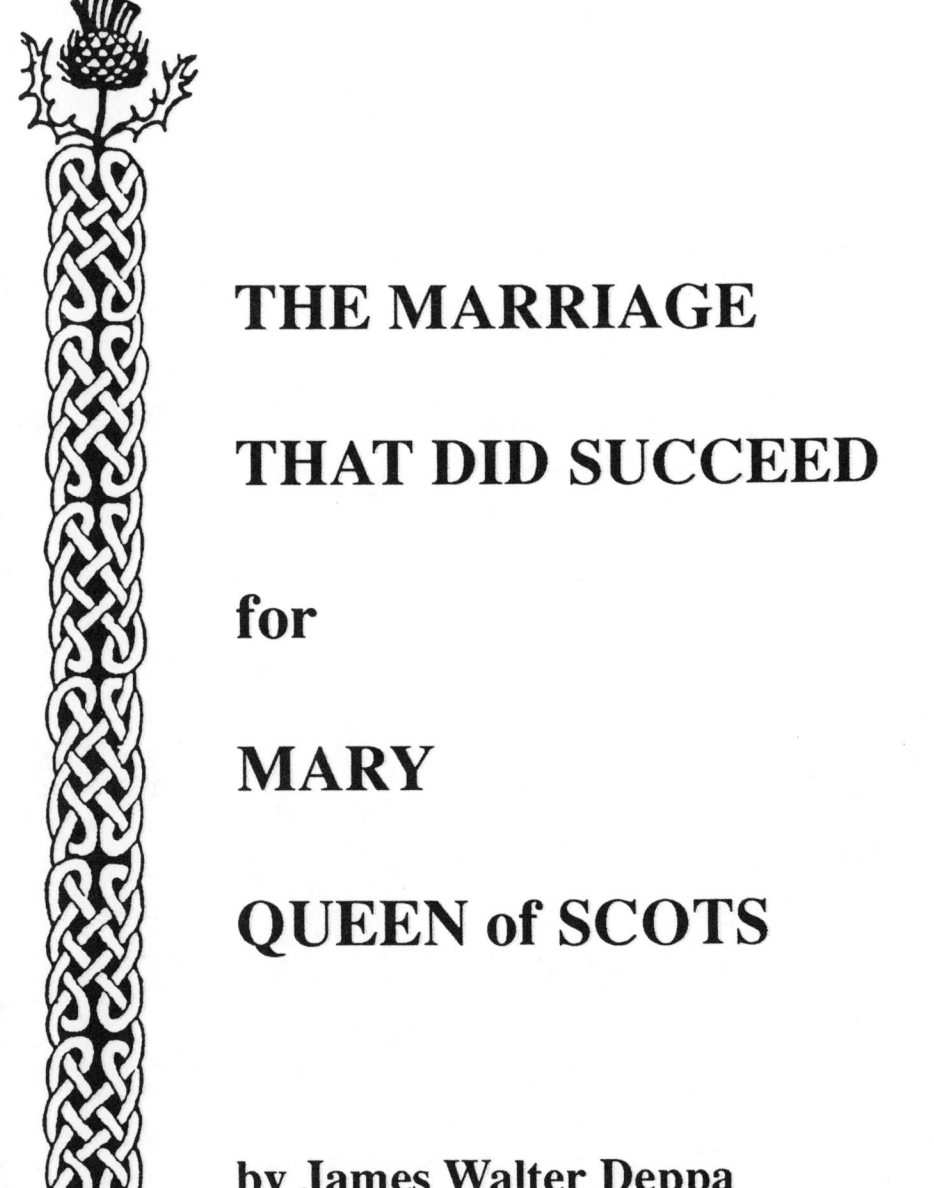

Copyright © 1990
by James Walter Deppa
All rights reserved

Library of Congress Catalog Number 89-81233
International Standard Book Number 0-9623620-1-8

IRONWOOD PRESS
20711 Warfield Court
Gaithersburg, Maryland
U.S.A.   20879

Printed in the United States of America

TABLE OF CONTENTS

I.	Mary Stewart, the Queen of the Deppa Legend	1
II.	The Queen and I	15
III.	The Sixteenth-century Lowlands	29
IV.	The Fench Connection	51
V.	The Magazine Story of 1909	61
VI.	The Accounts of the Lord High Treasurer of Scotland	81
VII.	The Stable-boy and the Lady-in-waiting	93
VIII.	Tracing the Steps of Our Dieppois	109
IX.	Queen Mary's Fifteen Ladies-in-waiting	139
X.	Melrose Abbey, the Home Base	161
XI.	The Regality Records of Melrose	183
XII.	Grist for My Mill	213
XIII.	Run-rig Agriculture	233
XIV.	Excerpts from Scottish Documents	259
XV.	Evolution of the Surname, Depo	273
	Bibliography, Grouped by Subject	305
	Index	315

THE MARRIAGE
THAT DID SUCCEED
for
MARY, QUEEN OF SCOTS

* * * * *

It Started a Set of New Surnames in Scotland

Dieppe	Dieppois	Depo	Dippo	Deippa
	Deippe	Deipo	Dippe	
		Dippie		
Deppo	Deepie	Dipo	Deipie	Depie
	Diepe	Deipy	Dipee	
		Diepie	Deppie	
		Deppa		

LIST OF FIGURES

Figure 1	Adaptation of a 1647 plan of Edinburgh	p. 75
Figure 2	The Borderlands	p. 97
Figure 3	Features of Stichill Estate	p. 125
Figure 4	The Seal of Melrose	p. 165
Figure 5	The vaulted ceiling of Melrose Abbey	p. 167
Figure 6	Calfhill Tower and Colmslie Tower	p. 201
Figure 7	Melrose Abbey Lands	p. 221
Figure 8	Pollock manuscript	p. 262
Figure 9	Transliteration of manuscript	p. 263
Figure 10	The Depo Family Chart	p. 277
Figure 11	The evolution of the surname Depo	p. 281
Figure 12	Part of the intermarriage network	p. 303

ACKNOWLEDGEMENTS

Two people of Edinburgh generously broke open the treasure trove of Scottish records for me:

Sheila Macbeth Mitchell, who was 95 years old when we last corresponded in 1986, told me where my progenitor was named in a manuscript of 1606.

Dr. Michael Lynch, of the Department of Scottish History, University of Edinburgh, responded to my numerous letters and provided key citations. His professional guidance helped me trace the faint but discernible trail of my first two ancestors, who had been in the service of Mary, Queen of Scots. It was my special pleasure, too, to meet him at the palace of Holyroodhouse in 1985.

Janetta Campbell Deppa, my grandmother, told me the family legend that I never forgot, and which is now recorded for the first time.

My son, Bruce Northrup Deppa, led me to break my vow never to touch a word processor. The manuscript would never have become a book without it. I learned to use three machines, with his coaching. He proofed and edited the text, printed copy, and helped me plan and hire work done. More thanks is due him than I can tell.

My wife, Louise, and all four of our children went to Scotland with me in 1985 so I could see the places my ancestors knew. I could not have made the trip without their help. They expertly arranged lodging, routes, and transportation. Roy, a kilted bagpiper, had hostelled all over Scotland. Martha had gone to Scotland and the Continent with us in 1969, For Ellen, our Speech Pathologist daughter, this was a first trip to Scotland.

My family and friends have waited a long time for me to finish. I thank them all. The bits and pieces of this story have been bounced off my Louise who has listened to me with infinite patience; and she has fed me well throughout. Now we can look back at more than fifty years of working things out together.

PREFACE

As a boy, I knew that we were Scottish, but I also knew that my surname did not bear that out. Grandma, though, was a Campbell, descended through several clans. Robert Deppa, my grandfather, had come from Glasgow in 1850 at the age of eight. His mother was a McKenzie. When I was sixteen and visiting my home town in Pennsylvania, Grandma told me that our name began when "a lady-in-waiting to the queen married a stable-boy." I never forgot these eleven words, which she told to me exactly as she had heard them many years before.

This book is not about genealogy, though a little about my family is used to anchor the modern end of a long chain that reaches back to 1561. The middle generations are ignored, for the object is to recreate a tiny episode in the queen's career when our fates intersected in the marriage that did succeed for Mary, Queen of Scots. This bit of Scottish history revolves around two people. All the others are supporting cast in the drama, but none are fictitious. Much of the book is about the lives of typical Scots of the late 1500s.

At the time, my family and relatives were there, and we probably discussed the meaning of this saying, but that was the end of it. It was a remarkable statement, neither understood nor questioned. Grandma must have learned it when she married Robert at the age of fifteen, an impressionable age for her, and for me, I know now. Her obligation to pass on the family story became mine in the same way. Such oral history can remain accurate for centuries only by rote. Formula repetition, without understanding, instinctively guards against the slightest change.

Much time has passed, and now after twelve years of searching I have found records that verify our legend. The *Accounts of the Lord High Treasurer of Scotland*, the *Regality Records of Melrose* and other old records reveal who the people were that our oral history "remembered." The stable-boy was hired into the service of Queen Mary in Dieppe, France, at the time of her triumphal return to Scotland in 1561. In typical unconcern for accuracy or interest in personal feelings, the man's name was recorded as "Depo" by a Scottish paymaster who asked this man and his two sons "where do you come from?" When he heard the word *dieppois*, he entered the name "Depo." That, in twenty variations, has been the family name ever since.

The lady-in-waiting was one of 15 Scottish girls in Queen Mary's train. Diluted by more than 400 years of intermarriage, our portion of French blood has been halved at least thirteen times. The centuries of unbroken ties to Scotland are far stronger than the original one-man French connection.

If I had not become obsessed with finding the source of my family tradition, several incidents in the queen's life-story would never have been uncovered. The reason is that only the name "Depo," derived through *dieppois*, reveals her presence and actions more than once. An uninvolved researcher would not have noticed that the name "Depo" was a tie to matters of interest to the queen. Although not directly referred to, she is there as the prime mover. My motivation has been to find that name and its connection with her.

The name is linked through very ordinary happenings: transporting her horses, the killing of a boy named Depo, a tenancy given to a stranger, a Frenchman, in an ancient agricultural abbey community. This tracing of the queen's stable-boy and the lady he married reveals events and places that add new material to the queen's biography.

My search uncovered three previously unreported bits of history, as well as a number of errors:

a. Mary's French horses were shipped from Dieppe, which fact may not be recorded as the port except in my book. Our name derives from this city, and the men, who were natives, provide the only proof I have seen that the horses left from Dieppe.

b. A royal horse farm was established at Stitchell, about thirty miles south of Edinburgh. I doubt this has ever been noted before. The fact that there even was a horse farm may rest solely on the recorded murder of one of the stable-boys from Dieppe.

c. Mary had fifteen ladies-in-waiting, though only four are mentioned in most writing, never the fifteen that I have documented here.

d. There are prestigious books that contain errors of fact. These became obvious only when the search for a certain lady and stable-boy led me into some obscure corners of Scottish history.

Mary, Queen of Scots, had ladies-in-waiting, horses, stable-boys and deteriorated abbey-lands, and a romantic nature that craved weddings and their festivities. From these elements a family emerged that became firmly established by the end of her son's reign (James VI and I, of Scotland and England). During these years, Scotland passed over a divide from an inconsequential position among nations to that of a more progressive 17th century state. An almost endless stream of books has been written about Mary. They can be skimmed through or conned minutely, but the basic facts have to come from a very few contemporary records by court officials and observers.

These originals were hand-written in the old Scots vernacular, and are unreadable by laymen today. A single page of the goose-quill script is in Chapter XIV, along with a "pony" that one can ride through the inky impasse. There have been scholars through all the years who were able to read these records, and there were scholarly clubs to foster efforts to save the documents and reproduce them in modern type. Up to 150 years have passed since this salvaging began, but the number of books printed then cannot fill the needs now, so that very few people can see this historic writing. The books are large and forbiddingly dry and complex to riddle through. I searched these books for any mention of the queen's horses and my stable-boy and his bride-to-be.

The records would have remained in the vaults at the mercy of bookworms and dry-rot except for the labors of the editors and their skilled copyists. They did their work well, and thousands of pages of ancient squiggles were transformed into verbatim transcripts. One particularly interesting restoration was made in 1833. Not much writing that old will be found in corner bookstores, but some is copied yet again in this book. The people who copied these records passed on a legacy or endowment for all to use.

One series, *Accounts of the Lord High Treasurer,* that began in 1877, was under the editorship of Thomas Dickson and J.B.Paul. The eleventh volume transcribes the fiscal records of the reign of Mary, Queen of Scots. Our ancestor, and his father and brother are mentioned twice. Although the bulk of the book consists of copied records, there is a 65-page preface to explain obscure matters. Everything else is in raw Scots or Latin, as written in 1560-64, when the record tells that a Depo boy was "slaughtered." These old records became so fascinating to me that it seemed important to pick some of them out of the public domain and make them come alive in a sort of detective story hunting for thirty horses and two people. Some new tid-bits about the life of Mary may be added by my book, I hope. At least the record will have been transferred from public-domain obscurity to public bookshelves, where those who are not historians and scholars can join the Mary club for a moment. For students who need to see the old Scots writing, I hope that my volume will be less forbidding and unused than the one I found that had its pages uncut and unopened. When I put it back on the library shelves, it had been used just once in this century.

CHAPTER I

MARY STEWART, THE QUEEN OF THE DEPPA LEGEND

Mary, Queen of Scots was born in 1542, and was executed in England in 1587 by order of her cousin, Queen Elizabeth. Both had descended from the founder of the Tudor Line, Henry VII.

Mary's husbands included Francis, the Dauphin of France who became King Francis II, Henry Darnley, her English cousin, and James Hepburn, 4th Earl of Bothwell. She provided the second and third of these with elevated titles before marrying them. All three of these marriages had disastrous consequences. This book tells of a wedding not her own, but of her own. Two people of her household, a stable-boy and a lady-in-waiting, married with her help, but an intriguing story led up to this wedding. Neither this story, nor the story of this couple's later life in the Borders of Scotland has ever before been searched out and put on paper.

These two became a part of history, oral history. The story of the marriage was remembered and repeated, generation after generation, in less and less detail, until finally only eleven words remained when my grandmother told them to me: "A lady-in-waiting to the queen married a stable-boy."

The many descendants of this first couple now live in Scotland, England, Australia, New Zealand, and the United States. The surname that is spelled "Deppa" in the United States is spelled "Dippie" in the other countries. Perhaps thirteen generations have borne the name, which began as Depo, and which evolved over 200 years through 20 variant spellings before it settled down to the present two.

The children of the first couple used at least five spellings. In those times, when writing materials were very scarce, and education limited to very few, the use of variant spellings was an accidental but helpful means of keeping family branches distinct. Though many people could at least write their names, it is evident that spelling was not one of their strong points. It is also clear, as I will explain later in the book, that these people found it virtually impossible not to jumble the double vowels of their patronymic, Dieppe. The first spelling, Depo, was an off-hand gift of the Lord High Treasurer's time-keeper, who enrolled two men from Dieppe, France into the queen's service in October of 1561. Most surnames have an origin in some distant unknown antiquity. Ours was put on paper by an officer of the queen in an instant so spontaneous, yet so important to our story, that the event will be re-created later in these pages in its proper setting.

For about the first two hundred years of our four-and-a-quarter century history, the descendants of this first couple were to be found near their origin, the Borderlands of Scotland, and in the Canongate suburb of Edinburgh some 50 miles to the north. The branch that settled on the spelling, Dippie, spread into English and Scottish towns clustered near Berwick-Upon-Tweed. Far fewer descendants were centered in the Canongate area. This discrepancy in numbers has special significance, and will be an important part of our study.

Until 1969, when I first visited Edinburgh and saw Black's *Surnames of Scotland*, I had no idea where my curious name had come from, although there had never been any question about our being Scotch (a perfectly correct term until a few decades ago, when it was changed to "Scots"). After that visit, my search ultimately became almost an obsession, but a very interesting one. In time, as my sources and information began to jell, I found that the queen's horses were beginning to nose out the queen as the center of my attention. Perhaps no one else has ever worked on the history of those horses so intently, but they were key elements in finding my origins. Enough is told in records we will examine that a novelist could easily write a fascinating story just about the horses.

In olden times, no one wrote about the common people, how they lived, what they ate, and how they managed to stay alive from sun-up to sun-up. But that is when our family started, in a very remote time. Our two ancestors were born about fifty years after Columbus discovered the new world, and my endeavor has been to enter their time frame as I try to reconstruct their lives and activities. This story could never have been written except that these two people were so closely associated with the queen that her activities, which were recorded, provided settings where our two can be seen rather clearly as they waited on their queen.

The records that were kept were scanty, badly done, and sporadic, with trivial matters given prominence, and important matters left out. Such criticisms are out of place, of course, for we have to avoid judging the past by the present. On the other hand, the 650 lines of verbatim excerpts I've included in several chapters, will show the truth of the comment. Even the written word of that time was a puzzlement, as our excerpts will show. The old handwriting can be read only by scholars. In the past century, many originals of these records, which are national treasures, have been printed in modern type faces, but even these editions are now old, scarce, and not to be found in many libraries.

To whatever extent the queen's activities were recorded, the presence of her servants and her personal attendants can be seen quite clearly as her reflection. Not to make a comparison, but our two stable-boys are visible in the same way in the records about the royal horses. It is really a fantastic piece of good fortune that I was able to find, after centuries of burial in big books, not only the names of the two stable-boys, but the exact date when they first landed in England just across the border from Scotland. We also know the day and hour when the young woman who married our ancestor landed at Leith, the port of Edinburgh.

Thus we are able to add a few lines to the story of Mary, Queen of Scots, but mainly I have tried to describe the way of life of her ordinary Lowland subjects, by looking closely at one family between 1561 and 1600. It became a game of the sort I enjoy, to unearth the old records and, so far as possible, travel the ground my ancestors knew. Only gradually did I come to know about the disastrous events that gruesomely littered every corner of Scotland. The burning of witches, reiver raids, war, famine and pestilence by-passed our first four generations, apparently. Our people lived in that environment, and must have shared in all the fears of the times.

So this book turns out to be as much a miniature of Scottish life, partly peasant, partly royal, as it is a portrait of our family. Perhaps the result is more history than genealogy. I had travelled to Scotland twice before I learned anything about the meaning of my name, or where my people had lived. After that my work began. I was startled and a little upset to find just how crudely life was lived then, but I could understand, for I had experienced the Appalachian backwoods, the life of the western Indians of the 1930s, and the campesinos of Mexico. It was not difficult to see the many similarities of lifestyle that were imposed by meager resources. More than once, as I saw that my work was digressing from a genealogical search into a study of life in the Borders, it seemed that the title should be changed to "Scottish Life," or even, "All About the Queen's Horses."

Queen Mary is the subject of a vast literature. One library file drawer I thumbed through was full of 3x5 cards of entries just for her. She appears to some as all but depraved, behaving like "a mindless zombie," and evil also, as events forced her abdication. She had an impossible role to play, and in other descriptions is treated sympathetically, with praise for her performance. Within six years after her return from France, she was destroyed by events she so often, and so foolishly, precipitated herself. That she was overwhelmed by the odds against her is tragic, but not surprising. She was not yet nineteen when she became queen regnant of turbulent Scotland. This girl was churned and chopped at by the cleverest nobles in three nations. Perhaps no one ever lived who could have done better, although she had a contemporary to the south who did live a lot longer. That queen, Elizabeth, evaded her own counterparts to the wily 4th Earl of Bothwell, but she also had a hard heart, which our fabulous queen did not.

Mary was only twenty-five when Bothwell's complicity in the murder of Darnley, her husband, was linked to her. She married the Earl, but not until after she had made him a Duke. (In chapter fourteen, an original handwritten account of this outrageous episode is reproduced.) Almost overnight, she discovered her people were outraged, and she was harried away to a 19-year captivity in England, then beheaded. Mary was as helpless to chart an unerring course for herself as Elizabeth was competent. There was no resemblance between the two, and Mary was beautiful.

Mary could not guide her realm. She could only create slight ripples in the flooding tide of Scottish affairs, and French, too, for she had the guileless directness of the child she really was. Before her final ruination she handled affairs of state, but she was at her natural best as a buoyant spirit with the riches and position to banish care, and to spread sunlight in the lives of the anonymous people around her, her own household.

The wedding which concerns us may very possibly be specifically mentioned in the archives of Scotland, but far greater matters are ignored, as is ruefully noted by the scholarly editor of the account books of her Lord High Treasurer. To Mary, the romance of a wedding was the peak of entertainment. It was also a very necessary charity that only she could provide. Without her sponsorship and introduction to life outside the palace, her lifelong companions would have been adrift in a forbidding city and land, where even their supposedly native language was all but incomprehensible. Her intimate ladies-in-waiting were all Scottish by birth, but their familiar speech was the French they had learned in the nursery, the school, and the royal residence at the castle Ste. Germain-en-Laye near Paris.

These young women probably were never identified in any contemporary document with the exception of the four famous Maries: Fleming, Seton, Beaton, and Livingston. All had been educated in the graces of the day alongside many children of the French nobility. A point to remember is that the Scottish lords would not have dared to send boys and girls of commoners to mingle with children of the French nobility.

As she matured in her active role as queen, it is probable that very few purely ornamental ladies-in-waiting were then kept standing around amongst her statesmen attendants, as they had when she was younger.

> Mary, Mary, quite contrary,
> How does your garden grow?
> With silver bells and cockle shells
> And pretty maids all in a row.

When she faced the problem of marrying-off her young women, and it fits all we know of her to believe she considered this to be her duty, she must have met a road block we can only surmise, not solve: there could hardly have been enough suitable young men, her pages, in her train. She must have enlisted the aid of well-placed families in her realm to provide the eleven anonymous bridegrooms that she needed. Later we will reproduce the records showing there were eleven of these lesser ladies-in-waiting. This information was found among the records of the horse's harness, which may be a peculiar place to count girls, but true.

When Mary and these girls were about six years old, the English had a strangle hold on Scotland, as history books explain. The solution worked out was to more or less trade Mary for French aid. She was to go to France without delay. Little Mary, the Queen of Scots, sailed from Dumbarton, the ancient stronghold on the Firth of Clyde, on the 29th of July 1548. King Henri, her father-in-law to be, had sent his own galley to carry her by way of the Irish Sea, a longer route to France, but safer than the North Sea. At this time, and through the years that followed, the lairds guarded the Scottishness of their queen. Young noblemen had routinely gone to Paris for their education. Thus it was no novelty to send the daughters and sons of noble families to the French capital. The children selected for the queen's train would play with her, be schooled with her, and be surrounded with a Scottish ambience that was vital if she were to remain a true Scot. In addition mature Scotswomen were made her personal attendants to constantly reinforce her colloquial language and patterns of thought. She did remain Scottish, but inevitably French became her primary language, which also was true of her whole party. They were immersed in the incredible extravagances of that royal life which had these children perennially visiting a string of magnificent estates and castles around France, at a cost that staggered even the royal treasury. One of the children in her train was to become the first mother of our family, and the heroine of this story.

Mary was born December 8, 1542, and since her selected attendants were undoubtedly approximately her age or younger, the actual child whose name I have not yet found could well have been born earlier in the same year. King James V, Mary's father, left her to be Queen of Scotland at the age of six days. He died with the bitter knowledge that he had no male heir, although he had left plenty of illegitimate sons.

We have not found the name of our heroine, but many indications throughout this account will place her family's residence in the Canongate, the same parish as the Palace of Holyroodhouse. It is recorded that a great-granddaughter of the little girl who went to France with her queen was buried in the palace cemetery. It is only reasonable to think that these connections were known in detail at that time. Do records of these families exist? It was appropriate and significant that a woman should be buried at the palace, whose great-grandmother had been married there.

There would never have been a Depo family, nor any records, except that the queen had certain needs that were filled by two people who shortly married. Also, the man had a brother, or a father, whose appearance in the official records was crucial to our search. This ambiguity will be considered at length, but it doesn't affect our lineage. Thus the most ordinary activities of very unimportant characters have made it possible to reconstruct a history that, amazingly, was not lost in the erosion of documents that went on for four centuries. The key was that they worked for the queen. Equally fortuitous was the unbroken chain of our oral tradition that connected the beginning and the end of these years.

Daughtering out of a line is an insidious process that has no cure, but we also escaped that route to surname oblivion through all those generations. My surname survived. It did not disappear in those ways but now I am ruefully watching my father's line become tenuous indeed even though he had three sons, and no daughters.

By and large, little effort is made to preserve family links with the past, nor are mementoes saved. This I can understand, and also know there is not room enough to save many things nor feel confidant they will be handed down. Thus cold vital statistics in some city hall may be the only record of a family, and that, somehow, seems less than a happy solution to the disappearing act. That a number of the palace staff were married by favor of our romantic queen seems a reasonable assumption, but only a half dozen instances, perhaps, have been mentioned by her biographers. There is a dramatic angle to our case that was unusual - the lady and the poor boy scenario. It was startling then, and still is. That is very likely the touchstone that kept the legend alive until I heard it and decided to find out its meaning, and to ferret out the beginnings of the Scottish family with the name that doesn't sound at all Scottish.

All of my life I have said my name was Scottish when asked my national background. No one ever argued with that answer, nor did anyone really seem convinced, either. We knew we were Scotch because my grandfather had been born in Glasgow in 1842. Also, Grandma was Scotch-Irish, all 98 pounds of her. That term, by the way, was used in America to separate the Scots who had lived in Ulster from the giant wave of native Irish that was flooding the United States. Her quick movements and sprightly voice with a slight burr left no doubt that we were Scotch.

Grandfather Robert, his brother James, and sisters Elizabeth and Marian, were brought to the United States in 1850. They started a farm in Briscoe, Sullivan County, New York. Deppa Road is still there, but only a cellar hole shows where the house once stood. They had landed in New York City and travelled about 100 miles northwest to Briscoe where there was a large tannery. Robert became an artilleryman, and was in eight Civil War battles. I prize his Union Army papers. When the war ended he married Janetta Campbell of another recent immigrant family. She was fifteen and a half years old. They did not remain in Sullivan County, but followed the retreating stands of Hemlock as the bark was peeled and used in tanning leather. When the trees were gone the tanneries moved on or went out of business, leaving ghost towns. Robert and his family lived for a time at Great Bend, Pennsylvania, where my father was born in 1876, the centennial of our nation, the fourth of six children. They moved once more, to Costello, Pennsylvania, another boom town with a big tannery (where I was born in 1908). This was about 100 miles west of the original homestead. The family had arrived there in 1886, again living on a farm, but also working on the side. My father was a grocer all his life, and his three sons all had considerable experience in that, and other retail lines, in later times and places.

While it is true that Scotch families can get together and talk up a storm, they are not what one would call loquacious between times. In fact, quiet contemplative chit-chat in a family, and with the children, may be a less characteristic mode than the laconic grunting of a yes or no answer to direct questions. Of course I am not really familiar with conversation in Scotland, where animated and kindly small talk may be the general custom. I do think that the Scottish "aye" is so lovely a sound to hear that one should take care to avoid questions likely to evoke a negative answer. The Costello Deppas were all of these things, but they no longer said "aye"; more often it was "no." The families that stayed in Sullivan County did not keep the legend alive. Its continuity as an oral tradition would have ended with my grandmother. In fact, it has now ended as a legend for it has now been written for the first time. Grandma was of Highland stock, and that must account for her tenacity in saving the family history. My grandfather's siblings all married Americans who did not have that Scottish compulsion to repeat family legends.

In the National Gallery in Edinburgh there is a painting, "The Legend," by G. P. Chalmers. It shows a Scottish grandmother holding eight young children enthralled by a tale out of the past that she is telling. Significantly, almost all the listeners are female, like the narrator. The two boys in the picture won't forget a word of what they hear, and in later years they may prompt women in their lives who stray ever so slightly in the retelling. They won't repeat the story themselves more than necessary to see that it is passed on. As a general rule it seems inappropriate behavior for males to appear to take an interest in old tales, although they may interpose objections if some detail strays from the accepted truth: "It was so told from such time that the memory of man runneth not to the contrary." So it was with the tale in our family which came so close to extinction. Grandma told a story that her daughter, my Aunt Lizzie, also told me, and I never forgot it. I really believe the tale went in one ear and out the other of all her children and grandchildren except three of us, but at least we remembered it. Nor, I have found, was the story ever told at all, or known, except in Robert's family. Grandma was the key. But I had a lively curiosity coupled with a less than robust constitution that led me toward the quieter activities. I puzzled over this seemingly meaningless statement, for none of us knew more than just a little grade school American history, and certainly nothing about Scotland. What did Grandma's story mean? Our name began, she said, when "a lady-in-waiting to the queen married a stable-boy." Just these eleven words.

After three score years and ten, as activities became less pressing, my curiosity nudged me into trying to find out how my peculiar name could really be Scottish. I had worked for years on my mother's Northrup, Wadsworth, Cutting, ancestry, tracing it back to Yorkshire in 1637. Tracing the Deppa side seemed hopeless to me. In 1969, at the offices of the Scots Ancestry Research Society, 20 York Place, Edinburgh, Miss Patricia Baxendine, M.A., handed me a copy of Black's *Surnames of Scotland*. There was an entry for Dippie, but none for my surname. Just how close does one's "pure" Scottish lineage have to approach perhaps the year 800 to be called a true Scot? If ancient Angle, British, and Pictish blood is acceptable in a true Scot, who may really be Irish-Celtic, circa 600 A.D., then perhaps a few drops of very old French blood should not bar one from the brotherhood. This boils down to the fact that "true Scots" are a duke's mixture of early tribes who were tough enough to survive in a tough land. Although surprised, I did not feel that my rating as a Scot had been lost when it turned out that my name had come from the French city of Dieppe. Moreover, Dieppe had been founded by Vikings, not Gauls (French). The history books tell that the Vikings left some of their blood, and thunder, too, in ancient Scotland. Thus, a man from Dieppe who went to the Borders to live, was moving in with his kinfolk to a degree, *n'est-ce pas*?

I had to wait until my third trip to Scotland 16 years later to find my surname in records there. Then the names of my immigrant great-grandparents, James Deppa and Marian McKenzie, and two of their fourteen children, John and Richard were found. These sons were baptized in 1834 and 1844, respectively. Annie and Richard McKenzie, and John Garkston were witnesses, undoubtedly the mother's sister, brother, and brother-in-law. These records were kindly supplied by a Local Studies Librarian, Miss Margaret Healy, of the great Mitchell Library of Glasgow.

Although I searched the virtually illegible microfilm records of Glasgow's Eastern Necropolis located in Camlachie, and also visited the cemetery, no records could be found of the graves of the nine

Deppa children that Grandma had told me were buried in Scotland. It seems that at that time, mass burial of cholera victims were often necesary. The use of the word lair, meaning grave site, in these records was a new use to me, but I find that it is an old Scottish usage. My family had lived in Camlachie, where my great-grandfather James worked in the huge industrial enclave just to the east of Glasgow. Those homes, and all of the iron, chemical, and other plants have recently been razed. The place looks like a war-destroyed city, with little left but two very high apartment buildings and the big old cemetery amidst acres of bulldozed rubble.

My 1860 map of Camlachie shows innumerable factories where James Deppa had found his employment. There was a famous forge there where the largest of 16-inch cannon were once made. That was labor-intensive work. Now Scotland is striving to build up a microchip industry. That is going from the biggest to the tiniest of products. I did feel strange being so near and yet so far from my great-grandfather, whose birthday was 102 years before mine. He bore my exact name, except that he had no middle name. He did not give his son, Robert, a middle name either, but Robert gave my father one. A daughter who did not emigrate became Mrs. Henry Dunlavy, but what may have happened to her is still a mystery. The gap between James Deppa and André (Hendre) Depo is 244 years wide, and I will probably not try to find the identity of the half dozen generations of my relatives who fit in that space. In any event, they all did their duty: they left male heirs so I could be born a Deppa in Costello.

Whether or not the Deppa children died in a true epidemic cannot be known, since many diseases were endemic. Cholera and typhus devastated Europe more than once, and Scotland was not spared except when Bubonic plague, the black death, swept through London in 1665 and 1666. Rat fleas carried the organism, *Bacillus pestis*, which killed the rats, and then the people, because they all lived together. When I worked with the Indians in New Mexico in the 1930's, I was startled to learn that the fleas living on common mesa rodents carried the black death organism, but, by sheer luck and separation, none of us caught the disease. Only when the animal host dies do the fleas use man as a substitute host, which is one of the reasons for not having rats around. In 1988, animal rights activists in a Washington suburb were protesting the killing of rats, and were urging that the city rats be caught and released on farms!

Through the four centuries of our family, enough escaped all hazards to carry on the name. The Deppas in Glasgow lost 9 of 14, or two-thirds of their children. One historian has said that of 20 children born in a family, only two might survive into the parents' old age. In the most terrible years of an epidemic a fifth of a population might die; in some cities far more. Non-existent sanitation saw children carried off year in and year out under the innocuous heading, summer complaint. The history of disease is not light reading, nor should one admit that it is interesting, I suppose. Thomas Malthus of the 19th century was close enough to the great epidemics to recognize the vulnerability of the human race. In the last two decades in Africa, population growth, food deficits, and war have agitated the World, yet hundreds of millions of people follow leaders who say go ahead and have babies without limit. Ironically, the medical, engineering, and sanitation advances of the past century have perversely made the Reverend Malthus a respectable prophet again, it seems. Women who have 14 or 20 children could now end up with grandchildren in geometric progression unless, as Malthus predicted, the four horsemen ride again.

CHAPTER II

THE QUEEN AND I

Volume III of *Regality Records of Melrose* contains information that started me on the trail leading to my progenitors, hidden deep in this and other old records. Our first father was a native of Dieppe, France. He would naturally have referred to himself as *un Dieppois* - a man from Dieppe.

Volume III also contains an index of Volume I of this large set of transcribed records. Court proceedings which I refer to in Chapter XI show entries for our man on pages 7, 22, 29, 39, and 68. His name was spelled Henry Depo in 1608. As we will see, his names in the records were all misnomers, which explains why our surname resembles Dieppe instead of the man's actual French surname. Volume III has an important entry for a John Dippo that I was unable to interpret until I had read a good deal of the history of religious persecution which came to be known as the "killing times." This story is in Chapter XV. These two volumes gave me the breakthrough that led to all the many references and personal experiences that finally put our family legend into the tiny niche of history where it fits like a long lost piece of a jigsaw puzzle.

The now defunct *Washington (D.C.) Star* newspaper of October 18, 1977 published an article which caught my attention. Later, a Jacques Cousteau television feature showed the details. Mrs.Sheila Macbeth Mitchell, of Edinburgh, Scotland, descended in Cousteau's diving vessel to see the *Britannic*, sunk in a Greek Harbor in 1916. She had been a nurse on this sister ship of the "unsinkable" *Titanic*, which the British had used as a hospital ship. One facet of this story moved me to action: Mrs. Mitchell, 86 years old, and her 91-

year-old husband, had recorded some 50,000 inscriptions from 20% of Scottish gravestones. When I finally got her address, and wrote a letter, this wonderful lady responded with pages of incisive comments and references that made me consult Harvard and Catholic University libraries to find three books not in the Library of Congress. Without her letter, I might never have found the key to all the other help and references that followed. Now, a decade later, this beginning has gone on to make a circle that fits our family into the Scottish picture. It has taken a long time for me to meet the queen, through her stable-boy.

It has turned out that my grandmother's family story was an eleven-word synopsis of Scottish records and history. Finding the records was not easy, but they have been in the archives all along, and certainly there are others that I have not found. Most facts fall through the cracks and crevices of history. Such is the case with the numerous ladies-in-waiting to the queen, one of whom was to become our ancestress, just as Grandma's legend had it. All the biographies of the queen tell of her four Maries, but apparently the names of the lesser ladies were never written down, except, perhaps, in their family mementos. I found them, though not by name, as I searched for every possible mention of the queen's fine French horses. This record is in Chapter IX. It seems ironic that in hunting for the horses that brought my ancestor to Scotland I found his wife-to-be, and her ten companions. Is it possible that these eleven anonymous ladies have never been identified anywhere except in the record we have analyzed, and then only by a lump sum number? There were eleven of them, plus the four Maries.

Marriages of these lesser people of the queen's retinue were frequent, we have read. In these weddings, the bride and groom may have been quite incidental, props almost, for festive entertainment. Everyone in the palace would have a good time, with dancing afterwards, and refreshments. The queen's sincerity and human interest in these people is above question, no matter that she dearly loved to stage weddings, and dance all night. In the pages that follow, we will see these newlyweds, our ancestors, as they find their place in the time of Mary and beyond to the time when the branch that went to the United States spelled the name "Deppa," while all the rest, apparently, spelled the name "Dippie." They live in Scotland in the greatest numbers, but also in England, Australia, and New Zealand. In the book, *Michigan Birds*, there is a report that one G. F. Dippie sighted Bohemian Waxwings in Toronto in 1895, but the current telephone directory does not list the name.

The two Depo men left a trail which would be completely unnoticed, incomprehensible, and without interest to anyone but a descendant of André Depo. That trail was unexplored until 1978. That odd name in the *Regality Records of Melrose* had probably never been really noticed by anyone until I went searching for it. When I found the name Depo in another source book written 42 years earlier, and not even in the same archives, then I knew I was not dealing with a coincidence. The startling vindication of oral history, beginning then, and ending now with this book, is an humbling realization. Eleven words repeated without change for 425 years!

We can be sure our prospective bride and groom were well known to the whole court, for they would have been habitually with the queen. The stable-boy of our legend, recorded as Hendre Depo, would have been called André, for that was the French name the Scottish clerk could not spell. Queen Mary rode every day, almost without exception. In this almost daily contact, he alone of all the hostlers spoke only French. She would have spoken to him with no constraint, for her informality with servants was something of a scandal. In Scotland, the stilted manners of other royal courts were missing.

Mary had lived for thirteen years in the hauteur of the French court. Queen Catherine de'Medicis, her mother-in-law, and others, were her exemplars, yet she never became like them in arrogance, nor could she conceivably have masterminded anything so terrible as the Massacre of St. Bartholomew's Eve, as Catherine did. Eleven years after Mary had left France and taken our progenitors-to-be with her, Catherine persuaded her weak-minded son, who had become King Charles IX, to signal the massacre. The church bells of Paris were rung at two in the morning of August 24, 1572, and the murdering began.

When Mary had her own Scottish court she treated people with the Scottish directness that was her nature. It would have been interesting to see her deal with foreign ambassadors, and others, for she knew all the European tricks for putting down presumptuous upstarts. Or did she? There were Darnley and Bothwell. She had been a self-confident queen of two nations. She was a Stewart, a Guise, and a very rich woman. The degrading, almost oriental servility that had been required of servants and lesser people in France was not for her in Scotland.

James Hepburn, 4th Earl of Bothwell, had an important hand in our ancestors' lives, especially the two hostlers from Dieppe. Even in France he would have seen Mary's attendants, for he served her as a high officer arranging for her return to Scotland. At Holyroodhouse he moved with complete freedom. In my opinion, the queen should have sent him packing early-on, for he destroyed her in the end. Perhaps it would be more accurate to say she destroyed herself through him. One can be sure he did not fail to ingratiate himself with the glittery bevy of young ladies-in-waiting. The background swirl of colorful, animated attendants had only the one function - providing center stage prominence for the queen. The four celebrated Maries were near royalty, only a step below the great Marie, their queen. Their privileged position was much more than to create a pleasant ambience, which was the function of the lesser ladies.

From our modern point of view, we can hardly comprehend a royal court of that time. Henry VIII and Queen Elizabeth of England were in competition with the magnificence, or degeneracy, of Spain, and of France, which was building toward the monstrosities of Louis Quatorze. In contrast, the court of Scotland was that of a poor and backward country. Even so, the Scots were proud of it, and of their queen, although some complained of her excessive show of wealth and giddy entertainments, as they saw things. It would be incongruous to think that the little people of the queen's household were wraiths who floated into nothingness after she was gone. Mary's biographers tell that her attendants married within the circle of the household. In fact, the thing that is most unusual about two of her people marrying is that, so far as we know, only one branch of the family, the one that emigrated to America, remembered to keep telling the story.

One has to do quite a bit of reading to gain an idea of the scope of a court, since tourists don't see 16th century courts in action. I have been able to visit a number of great houses and palaces of that era. One, near Halifax, in Yorkshire, more than many much larger ones, had within its walls the independent living capability of a village, a fascinating array of craft shops ready for the workmen to arrive in their picturesque garb. At Holyroodhouse, craftsmen from the adjacent city supplied the Palace, but Mary had an apothecary, and other special craftsmen, and the only priest legally in Scotland. She had Riccio, her Italian secretary, one of her less wise selections. She had Sebastian, who was an especial favorite, and one of the valets of the queen's chamber. He had "great cunning in musike, and merrie jesting." He married Christely Hogg, and it was to his wedding's masked ball that the queen rode, near midnight, as the king was about to be murdered - a piece of business one really should look into, but not here.

Although we are little interested in Darnley's role (he was her unwisely selected husband), he had three king's "pages of honour and two lacqueys" all costumed in the royal colors of yellow and crimson. Each page was waited on by a "gentleman's gentleman," also in livery. The pages' clothing was too incredibly stuffed with bulging padding to be believable. Apparently they were almost as round as beach balls. Five "sangistaris" were dressed much like the pages, but one wonders how the quintet could sing in their hot, bulging costumes.

The best surgeon in Edinburgh was on call. In one case, he was successful in "curing and mending of tua fals noteris quhais handis was strikin of." (The "is" suffix demonstrated formation of the plural). As I am not a linguist, it is not clear to me why so much of the old Scots speech reads so much like contrived obscurity. It has incorrectly been called a dialect of English, and these pages will be full of it, for we are now immersed in the mid 1500s. Remnants of archaic dialects may still be heard in the Eastern Shore region of Maryland, and in the Appalachian Mountains. In any event, the cutting off of four hands of two deceitful notaries would be considered unnecessarily harsh nowadays.

The queen had many other personal attendants: ladies of the bed chamber, her horse groom, and Nicolas la Jardiniere, a female "fule." There was at least one other female fool in the royal household. It is recorded that Nicolas needed a "gouvernante" in the person of one of the bedchamber women named Jacquelene Critoflat. This fool got a grey cloth mantle trimmed with green. Jonet Musche, the other "fule," received a suit costing L4 (4 pounds), 5s (5 shillings). The king had two male fools, one of them outfitted with a very expensive coat costing L27. The other apparently was Scottish, for his name was James Geddie. Both were provided with "keepers." It is more than likely that their jokes and antics needed firm termination capability near at hand when they no longer seemed amusing to royalty, nor would it have been in keeping for the crowned heads to cut off their foolishness personally. They did have a fool's license, but it was subject to instant cancellation; ergo, the keepers. Humor in those times could be very sly, and subtle, but it varied up to broad and bawdy, distinctions that could not be left entirely up to the jester's judgement.

At the center of this hodgepodge was a very compassionate and sentimental monarch with virtually absolute power within the palace. In other matters she had great power also, but there was a circle of wolves in the clothing of noblemen out there, and a watchful population. Perhaps her giddy entertainments, and there were many, were her defense against impossible obstacles. Then there was her virtual obsession with horseback riding, when she could escape all the problems for a time, at least. I have a sentimental affection for the queen, for she was the vital instrument that started my family.

In reading the Lord High Treasurer's accounts of expenditures for "fules", for coats, hats, shoes, "seidis" for the royal garden, 15 saddles, 45 palace beds, etc., *ad infinitum*, it begins to register that these are all government expenditures. Even gold chains costing 1400 Scots pounds, to present to departing ambassadors, came under that category. Less important personages got cheaper chains. Nowhere have I seen a record of a gift ring, bracelet, necklace, wedding gown, new coat for a bridegroom, cooking pot, table or anything for keeping house; yet it is generally recognized that the men and women of Mary's household married each other. Apparently many of them married. The queen, possibly, was richer than the national treasury, and she had her own chamberlain to manage these ample assets. Thus we encounter a blank when looking in official records for gifts to her dearly loved little friends. How well she must have realized their vulnerability, and acted to give them a future in this land which was strange to them. New attendants could be procured very easily, with the added advantage of placating local jealousies. As Mary well knew, her court was much too frenchy to please the Scots, especially in the almost total use of the French language. The whole arrangement was vilified by her vituperative critic, the Reverend John Knox, half a mile up High Street.

As her original ladies-in-waiting, pages, and servants slipped into oblivion through lovely and entertaining palace marriages, Mary, the warm-hearted queen, not only gave these dear friends this greatest possible gift, she also poured oil on her turbulent political waters, for she would then be able to replace them with substitutes from the local political scene. It would be incongruous to suppose that Mary, who loved above all to go to weddings, did all of this on the cheap, but from a practical, cost effective viewpoint it would still be cheap entertainment no matter what wedding gifts she might dispense.

There were the palace, the chapel, and the great hall with its built-in catering service. There was even a Presbyterian minister, Mr. John Craig, whose record book of marriages I have tried to locate, with dubious success, for few people were rigorously systematic about records in 1562.

I am often amazed to find that archives hold material to this day that one would swear must have crumbled to dust. I don't know why, but these detailed curlicues out of antiquity are fascinating to me. When it dawned on me that the palace minister would almost certainly have marriage records, I asked my Scottish history savant, Dr. Michael Lynch, of the University of Edinburgh, if such a record might exist. Part of his reply is quoted, to show how simple such an investigation is not:

> "The Register of Marriages for the Canongate does indeed start in 1564, and the early part of it, from 1564-1565, is fully printed in *The Buik of the Kirk of the Canagait*, A. Calderwood (ed.), 1564-1567, but there is, unfortunately, no trace of a Depo in it. There is, however, a complication about the minister. John Craig had a complicated career. He was minister of the Canongate 1561-2, but then left to become second minster of Edinburgh about April 1562. (John Knox, of course, had been the capital's first minister since 1559). So whether he performed the Depo marriage service in the separate parish and burgh of the Canongate depends on how early in 1562 the ceremony took place...The full details of Craig's career and of Canongate parish are in: *Fasti Ecclesiae Scoticanae*, ed. H. Scott (Edinburgh, 1915). His successor in the Canongate was John Brand until his death in 1574."

Although it was interesting to learn in what detail these records were retrievable, the news was disappointing. I also learned from another letter that many records were not started until 1562. That means that when Mary took charge, she tightened things up in only four months. Now back to the wedding performed by a minister whose name and records we don't have for a certainty.

The dozens of palace attendants and servants of all degrees would have flocked to the wedding of their own daily companions. This sparkling scene, with Mary and her four Maries at the height of enjoyment, was repeated many times. It would hardly be credible that Mary allowed her lifelong companions to drift into an intolerable spinsterhood through loyalty to herself. Our crystal ball is too dim to reveal who gave the bride away. Was her father alive to be there? We will see later that there are many reasons for believing that her family lived in nearby Canongate. There could have been brothers or uncles to see her safely married. The documentation I have found for the origin of our family name fits perfectly into the history of Queen Mary's reign. The wedding she sponsored was our beginning. That is not a pun around the motto of the queen herself. One of her last acts before her beheading was to embroider: "In my end is my beginning." Looking for my family roots started out along the usual lines of a genealogical search, and it was only that, until I hit a stone wall.

The recording of vital statistics is a rather recent innovation, especially their indexing. 1855 marks the beginning of many Scottish registers. Addresses of ancestors are rarely available to a searcher, yet they are needed in order to pry open the census books. Wills connote some wealth and compliance with legal procedures. Directories were for the more important citizens. My inquiries soon revealed that before 1855 the records were kept by ministers or clerks of more than 900 parishes in about 4000 unindexed volumes. All I knew was that my grandfather came from Glasgow as an eight-year-old boy, and his father had red hair, more than that really, but not much. By innate stubbornness, and using time, paper, money, telephone, and travel, I found skilled correspondents who were generous with their expertise. The blank wall was cracked open, as I could never have foreseen. Now I knew where my great-grandfather had lived with his family, and his occupation. In the fall of

1985, my wife and I took our four adult children to see where their great-great-grandparents had lived, as well as the other places in this story.

Curiosity about people of long ago led to my first interest in ancestors. Then a high school course in ancient history, augmented by two years of Latin, got me started. My main interest had always centered on nature and the outdoors, and that has continued to this day. Forestry and conservation became the profession which I followed along many varied byways after 1932. I have instructed my children, if they ever find me on my deathbed, to carry it out to the woods, and I will recover, telling them about the trees.

Reading has taken me in my armchair to many places, but the constant theme has been man's niche in the world, a mixing of history, conservation, ecology, anthropology and more. These big words boil down to assessing what man does to his environment. We seem to believe that if we don't wear the planet down to bare rock, who will, so why not get on with it? No other creature knows how to do it. We have become experts in this century. Some, like elephants, seem to be destroyers, but they never exceed the recovery potential of their niche. It is particularly ironic for me to investigate ancestors four centuries back in time. My tendency to cast an appraising eye four centuries or four millennia into the future is *prima facie* evidence that I hunt ancestors for the fun of it, not with any expectation that my chronicle is anything more than a slight paragraph in the record of a few transient sojourners who seem to be marching toward the edge.

In 1933, with freshly engrossed sheepskin in hand (Michigan State College), I joined the U.S. Forest Service, in Arizona. Later, in the new Soil Conservation Service, my employment put me into the midst of the Navajo Indian Tribe. Their 17 million acre homeland surrounds that of the Hopi Indians. Another move put me on the 37 million acre Rio Grande Project of the Soil Conservation Service as District Forester. There were 13 other tribes more ancient than the Navajo in that watershed. West of Santa Fe, New

Mexico, the ancient cliff dwellings now called Bandelier were on the edge of the huge Ramon Vigil Spanish Land Grant. I went there frequently, supervising a timber operation, until suddenly the whole mesa was closed to access, and our cartographic division was put under guard - the Manhattan Project, we were told. There is a city up there now. They call it Los Alamos. When I knew Los Alamos, it was a boy's school so exclusive that an alumnus would enroll his son as soon as he was born. Charley Shearer, a ranger on my staff, and another man, had founded the school years before as a wilderness camp.

Scientists made a bomb there that they took to another of my favorite spots and changed the history of the world. I don't suppose the calcium sulphate sand dunes that lie cradled in a vast field of lava sparsely covered with extra large prickly pear are much changed because of the explosion of the first atomic bomb. The hot blazing white sand still generates miraculous mirages, I suppose, that force you to imagine you might be dying of thirst and futilely travelling toward lakes that become heat waves, and vanish as you go toward them. Even the first atomic bomb couldn't much change that wonderland in New Mexico.

The White Sands are granulated gypsum no different chemically from the wide gypsum layers, or strata, in cliffs 200 miles to the north near Los Alamos, The Cottonwoods. Three hundred miles farther north past most of the Colorado Rockies, the gypsum takes on its classical, elegant, translucent nature; the treasured material carved for the pharaohs. Near Fort Collins, alabaster carvers like to sell you lighthouses three feet high with an electric bulb inside. They are pretty, but my souvenir piece is a three-inch bowl nice enough for any pharaoh.

The Conquistadors missed all of this except the White Sands, and they did not appreciate those dry dunes. About the time Mary Stewart was born, the Spanish were moving from Mexico through *el paso del norte* to Christianize the seven cities of gold, but they named the route between *el Rio Grande* and the Sacramento

Mountains, *el Jornado del Muerto*. In an air-conditioned car, the Journey of Death is now part of New Mexico's "Land of Enchantment." Fifty years ago, air conditioning for cars had not yet been invented, especially for government cars. This gave me an appreciation of the black side of the White Sands.

The Hopi villages which the Spaniards thought were full of gold, were contemporary with the later Cistercian occupancy of Melrose Abbey. Very possibly, the Hopi had a higher standard of living than the Scots then. There is little doubt that the Borderers, and certainly the Highlanders, lived a more squalid, starved and mistreated life up into the 18th and 19th centuries than any of the Pueblo peoples that the invaders so despised. But the white men had the firearms, and the injunction to go forth and rule the earth and the inhabitants thereof.

If I had a Scottish coat of arms, I have found nothing to indicate it should depict a cattle thief couchant, a V.I.P. in any posture, or a bar sinister. In fact, the English coat of arms I might claim has nothing to do with my deeds, but rather the deeds of an ancestor on the battlefield of Crecy in 1346. Coats of arms were great for the people who earned them in the days of chivalry, but I am not sure it proves much to hang a mass-produced placque by the front door in the 1980s. Few people are at all interested in writing something down about their recent ancestors, I have found, even though that would add up to a considerable history before long. In the old days, many simply could not make any such attempt. After reading a great deal about early Scottish life, I am more than sympathetic with those who were lucky if they passed on life itself to their children. People have to be concerned first of all with their daily problems. But when this *de minimus* thought controls lives for generations on end, the family as a known quantity is obliterated. This is like the blip on a computer screen; when the power goes off there is a blank - like a family without records. It seems reasonable that each person should leave some record behind. Just a note naming one's parents and grandparents along with dates and places would do the trick. Only a few hundred generations of that would have told all of us just how we had descended from Adam and Eve. Let me add "joke" to that comment, for I well know just how ardently that very project is now being pursued, with vast expenditures, by those who believe without question that the beginning was just 4004 years before Christ.

CHAPTER III

THE SIXTEENTH-CENTURY LOWLANDS

It is true that in the history of the World our man from Dieppe and the lady-in-waiting he married are of small importance, but even so, I feel that the puzzle of our origin as a family should be put together. The jig-saw pieces have lain jumbled in scattered record books too long. It is time, just for the sake of decency, to fit them together. Obviously I am writing much more than a line diagram of my family with the barest of footnotes. That is what I intended at first, but my own interest in looking behind the scenes took over. The Scotland of long ago had to be investigated for a new reason.

Hundreds, perhaps many hundreds, of individuals must have borne our name while daughters entered other families. Early in my research I began to realize that the span of time was so great that our beginnings had been in a strange and dim antiquity when Scotland was just beginning to emerge into a role that was new to her. Although this is hard to admit, she was just beginning to be a civilized nation. The more I read and wrote, the more it seemed to me that other people might share my interest in the customs, agriculture, language, and people of those times. I ended up writing more about the stage than my people on that stage. As a result I feel certain that the queen's horses and her ladies-in-waiting have received attention that they have never had before.

The abbeys, built before the dark ages had passed, the earliest inhabitants of this land, the destroyers, the defenders; this history enticed me into reading more and more. A chart of my family line omitted too much that I wanted to know about how lives were lived in that long ago time. My first few paragraphs grew to include many things that needed to be said, and others that I just wanted to say. More than once, in the morning, an insight would practically jump into my head as I awakened. One puzzle that baffled me from the beginning was why my family in America had an ancestry legend, and the branches in the Borders apparently did not. One morning the answer hit me like a thousand of brick: secrecy. In the Borders, secrecy was a way of life. Not just because of the reivers, who were a species of robbers we will tell more about, but because Scots minded their own business. As we proceed with our story, it will become obvious why these stoic people kept their thoughts to themselves.

The mechanics of living in the sixteenth century can but dimly be imagined by anyone who has always had electricity, communication, transportation, kitchens, bathrooms, and grocery stores, and who never knew anyone not so blessed. My search for an ancestor took me into that century and into the Scottish Borders - a term that meant nothing to me at first. As I read and uncovered records of people with names much like my own, new perspectives were opened. The simplest of statements called for more reading, writing, and even travel.

An example is the case of John Dippo, and his servant, William Purvis, each of whom was fined 50 pounds(Scots) for contumacy. I didn't know that word had been given a vicious special meaning in those times of religious persecution. I assumed that John and his servant had perhaps given a judge some back-talk, and been fined for contempt of court. What I eventually found out was that these two had been caught up in one of the most horrendous of Scottish nightmares. I thought if our family had been through that, it was up to me to write about it and help acknowledge the heroism of the thousands who lived and died in the "killing time." (The details of the story of John Dippo and William Purvis are in Chapter XV).

The Sixteenth-Century Lowlands

The year 1561 brought our two key ancestors together. The event was the return of Mary, Queen of Scots, after 13 years of absence, during part of which time she had also been the Queen of France. This was such a dramatic situation that no one noticed our two people, so important to us, but of no special importance in the palace, or in history. The bridegroom-to-be, a palace stable-boy, was one of three family members who had left Dieppe to care for the Scottish Queen's horses. One, Alexander, was either the bridegroom's brother, or his father. The ambiguity cannot be positively solved. More than once the old records fail to convey a clear message. Nonetheless I am so pleased to know by the record of the Lord High Treasurer that the Depo name was recorded in Scotland in 1564, that the exasperating muddle of words and meaning can be overlooked. This situation will be left up in the air for now, and carefully looked at later.

Almost certainly it was the family of the bride who talked among themselves about the wedding, and who initiated the family legend. Almost certainly their new son-in-law only spoke French. Whether they fully accepted him mattered not, in the long run. The salient point here is that descendants of the city girl's family passed on a record of the event by telling that "a lady-in-waiting to the queen married a stable-boy." An average of three generations per century for over four hundred years repeated that story without deviation. Try to imagine all the tongue wagging that went on for the first fifty years among the people who actually knew the principals. Everyone within earshot had his say, we can be sure. A French son-in-law? The queen's mother had been French royalty, almost, and French people were commonplace in Edinburgh. No problem about status, unless some choleric uncle or other had a cat-fit about a foreigner in the family. After the flood of discussion had subsided other news crowded out the old. People died, and were forgotten. What happened very soon to the queen herself was so shameful, and the aftermath so painful, that people doggedly pursued their lives thankful for sustenance, not romance. The story of the maid and the stable-boy persisted through it all in one Canongate family. During these end-of-century times there was no war, but the newness of the Reformation, the turbulence of government, trade, and living conditions make it impossible to guess what may have been transpiring in the family of the once-upon-a-time bride. Her parents must have had a noble name for their little girl to have been chosen to attend the queen. But noble titles were so indiscriminately acquired in Mary's time that her regent may even have bestowed one on the father of a pretty little girl who lived just outside the palace walls in the Canongate, just so she could attend her little queen at the French Court.

This girl, in the course of time, had numerous children, and much of our story is about them, and the way they and their neighbors lived. Evidence shows that one daughter as well as one or two brothers lived with her mother's family, in the Canongate. The daughter's surname, Dippo, of course disappeared, as maiden names usually do, but not so with her brothers whose surname, in many variations, survived in the Capital city. They, and their wives, and their sons and their wives, and their grandsons and their wives, distilled a story which was growing more and more remote with each generation, but they were all proud of their romantic origin. So the tale became a legend without specific meaning, but repeated without change until I heard it without the slightest comprehension. I didn't even know about any queen of Scotland then, but I knew it should be passed on just as I had heard it.

Descendants of one Canongate family passed down this story; meanwhile there were many other siblings living on an allotted farmstead not far to the south, in Melrose. They and their descendants spread far and wide, mostly in towns, in both the Scottish and the English borderlands along the river Tweed, to the east.

The two situations were simply different. A story was repeated in a Canongate family, but not in any of the others. Eventually it was perfectly natural for the families in the Borderland to associate their name with the flight of Huguenot refugees from Dieppe. That story was apparently settled on in the 1700s, and became firmly

The Sixteenth-Century Lowlands   33

entrenched as fact in the following years. When one thinks of all that can happen in one long lifetime, it can boggle the mind to consider the confusion of events possible in a dozen or more lifetimes, and none of it written, except when some official record is left. We wish there were more, but at least there are records that place the bride and her stable-boy in the queen's household. We go on from there.

I am proud to be of Scottish heritage, but it would be chauvinistic to gloss over the fact that the 16th and 15th century Scots were barely emerging from an unenlightened past. The glories of the renaissance, in Italy for instance, had not found a home in Scotland, which was more noted for its crudities. We can well believe that the level of living, the culture, was minimal. People lived without much mental stimulus, and under a heavy burden of ancient customs to be followed without deviation. Many people were so backward as to be nearly inarticulate and bungling among their fellows. Only the most commonplace of utterances in a thick brogue barely understandable to those they lived and worked with would be conceivable for those times. Very few would have been even slightly learned in the world of books or speech, but that is not to say that they were lacking in potential. An easy flow of conversation or general give-and-take between people should not be visualized as we try to imagine life in the Borders throughout the 1500s. Not until the next century would reading and writing be taught in small schools.

The capital city probably had a population in the range of 20 to 25 thousand, including the Canongate, which was a suburb outside the northeast wall of Edinburgh. The one thoroughfare was High Street, now called the Royal Mile, which ran rather steeply downhill from the ancient castle to Holyroodhouse, the Palace. This mile of history is so important that we make no apology for stressing various incidents and descriptions more than once. My foreign travels came late in life, but besides this street, I have been on the great streets of London, Paris, Rome, and in the city of Montezuma, have walked where St. Paul walked in Jerusalem, Athens, and Corinth, where

Rameses II glorified himself in Karnak and Abu Simbel, but High Street remains special to me.

Centuries before the building and rebuilding of Holyroodhouse, a magnificent Augustinian Abbey was on the site, surrounded by forest, long gone even as a memory. The adjacent Canongate had religious significance, but developed into a residential area where condominium-type tall houses surrounded "closes," which opened onto High Street, and which had gardens in the rear. This pattern of building was repeated up High Street to the Edinburgh city wall, where Netherbow gate stood guard. The palace chapel was also the parish church of the Canongate. I am convinced that two or three children of our first family came here to live with their grandparents. Many of the better-off families lived in apartments on these closes, and numerous indications place my people in this location.

Our story will tell how the Depo family lived on a Melrose Abbey farm where the father was a *feu* or fee holder, a *feuar*, or renter, a vassal of the recently secularized Abbey. These terms had been carried down from feudalism, and were in the process of becoming archaic, but they show what a long-ago time we are dealing with. "Vassal" is used in the court record that I cite, but it was not really correct for Depo because the land was no longer owned by the church, or by a feudal lord, but held by a commendator at the pleasure of the monarch. The old terminology was slow to fade away. This use of the term vassal did not have the meaning of serf, as it once did when either term would have meant that the children, through elaborate rules, would have been virtual slaves to the overlord. These children were free, but they had almost no choice but to move away when they were grown, for there was no land for them there. Many indications point to villages and towns, trades, and crafts as the destiny of these ancestors and relatives. Through the generations these people were healthy and prolific, or such numbers could not have multiplied. The unusual surname became a remarkable tracking device, for there is no confusing it with others, a problem the Smiths, Thompsons and many others have.

The Sixteenth-Century Lowlands

Dr. T. C. Smout, in his *History of the Scottish People from 1560 to 1830*, describes many facets of life in Scotland, and in interesting detail, always distinguishing between the Highlands and the Lowlands. It is often difficult to be sure that a written account applies to the part of Scotland where our people lived. In many details, two nations could hardly have been more different. He points out the extreme scarcity of information about the lives of country people at the time of Mary. Eyewitness accounts of living conditions then would jar the equanimity of anyone whose ideas of Scottish life came mainly from watching St. Andrew's Day parades, and perhaps touring various Scottish castles.

As much as 200 years later than the first Depo, and in the more prosperous western Lowlands, the typical house of an established *gudeman* (farmer) was about 30 feet long and 14 feet wide, divided into two rooms, separated by a "box-bed" for the gudeman and his wife. This was a box-like enclosure that held the bed, and was entered from the private side of the house, which was called the *ben*. A sliding door gave access to the box-bed.

The other half of the house was called the *but*. Everyone, including passing beggars, made use of this room. Food was prepared here, but the gudewife also had cooking and eating arrangements in the *ben*. At night the women workers and the older daughters slept in the *but* on board bunks or wherever they could find space. Sometimes a loft was floored so young boys could sleep overhead. If the wind blew too much smoke down the *lum*, and the *but* became unbearable, the women would go sleep with the cows in their attached shed. Maybe the boys then came down and took over the vacated spaces, for the smoke up among the rafters must have been even worse.

Men who were permanent workers on the farm, and grown sons, slept with the horses in their attached shed, or else in the *bothy*. This structure was a very crude bachelor's quarters where a small cooking fire might be kindled against an end wall of stone, with or without a *lum*. As in the Highland "black houses," smoke was often left to find its own way out through the thatch and crevices. Habitations all over the world used to come with and without chimneys.

The milk cow was kept in the house, according to one witness who wrote that his mother knew it was time to put the porridge on the fire when she heard the cow standing behind her pass water for the second time. I hope the witness was lying. I have to guess that the cow was not in the *ben* itself, but rather in the attached cowshed portion of the motel-like structure. Maybe the partition was very thin, or even had a dutch-door sort of closure.

> Wi'kindly welcome Jenny brings him (into the) ben.
> A strappin' youth; he takes the mother's eye;
> - - - But now the supper crowns their simple board.
> The halesome parritch (wholesome porridge), chief
>   o' Scotia's food;
> The sowpe (milk) their only hawkie (cow) does afford,
> That 'yont (beyond) the hallan (partition) chows
>   her cood (chews her cud).
>
> The Cotter's Saturday Night
> by Robbie Burns - 1785

Crude as they were these living arrangements which made use of the animal heat to temper the winter cold and were on some of the best arable land, were a century later than the more crude habitations of Queen Mary's time. We will catch further glimpses of daily life as we try to pick out our ancestors from among the largely barefooted women and hard driven men keeping body and soul together in the sixteenth century Lowlands.

There are numerous reasons to believe that our people were better situated than the average Border family. For example, both the mother and the father had sophisticated backgrounds and experience which no Border farmer could equal or even understand.

The man, raised in Dieppe, was city-wise, and had seen some of the best tradesmen and craftsmen in France at work. The mother had an education unequalled among the "farmtoun" women, or even among the Edinburgh women of her day. It does not trouble me to believe that both of these people were capable of adapting to the diminished status of farmer. In that century, life was what it was, and frills were never guaranteed. If we were to make comparisons with the United States of today we would not come out so well, considering the millions who can neither read nor write, nor have a family to live with. There was muscle-work aplenty then, but now hordes of people find themselves useless in our technological labor market.

Most rural Scots were properly described as peasants, but they often lived by increasingly higher standards of principles and education, especially in later decades. In these rudimentary dwellings, the *gudeman* read books, the Bible in particular. The children had their own little moralistic tracts, and the *hinds*, who were skilled farm-hands, often had cheap pamphlets called chap-books bought from travelling chapmen. Some would read aloud, and debate fine points with vigor and skill. Perhaps disparity describes humanity, and it is impossible to tell about the best, the worst, the drunk and the sober, and come out with a true picture. The best we can do is lay out some of the elements found in those times. The changes from decade to decade were not great, but the speed of change and improvement was accelerating as never before, and a lifetime could make a difference. In the dark ages a lifetime didn't make a particle of difference; lives were lived in timeless monotony. Later, reading materials, which had always been very scarce, became plentiful as paper-making and printing shops opened up. In time, Scotland became the envy of Europe in agriculture, education, and fastidious dress, besides leading all in shipbuilding and other commercial pursuits. Over-compensation was at work.

Prior to their marriage in the palace, the bride and the groom occupied an in-between world comparable to that of servants in any grand mansion. A lady-in-waiting was not in any true sense a servant, but she was there to perform a service - highlighting and reflecting the queen's moods, a delicate ballet. The stable-boy, too, must have served expertly in his role with the queen's horses, where he certainly wore distinctive livery. Thus, they were well accustomed to the ways of the great people. Outside the palace, they had no special status, but it would have been very strange if the young woman were not identified and well known among upper class families. It could have been possible that her family had very limited resources. There were very rich people in Scotland, and there were very poor noblemen, too.

The clans, tartans, kilts, bagpipes, crofts, lochs, clearances, and the beautiful Highland scenery and the Gaelic language are not part of our story. I learned this definitely when I searched Scottish directories for the name Dippie in 1985. I found one in the Highlands, against some twenty in the Lowlands. In the long ago, we were more enemies than countrymen. My grandmother said we were Lowlanders, and that was the first time I had ever heard the word used. She was undoubtedly quoting her father, Charles Campbell, telling her about the four clans in her own family, besides that of her new mother-in-law, a McKenzie. She told me stories, one of which I especially remembered: her Grandfather, William Munro, an Orangeman, had been beheaded in Ireland.

In 1561, when Mary returned, almost no Scot had been to the American Continent and returned to tell of his experiences. Spain, Holland, and England, but not Scotland, sent out most of the expeditions. There were Scotsmen still alive who could remember hearing that Spanish ships had gone to India by sailing west, not east, and that they had returned. It had been good news to learn that they had not fallen off the edge of the world. The Vikings, of course, had gone to the new world 500 years before Columbus, but even we didn't learn about that for another 300 years, for they left barely a trace of their presence to be discovered in the 1800s.

By the time of Mary, Edinburgh had long had a protective city wall, making space for housing very cramped as the population slowly grew. The city was less than a mile long, and much narrower. Some of the worst wooden tenements in Europe were jammed on the rocky spine that held the ancient castle high in the air above the whole city. High Street, now called the Royal Mile, ran rather steeply down through Nethergate in the wall and through Canongate, to Holyroodhouse a mile from the castle. Water could quickly run off this ridge, but stinking piles of solids accumulated, to be worked over by dogs, but seldom by men with shovels and carts. There were a number of French people living in these tall and noisome tenements. They presumably brought a new sense of refinement to their neighbors, for a warning in French began to be heard. The Scots picked up the cry, and before throwing their slops out the window would shout "gardy loo" - their vernacular for *gare l'eau*, "watch out, water." Pedestrians could jump, or else. So Scots learned some French. For the tenants upstairs, a more convenient disposal method was invented which was less likely to soil the walls of their house. A booth could be built projecting out from the apartment. The alley below, which was called a *wynd*, was deluged without the *gare l'eau* warning. Men could be hired to thread their way through these sewer-like streets, and *wynds*, carrying a sedan-chair passenger. Edinburgh, now one of the world's most refined and beautiful cities, was often devastated by disease in those terrible centuries.

The history of the Romans in Scotland began before 100 A.D., and it is very interesting. The way we like to have it told is that Hadrian built his fortified wall from Newcastle to Carlisle, from sea to sea, in the years 122-128, to hold back the Scots and Picts who were too fierce to conquer. That may do to tell, but is not the whole story. These native people were fierce fighters, elusive, courageous, extremely hardy, and intelligent in learning from their culturally advanced enemies. The legions did find these northern barbarians difficult, but since they had nothing that the Romans really wanted, the soldiers built the wall mainly to avoid fighting all the time. The legions were filtering back to Rome from all their frontiers as their empire disintegrated throughout the fifth century from the rot in Rome, itself. Among the things they left behind when they withdrew were five tons of new nails, a million, a portion of which I saw in the National Museum of Antiquities in Edinburgh. A singular revulsion at the sight took me again to Golgotha, and to the Colosseum. I had been to these places where the Romans had used spikes like these but not for building. The Border people had never experienced peace and quiet for any length of time, nor would they until nearly the 18th century.

Various animals, including horses, were undoubtedly legacies of the Romans, just as American Indians who had never seen horses, sheep, or goats, built up big herds from those that strayed or were stolen from the Conquistadors about the time Mary came home from France.

Derision has often been focused on the Scot's thriftiness, but such mean remarks about his tightfistedness and canny dealings may be tinged with jealousy. The fact is that most Scots had little or nothing in their fists. If one did, it was because he had been canny and hard working. They were "cute" as my father said, meaning shrewd. When my schoolmates said cute, they meant a pretty girl. That word acquired two meanings for me in 1920, as I began to be aware of words my father used differently. Scots were cute by his definition, but definitely not cute the way my schoolmates had it. There was charity in Scotland, but in general it was cold charity. Thriftiness was an essential trait. If you botched up, or your plans failed, or your food ran out, you found your own solutions, or you could very well weaken and die before March was out and green weeds with their vitamins began to provide a bit of sustenance.

Just as the sewerage system in Edinburgh no longer depends on gardy loo, so too the legal system has evolved. In trying to learn how life was in mid-century, when the queen returned, I found one example forty years in the future to illustrate Scottish jurisprudence. In 1600, the famous Gowrie conspiracy transpired. Three years later, the bones of Sir Robert Logan were exhumed, placed on trial for high treason, convicted, and a sentence of forfeiture was pronounced. By this legal procedure the crown seized the assets of

The Sixteenth-Century Lowlands 41

the estate. No one to this day knows if there really was a conspiracy, or where blame lay, but a "just" verdict was rendered, and the assets turned over to the Lord High Treasurer.

Everyone lived under a pall of superstition observed today only by followers of the 3000-year-old pagan worship of stars and planets called astrology. The old Scots had their own mumbo-jumbo. They did not live under as black a cloud of fearful beliefs as did the Romans, who were completely under the control of "fates," but they were beset by fears at every turn. One element of their superstition had its roots deep in antiquity: witchcraft. There were also rites to foster fertility in crops and livestock.

The persecution of witches was a fact of life that began and ended almost exactly within the lifetimes of our first Melrose family. Starting the year before our stable-boy came from Dieppe, and ending at about the time his great-granddaughter, Euphemia, died, the murder of witches was justified by the new church with its Old Testament emphasis. In Scotland, from 3000 to 4500 witches were burned. Burning alive was preferred, but there were other horrible ways. In England, with five times the population, perhaps one thousand were killed, and in New England, only about six.

Things were even worse in Holland. In the weighhouse in Oudewater, south of Amsterdam, I saw records of 20,000 death warrants signed by one official. Some warlocks were killed, but almost always it was old women who had babbled in their poverty-stricken dotage. Perhaps they had tried to get paid for a proverb or a cure. We were told in Holland that family members were sometimes the accusers. During our visit there, my wife got a certificate from the weighmaster showing that her weight proved she was not a witch.

In Scotland, this blot, not on some savage tribe, but rather on Scottish Presbyterian leaders, came from theologians interpreting the Bible, and this _after_ the Reformation had cleansed the Church. This was a "forward" step, since it led to the "enlightened" present time, where we only destroy entire ecosystems. The witches were almost always poor country women, not the better situated city people. Probably no prominent and well-off citizen was ever burned as a witch; their role was to act as judges. Treason and other crimes were punished by fearsome means that were all part of the social atmosphere of those times. In Canongate, this fear was unquestionably less than in the Border villages and towns where most of our family remained, keeping their thoughts to themselves.

Superstition seems always to involve fear of some kind of harm, as well as a means of averting the harm. Little is now remembered of such beliefs except in a joking way. Black cats, walking under ladders, and saying "bless you" or "gesundheit" so the devil can't snatch away your soul during a sneeze, are some of the old precautions still in use. In the Highlands, but to a degree in the Lowlands of the sixteenth century, the Beltane fires, kindled with elaborate ceremony, preoccupied the attention of all country people, but especially herdsmen. One can judge the extent of these ceremonies by the fact that they were still prevalent into the eighteenth century. They were part of the Easter celebration, but buried not very deeply in the symbolism there were traces of human sacrifice by burning, once believed to help secure a good harvest.

The Beltane fire had to be kindled by friction of a wooden spindle twirled against an oak board by three-times-three men or three times nine; there were many variations. (In starting a fire by friction, as a Boy Scout, I preferred cedar and elm, or even yucca, for my spindle and hearth.) The Beltane observance required that ceremonial oat-cakes be eaten. These were ordinary bannocks, but made with special knobs on them that had some ancient meaning. There were many other ritualistic procedures. The celebrants spent the first two days of May at these rites, which were carried out on a hilltop where a trench had been dug around a table-like section of undisturbed turf so people could sit with their feet in the trench and eat food placed on this table. Harking back to heathen times, there were ceremonies of leaping through fires to symbolize human sacrifice. These people didn't know what all these antics meant.

They just knew their ancestors had taught them to do so on the first of May. Tradition, more accurate than script, had passed down the formula, and for how long? At least 1000 years, but with the modification that people were no longer actually burned. I believe the Beltane fires have not burned now for a long time, but our ancestors at least knew about them. When I was a boy and visited my grandmother in Pennsylvania, all this had simmered down to leaving wildflowers on her porch on Mayday, and then hiding until she came out her door.

These ritualistic observances were noisy and competitive, as a "victim" was selected who was to be a pariah through the following year. Such rough celebrations became annual times of play. There had to be some form of relaxation for the young men and women, too. On Sundays, after church, rough horseplay often served to work off the boredom and stifling strictures of the workweek routines. Besotted drunkenness and all degrees of inebriation incapacitated far too many men and women of the time. The making of ale at home was given a high priority, and it consumed a large share of the agricultural effort. The barley, or *bear*, was largely used to make ale.

An era in Scottish history that had a profound influence throughout the Lowlands coincided with the advent of the surname Depo. Hendre and his new wife became Border people when they were settled on land of Melrose Abbey. When they arrived they could have had no notion of what it meant to be Borderers. War with England had subsided into Border skirmishes, as often as not instigated by the Scots raiding in England. London was far away, and merely noted the sectional strife. Edinburgh was not able to intervene effectively, so these people were left to fight among themselves. Sometimes men from both sides collaborated, and sometimes marriages occurred, which made it awkward if a blood feud was in progress. These raiders and reivers had the upper hand for generations on end, but slowly came under control about the time Hendre was in his sixties, and his children had families of their own. The word reiver will not be found in many modern dictionaries, but the root "reave," of bereave, shows that these people were plain and simple robbers, in spite of any mawkish sentimentality about their heroics. They would burn down a widow's hut with her in it if her village needed to be given a lesson. And they would sleep well that night.

Three dozen of the great Border families that are named in *The Steel Bonnets*, by George M. Fraser, were notorious raiders, or, as they said, riding families, for the words "raiding" and "riding" were synonyms, as were "road" and "raid." Of all these families, the Armstrongs were the most powerful and dangerous, for they could assemble 3000 mounted men. The Elliots, with their name spelled some 70 different ways, sometimes allied with the Armstrongs as masters of the territory surrounding Liddesdale, Eskdale, and Annandale. This is next to the border, south of Melrose. These and more than thirty other notorious "ever riding" families never ceased their forays. Most of the raiding was done in the winter months. It was indeed fortunate that our new family was on land more than twenty miles north of the most destructive reiver activities. None of the predatory riding-families were within convenient cattle or sheep driving range of our people. Defenseless cottagers from sea to sea dared not mention a name, or complain. If children grew up to be taciturn, this was one of a number of reasons, for this mode of living had lasted about 300 years, until the kingdoms were united under James, the king of both. As we all know, he was the son of Mary and Darnley.

There has long been a notion that the reivers did not like to kill a man. When you read the record, the reluctance turns out to be just a fable. Horses and cattle were favorite targets of the thievery, but gold, silver, and even the smallest hoards of pence and shillings were never overlooked. In the process of searching, thatched roofs were set ablaze to keep up a desirable level of fear among the population. Bandit and robber are blunt but correct terms for these lawless men.

The raiders could cover forty to seventy miles a day when necessary. There is abundant evidence that reivers, both English and Scottish, could be armed and riding quickly. John Maxwell, of Herries, said that 350 could be assembled in thirty minutes. Working alone, or in twos and threes, they would steal cattle to feed their families instead of farming and risking loss of their crops to other robbers. Such routine thievery was commonplace even among acquaintances. Blackmail as a virtual insurance policy forced peasants to pay what amounted to double rents. The Grahams, who were notorious blackmailers, had bands of riders and enforcers working for them. They defined their demands for protection money in the Latin phrase *pro clientalia*. The poor who were unable to pay were "daily ridden upon and spoiled." The reiver's biggest hauls though, were often coups, wherein they stole from each other. Referring to *The Steel Bonnets* for a slight idea of what was meant by "riding," we find that in one example, thirty Elliots stole a widow's four oxen, six cows, her one horse and all her possessions. Later, another woman's husband and another man were murdered, and her herd of forty driven off by the same reivers. Dickie Armstrong and one hundred followers drove off two hundred head of Hecky Noble's cattle. They also destroyed nine houses and burned alive her son John and his pregnant daughter-in-law.

The Grahams, with both English and Scottish roots, were top-ranked despoilers, but specialized in blackmail, extortion, and intrigue. When Queen Mary's son became king of both countries, the Grahams were savagely dealt with, perhaps partly because they could be relieved of some of the best properties in the Borders. Their persecution became an epic of banishment, executions, confiscation and harrying never equalled for cruelty in British history. But they always tried to get back to their homeland. Under assumed names, including their name spelled backwards, they returned often, to their deaths, or to re-transportation. They were transported to the Low Countries, and then to southern Ireland, but few stayed. The story of the Grahams makes your blood run cold - first for their victims, then for them.

I have to use restraint in describing the Border people, for my connection is too remote to give me much license, but I do claim some. The author of *The Steel Bonnets*, though, is a native who tells the story without hedging. His harsh summary that no man could walk unarmed or trust that his beasts and goods were secure is believable. Until about 1625, these people had "lived in a jungle by jungle rules" for some 300 years. To put it mildly, he says this experience had a lasting effect on the people who lived there. While the young Shakespeare was writing his plays and England was relatively calm, the peasants on both sides of the border were dominated by fire and sword. The reiver was a professional gangster of superb skill, posing as an agricultural laborer, or with gradations of status up to a peer of the realm. George MacDonald Fraser, the author, says that the credit side outweighing all the rest is the Border virtue of staying power. The ability to endure unchanging is to be found in these people. In spite of everything, they have survived and carried their tenacity to every part of the globe. If the Borderer seems close, tough, and dour even today, remember that he lives in the shadow of ancestors who survived raid, theft and bloody murder.

This chaotic turmoil ruled throughout the 1500s. Borderers, great and small, but especially the helpless small people, lived under the constant threat of the reivers. Robbery, burning, and sometimes death at the hands of neighbors and lairds instilled continual fear. This among people who were self-respecting, but virtually paupers, barely subsisting, eking out a tiny oat and sheep crop by selling a hide, catching a fish, earning a few pence, and by contriving in ways we cannot even imagine.

Neither Queen Mary nor her father, King James V, nor her son, King James VI during his regency, were able to suppress the banditry and establish order in the Borders. The highwaymen ruled at night, and the smoke of burning was their signature. Keeping your mouth shut, your possessions hidden, and escape routes for cattle and family planned beforehand were the first rules of life.

The Sixteenth-Century Lowlands

> Through Solway sands, through Taross moss
> Blindfold, he knew the paths to cross
> Alike to him was time or tide,
> December's snow or July's pride;
> Moonless midnight or matin prime.
>
> - Sir Walter Scott

A settled and reasonably secure existence had never been experienced by the people of this sparse, barely habitable land. Perhaps if they were not effervescent, exuberant, and profligate in spending, the reasons are not difficult to discern. Where else, for instance, are thistles for food a cherished memory, kale a luxurious vegetable, and the discovery of turnips just a few generations ago, utter bliss?

If this environment made the Borderers hardy, it also made them fiercely independent, some say stubborn and contentious. Be it noted that the people of Europe were not in the midst of a golden age either. There were unspeakable atrocities on the continent, but with a difference. Aristocrats of various stripes there inflicted personal wars and depredations on the helpless populace. For an example, ride down the Rhine and observe the robber barons' castles. Scots fought, but not often to satisfy their ruler's personal greed. That was a vital difference that helped the Scot stand up like a man. Scottish industry and inventiveness came to the fore in the next three centuries, as history and literature show.

Our unsuspecting young Frenchman and his lady were dropped into the midst of this chaos in the Borders. Those who are their descendants should note that very important facts apply to this family, and in some ways to it alone. They were outsiders. They had no centuries-old family feuds or family connections hanging like millstones around their necks. This meant that they were not especially marked for pillage, theft or murder. Perhaps it was recognized that not only the queen, but, even more importantly, the Earl Bothwell, had a custodial interest in them. He and his confederates were fearsome, and not to be crossed for some trifling gain.

Looking at the riding families geographically, their depredations were greatest from Liddesdale west toward Carlisle. East of Bothwell's Hermitage Castle in Liddesdale, reiving went on, but the anarchy seems to have been on a lesser scale. Some governmental efforts at control had been exercised through these centuries in that area more than in the western marches. The English had also made some impression on the raiders, for Newcastle and Berwick were important to them. Even a slight perspective on the relative safety of west versus east fits the new family into a certain niche in the history of the Borders. The children and grandchildren left the Melrose farmstead, and went east, never west. There are records, especially in the Dippie/Dixon family, that place them in these Northumbrian towns: Ford, Etal, Wark,and Wooler; as well as the border towns of Berwick, Tweedmouth and Coldstream. They also lived in Chirnside, Coldingham, and Duns, which are Scottish towns just north of Berwick-on-Tweed. These people made their living in towns, but in doing so they conform to a well-recorded migration. Thousands of Scots had settled in Northumberland, England, by 1587, especially on the very borders. Our people were there among them. Some English towns had more Scots than English. Furthermore, they engaged in merchandizing, as did our people, giving severe competition to the English. As we have taken pains to document elsewhere, the Canongate and Edinburgh were the home towns of a daughter and two sons and their descendants who never spelled their name Dippie. In the course of time, however, that spelling eventually displaced all others. This distinct separation of the family Depo into what might be called two regional divisions fits perfectly into the history of the times. The father and mother must have been appalled as they found what a lawless environment they had so graciously been set down in. Three of their children were sent to live in the capital, and the rest married neighbors or at least stayed in the Borders, especially in the area near Berwick.

It may not be immediately obvious, but everything we have outlined was carried out in a religious atmosphere. Perhaps what we have said can even give an insight into the conduct of church affairs at that time. When the Presbyterian reformers did away with the Catholic Church, they then specified inflexible rules of worship. Those who didn't conform were subjected to intense pressures. The stocks were used routinely. If that didn't "learn them," as the Scotch I used to know would say, then the women, especially, got their *craigs* (necks) put in the *joug* at the church door. Others were induced to improve their worship by having a *lug* nailed to a post. If having a hole in your ear wasn't sufficiently Christianizing there were the pit and the gallows. Since it was un-Christian to hang women, the worst offenders were drowned in the pit. Gallows were prominent everywhere, usually on Gallows Hill. These features of Presbyterianism were so revolting to the tough soldiers of Cromwell's army when they came through the Borders, that they destroyed these religious accessories. So things got better gradually, for the advance of religion is a picture painted with a broad brush. Fine details don't show. Cromwell's soldiers and the "killing time" of the late 1600s were steps ahead, though many were hurt along the way. High school kids who learn all about why there is a Bill of Rights in our Constitution may not understand all they think they know about freedoms, but the writers of that document knew almost at first hand, or from grandparents, what it meant to have freedoms denied.

CHAPTER IV

THE FRENCH CONNECTION

The Protestant Reformation begun by Martin Luther in 1520 spread rapidly across Europe, and in each country the breakaway from the Roman Catholic Church had a leader. In Scotland, the firey John Knox was the man. The often atrocious events of the Reformation lasted for many generations. Religion drove the politics of those times. The Earl Bothwell, who forced Mary into a squalid, but Protestant, marriage to him, was completely indifferent to religion. He simply wanted to be king. Mary was putty in his hands, and she let him lead her to destruction.

In August, 1560, three acts of Parliament had abolished both Papal jurisdiction and the Mass in Scotland. Exactly a year later the teenage queen could not have comprehended the full import of her going into such an upheaval, and she a Catholic. John Knox, the Reformer, must be kept in perspective. He had received the education of a priest, had been sent as a captive to the French galleys for very little cause, was liberated through English influence, and was made a Royal Chaplain in 1551. When Mary got to Scotland, she alone was permitted to have a priest in her private chapel. Very likely, all of her attendants and servants converted. An interesting conjecture is that every one of them, except two hostlers from Dieppe, had always been Catholic. We can be practically certain that they were Huguenot, or Bothwell would not have chosen them to go to now Protestant Scotland, but that is another chapter. No one in Scotland had any choice about his denomination unless he chose to be outside the law. The Highlands, as always, were a law unto themselves, and some sort of Catholicism persisted there, unreachable among the crags and fierce clans. One can only wonder how this switch in thinking and ritual was accomplished throughout the land, unless, of course, one chose to read dozens of books on the depressing subject. Only Mary's priest was exempt from the threat of death for saying the Mass.

The Reformation included the expropriation of Church property, including the riches and extensive holdings of Melrose Abbey. Its adminstration and income were in the hands of a secular commendator. A bailey court, which convened twice a year, gave him powers of enforcement. Many individuals farmed the land, and paid rent as their forbears had paid their Abbott. The new couple from the palace started as renters at Melrose. They and their children became part of the tangled web of history, like a few fibers in a coat, not visible, but there nevertheless, helping hold the fabric together. History books spin out the generalized web, but rarely notice the little fibers in it. The biographers of Mary all but mention the three people who were our beginning. The three of them were playing their bit parts on her stage, helping to keep the spotlight on the prima donna, but only for a year or two. Alexander Depo played more than a bit part, for he was reported murdered, or was it his young son? That story has to wait its turn.

It was also in 1560, on December 5, that Francis II, the seventeen-year-old King of France, died. His eighteen-year-old widowed Queen was Mary Stewart, or Stuart, as it is spelled in French. We have told how Mary had been taken to the French Court at the age of six with all ceremony, and was trained to become the bride of the Dauphin. Her mother, who was her regent in Scotland, visited her in France when she was eight, but they never met again.

In the course of events, Mary became Queen Matrimonial of France, but her Scottishness was there under the veneer of French sophistication. The Scottish lords had never relaxed, for they knew the possibility existed that she could become their Queen Regnant. Thus, as her leading biographer puts it, there was "an endless string of ladies-in-waiting, maids-of-honor, and equerries" in attendance.

Her train of Scottish noblemen's sons and daughters was matched by an equal number of children of the French nobility, a train of perhaps thirty to be educated together. Mary was the Queen of Scotland and the intended queen of France, and thus the focus of attention and deference in this group, including its adult staff. She even had an uncertain claim to the English throne. She alone had special tutors and royal treatment almost beyond modern comprehension, for this was France at the height of extravagance. The education of the Dauphin was not neglected, nor should he have been lonesome, for he had an entourage of thirty-seven pages of honor. Incredible expenses were incurred in the royal French establishment, and unseemly economy could not be practiced by the Scots. This was a bilingual world for the Scottish children, but French became their more natural language. Mary was perfectly fluent in colloquial Scots, the language she had learned as a child, and which she was never allowed to forget.

The incredible luxury of Mary's upbringing from the age of six to eighteen needs to be factored into any astonishment one might have that in the future she favored one of her ladies-in-waiting with a wedding, and the gift of a farm tenancy to the husband who had brought a touch of French manners with him as he brought her French horses to be ridden. Such gifts could have meant no more to Mary than mere gestures, yet the sentimental connection with these little people was the essence of her inner nature. In her dealings with powerful people she was wrong too often; consider Darnley, Bothwell, Queen Elizabeth, and the good advice she would not take, especially when she insisted on throwing herself on the mercy of the English queen. She found no mercy there. She was at her best giving happiness to unimportant people, dressing up, and dancing the night away after some light-hearted frivolity such as a household wedding. This she did with the censorious John Knox only half a mile up High Street, poised to thunder denunciations from his pulpit. Her "French fillocks, fiddlers and others of that band" made the place more like a brothel than a place for honest women, he preached, but he could scarcely denounce weddings between palace servants.

Mary's familiarity with luxury beyond comprehension is not only interesting to read, but needs mention if one is to understand the jolting comedown when she came to Holyroodhouse. When she was nine, her nursery had accommodated twenty-two lap dogs, and four big ones. There were falcons, birds and always horses. Two bears were sent to her as gifts, and the children were provided with a veritable zoo. Actors and acrobats entertained them. Every few months the children were moved from castle to palace in a continual game of musical chairs. One palace of 400 rooms was overwhelming; but it and five others dwarfed what Mary found when she moved into her Scottish palace, where she was queen in her own right.

Thirteen miles from Paris, down the river Seine, the castle Saint Germain-en-Laye, situated on a hill, was begun around 1124 A.D. Many kings lived there through the centuries of its building, razing, and rebuilding. More than 10,000 acres of forest bordered it; now it is engulfed in upscale residential developments where my son Bruce enjoyed a holiday absorbing the realization that an ancestress had lived in the castle for years. It was a bit unsettling to me when I read, in a famous biography of the queen, that this castle is in the Loire valley which is many miles from Paris and the Seine.

Henri II and his wife, Catherine de'Medicis, lived there with his mistress, Diane de Poitiers, in the apartment just below. She became a second mother to the royal children and to Mary's Scottish ladies-in-waiting. Three future kings and their sisters, Elizabeth, Claude, and Margaret, also lived in the labyrinth of rooms, corridors, wings, courtyards, and vast gardens, grounds and lesser residences. Mary, the tiny Queen of Scots, was absorbed into this menage where the only familiar forms for the first years were Scottish children, one of whom we shall follow with especial interest, for she subsequently met and married her queen's stable-boy. The royal sons, Charles and Henri, became Kings IX and III, respectively, after their older brother had married Mary, had become King Francis II, and had died, all before he was 17.

The French Connection

After the death of the young King there was no place for Mary in France. After thirteen years absence she would go home to be reigning queen, leaving the malevolent Catherine de'Medicis, her mother-in-law and niece of the Pope, to deal with the French situation. Both were widows of kings, but Mary was still the Queen of Scots, and her countrymen rejoiced to know she was returning. Eleven years later it was Catherine who ignited the massacre of St. Bartholomew's Eve, using her deficient son, Charles, then king, for the authorization. Within a few weeks, upwards of 10,000 Protestant Huguenot men, women, and children would be killed by rampaging French Catholic mobs in a madness that would not cease in that century.

An eight-month mourning period was observed after the death of Mary's husband. Then the extremely able Lord High Admiral of Scotland was placed in charge of managing the move to Mary's native land. He was James Hepburn, 4th Earl of Bothwell. Months of preparation culminated in the departure of Queen Mary from Calais on August 14, 1561. Her two shiploads of horses were shipped from Dieppe.

The best report of her departure and travel through the North Sea is in a letter that the English Earl of Rutland wrote to Lord Cecil for the information of Queen Elizabeth. She had delayed giving a safe conduct to Mary in advance of her departure, so the fleet sailed expecting to be waylaid. As we shall see, Mary's two shiploads of horses were impounded, but that was probably an unconnected incident. Rutland's letter reported:

> "...two great galleys, the greater being all white, the other colored red; she bare a blue flag with the arms of France, and in her stern another white flag glistening like silver. At the same instant there appeared, a good distance from the galleys, thirty-two sail of tall ships and shortly after further off twenty-sail...P.S...Is credibly informed that divers ships laden

with the Scottish Queen's provisions are landed at Inchkeith and Dunbar."

Sir Nicholas Throckmorton, a sort of minister, often without portfolio, wrote more precisely to Elizabeth: "The writer's servant coming by Calais, saw the Queen of Scotland haling out of that haven on the 14th instant, about noon, with 2 galleys and 2 great ships."

This expedition moved with both sails and prisoner oarsmen. The trip of 600 miles took five days rather than the customary seven, even though Mary forbade that the rowers be whipped as was usual. The ships carried magnificent furnishings for her palace: furniture, turkish rug, utensils, and fine materials of every description. Mary's jewels, equal to a national treasure, she kept with her, saying that if she were safe to go to sea, why then so were her jewels.

As I watched television coverage of the closing ceremonies of the Statue of Liberty Centennial festivities on July 4, 1986, there was an exhibition by a French equestrian team that fascinated me. Just then I was writing about the thirty horses Queen Mary sent to Scotland. I do not know, but I suspect that this present day team was performing a routine that had entertained a royal party 417 years before at a tournament where King Henry II was wounded, to die on July 10, 1559. The Dauphin became King Francis II that day, at the age of fifteen-and-a-half. His father had already jousted, but late in the day insisted on one more passage-at-arms with a friend who reluctantly agreed to the order. Wounded in eye and throat, the King could not live, and so precipitated the history of Mary in Scotland, and all the events we write about, including creation of our family.

On the television screen there were, as best I could make out, thirty beautiful, big, matched, chestnut horses. The helmets of the riders trailed bright plumes falling to the saddles. The uniforms and caparisoned horses seemed straight out of a medieval pageant, which was indeed true. The riders sounded horns, and a strong drum cadence came from large, flat pairs of drums fastened astride some of the saddles. Four spokes, of five horses each, rotated in perfect formation around a hub of horses, then the pattern dissolved into a series of other figures. The horses were perfect performers, and I wondered how they had come 3000 miles from France; not on slow Dutch freighters, I was sure. They flew, I suppose, for Pegasus flew, I had learned in grade school.

In the account I was writing, Mary's horses were just as beautiful, we can assume, but trained for riding, not performing; nor would they be meticulously matched. Some would stand out as individuals, for she would have had special favorites for processional duties, for hawking and cross-country chases. Each of her ladies, too, would need to have her favorite taken to Scotland. There would have been two carriage horses, and mules to carry picnic hampers and to demonstrate their utility to the Scots. Brood-mares would be taken with an eye to the future. Quite a lot of thought went into choosing which horses were to go. Saddles and gear were to be made in Edinburgh.

Taking the horses from Paris to Dieppe must have resembled an exhibition performance. Perhaps for three days the procession must have created a sensation through the countryside, with advance men arranging for feed and overnights as needed. Possibly the half dozen or so hostlers rode their own horses, with each one controlling five of the herd. However it was done, it was a brilliant show. At the port, the Earl and his agents must have been arranging for ships with stabling to be installed, and hay, grain, and water stowed. The horses coming down the road were responding to the commands of their French Catholic hostlers, but after embarkation they would be responding to French Protestant, Huguenot handlers. The demarkation was hard and fast. Two able men had to be engaged who were not only competent, but Protestant, for they were going to Scotland, which had changed its religion in 1560, and this was 1561, in August.

The Huguenots numbered between three and four hundred thousand. A large proportion of these were in the skilled occupations, largely city people in trades, commerce and manufacturing. The people of Dieppe, especially, favored the new religion. Bothwell, who had been educated in Paris, was fluent in French. In this busy port city he and his agents would have had no difficulty in finding qualified men to handle the horses on each of the two ships needed. It will be seen that events in the future often turned on the use of the French language. On many occasions apparently insignificant matters developed important consequences for our family. For instance, our very name was given to us by a Scot who knew no French, as I will explain later. If that man had been able to converse with our men from Dieppe he would not have entered their name in the official record book as Depo, but rather their actual French surname, and that would be our family name today. In that case, we would be hard pressed to convince people we were not French, no matter that, for nearly four hundred years, only Scots married into the family.

Later we will quote a contemporary account that all but states that one man was assigned to each ship to care for its load of animals, and that fifteen horses were carried on each ship. We call our ancestor a Frenchman, but might more accurately think of him as of Nordic blood, descended from Vikings that raided and settled along many shorelines at about the turn of the millennium. The river Arques breaks through the high white cliffs of the French coast to enter *La Manche*, the sleeve. (The French do not border on the "English Channel." They live along a body of water they called *La Manche*, for they did not need English help in naming their waterway). The Vikings and later the Normans found the deep channel scoured out of the constricting chalk cliffs to be one of the best of harbors. This outlet of the river was *diep*, in their tongue, and Dieppe became the name of the town built at this sheltered port, and it became our name too.

It would be strange to suppose that this man of Dieppe who became our ancestor had no family. All who sailed knew they might

The French Connection

never return. Those on the ships and those on the dock would have been full of assurances as they said their good-byes. As these people watched the animals gotten safely aboard, then saw the final casting off with the tide, what were their thoughts? None of them had an inkling of the terrible things that were to overwhelm those left behind just a year later, and again eleven years later when the Catholics descended on the Huguenots. Did the relatives and friends perish? Dieppe was especially hard hit, for it was strongly Protestant, and a thriving city ripe for jealous pillage.

Europe was erupting in wars of religion with even the Moslem Turks threatening from the Mediterranean. The March 1988 issue of the National Geographic sheds light on the scene in Dieppe. A year after our ancestor left, one of his townsmen, the famous Huguenot sea dog, Jean Rebault, came back to Dieppe after settling a colony on the coast of northern Florida. He found his city under seige by a Catholic army which captured it. Thus our ancestor escaped, but without doubt he lost relatives and friends in the fallen city.

The best we can hope for is that the very experience of the parting may have induced others to leave everything behind and escape without fatally delaying until St. Bartholomew's Eve. There was time, for that was in Paris years later, and a hundred miles away. The persecution and killing went on through generations of families, and we can hope that if we had any remote ancestors left in Dieppe, they went to Holland, England, or somewhere safe; no one would ever know, not even the ones who went to Scotland.

By working backwards from Mary's age of 18, we can guess her ladies-in-waiting were 17 or 18. She who married the French stable-boy would likely be younger than he. This would make him, and his name was André, around 19 or 20. Bothwell would not have hired him if he were married, for he knew, even if the young man did not, that a return to France was not in the cards. The French horses were more important than the man, and they needed their familiar care, not Scottish handling. The young man would not have been thinking about all of this, but would have been excited about working with the queen's beautiful animals. The not-married status makes it probable that André was close to 20 but not much less, for it was a very responsible job. Those people were very precocious about work. Very few of them lazed through to adulthood with neither an education nor work experience.

The other man, Alexander, is critically important to us because his name was recorded by the Lord High Treasurer of Scotland in 1564. This will be carefully studied later, for it establishes by the queen's own officer, that our name was in Scotland then. That, of course, is of no great historical importance, but this record, tied in with others by the same official, reveals many activities that are of historical interest. These are matters of Mary's reign that I have not seen recorded anywhere. It would be a digression here to do more than mention that a surprising puzzle has to remain unsolved about Alexander. The language of the report of his death is too ambiguous. It will be left to a later chapter to explain how this man may have been either André's brother or his father, but the ambiguity leaves room for thinking that André had a much younger brother who travelled with his father in one ship. Alexander could have been a widower taking his two sons to work with the queen's horses. Could he have surmised the danger that was overhanging the people of Dieppe? Was he so well qualified about horses that Bothwell would have no other? If the mother of the boys had died, was this an opportunity for them to leave some of the sorrow behind?

These surmises are important to the belief that our family tradition is compatible with history. It is rare good luck that records reveal so many data points of our beginnings, bench marks permitting us to reconstruct the in-between territory with considerable confidence. Reasonable projections beyond, and interpolations between, recorded data give a generally accurate picture of our family, just as in the construction of graphs one can legitimately fill in details between the hard data points.

CHAPTER V

THE MAGAZINE STORY OF 1909

Of all the people who returned to Scotland with the queen, our interest centers on one, a lady-in-waiting, one of many in the queen's nearly anonymous household who were all overshadowed by the four famous Maries. Nonetheless, as we have pointed out before, her family had to have been of the nobility. Scotland was top-heavy with nobility accumulated through a thousand years. A few were very rich, but mostly their fortunes varied all the way down to poor, and a good many were unscrupulous, to put it charitably. The many girls, as well as boys, surrounding Mary were truly her companions and playmates, for they were children together for a dozen impressionable years. The girls were her ladies-in-waiting, and the boys pages; none were selected or placed for political reasons except, perhaps, as a favor to the parents.

In no other court in Europe, such as that of Elizabeth of England, would such familiarity with the queen have been even imagined. Childhood, in those times, did not really exist as we know it. Babies were, of course, helpless, but the youngest children were put to work in the home or in commerce as incompetent adults, who were expected to improve in performance as they grew bigger and stronger, if their minds were not permitted to wander from the job they were set to. While there was no physical work for the children of the court to perform, they were certainly held to rigid forms and protocol. Edinburgh families undoubtedly provided many of the men, women, equerries, and other members of the young queen's establishment.

Later we will cite records of marriages and burials close to, and at, the Palace, which barely miss revealing the name of the Edinburgh family that we feel certain sent its wee lassie off to France to be a companion to her wee queen, eventually becoming the progenitress of our family. Sometimes such information is written down, but to this day, keepsakes, letters and pictures are thrown away because no one knows aught about them, or worse yet, someone considers them rubbish, and their ancestors as well. Agnes M. MacKensie comments in her book, *The Scotland of Queen Mary*, that "no fewer than eleven writers of the 15th and 16th centuries, with reputations, are sunk without a trace, not a line of their work (in Scots), survives."

When I began my search to discover how my name could possibly be Scottish, I had no expectation of finding any source material. Scotland is far away from Maryland, to say nothing of the other five states where I have been a resident, endeavoring to make some progress on this project. After a great deal of reading, and also travel in Scotland, I learned that fine distinctions are made between the Scots of the Highlands, the Lowlands, the Hebrides, the Borders, even between Dundee and Edinburgh. Their speech, values, and outlook, now, and in times past, show many variations. If the Unites States is a melting pot, Scotland is a stew kettle, except that the pot may now hold more Scots than the kettle. Most American Scots are probably only dimly aware of their ancestral homeland, proud as they may be to say they are Scottish.

Education in Scotland was ahead of England, the *Brittanica* says, with four Universities founded as early as 1411. Women in those days held a position alongside men far more equal than in other countries, yet much of my problem lies in the fact that women's names were not often written down, nor many records kept. Still, I can scarcely believe how many citations were generated by this family with its brand new name in Scotland. That very newness must have been significant in a neighborhood where a family name could be ten centuries old, and practically none were new. Ironically, and with characteristic conservatism, a prominent

Scottish genealogist informed me that my name couldn't be Scottish since it was not in Black's bible of surnames. This, after he gave me several useful citations of our name variants nearly 400 years old. Apparantly, a dozen generations of intermarriage with "real" Scots could not dilute the drop of blood of one Frenchman who gave us our name, at least not in his opinion. Ironically, Black, with no incentive to trace our name to its beginning, had only the erroneous information gleaned from an unsigned magazine story to put in his book of surnames of Scotland.

A lady-in-waiting and a stable-boy provided the entire motivation for my many years of search for the hidden meaning of a very simple statement. When I was 16 and my grandmother told me that our name started when "a lady-in-waiting to the queen married a stable-boy," I realized, even as a boy, that this family story had been handed down for a long time, and was very strange, but none of us thought of this in terms of transmitting a legend. I had never heard of Queen Mary. Kings and queens were foreigners. I was two generations removed from Scottish life and busy just trying to learn the names of our own Presidents. I knew nothing of the traditional obligation of grandparents to pass on family history. Grandma was of Highland stock, a Campbell, but she said her husband's people were Lowlanders. I know now that they too felt responsible to pass on this story, else it never would have survived. I would give anything to know details of which older person passed it on to which younger one. Obviously, far more young people heard it than passed it on, but a viable chain survived, link by link, in one branch of the family. Perhaps the very fact that this one family left its familiar home, and went to strange impersonal Glasgow, and then to the United States, made this story a comforting attachment to the past they were leaving. Through all the years, centuries, as a matter of fact, the chain held, and the statement survived.

No one that I have ever known had the powers of recollection of Grandma. I had just finished Ancient History in the ninth grade, and started to chart my mother's family as my history book charted kings. Then on one of our annual visits to Grandma and the relatives, I quizzed her, and recorded the things she told me on a chart that I still have. The chart is on a piece of butcher paper torn from a roll of paper washed three miles down to our house in the flood that destroyed the town where I was born. The Bayless Pulp and Paper Mill dam broke during the afternoon of September 30, 1911, at Austin, Pennsylvania, and devastated both Austin and the downstream town of Costello where we lived. I was three years old, and remember leaving our house, and walking with Mother, and my brother, Lawrence, to Grandma's, out of reach of the flood. I remember the mud left in our house, but not the water. The flood had moved our house, crushing the house next downstream. Many escaped because a man rode his bicycle ahead of the water for three miles shouting the warning that many had expected for years. The pieces of the huge dam, 50 feet high, still stand like open gates to testify to the criminality of its building.

THE AUSTIN FLOOD

> On the 30th day of September,
>   and such a pretty day,
> Without a moment's notice,
>   the Austin Dam gave way.
> With mighty force the waters rushed
>   toward our little town.
> The houses fell like toothpicks
>   and parts of them torn down.
> Now when I think of the disaster,
>   it nearly chills my blood;
> For I think of the wives and little ones
>   that perished in that flood.
>
>   [by an unknown balladeer.]

The names that I put on my first chart in 1924, were given to me by this septuagenarian woman without notes or hesitation. There were nine children in her family, all given in order. Her Father was Charles Campbell, and her mother, Isabella Munro, whose brothers and sisters I have in correct order. Charles had two brothers, and a sister, Isabella Craig.

My great-great-grandmother, Isabella Munro, (circa 18th century), was my grandma Janetta Campbell's grandmother. Isabella had married William Munro. They had their eight children, obviously before he was beheaded, but written history has to step in here. I have no dates, but Grandma said he was an Orangeman, and he was beheaded. This is part of the Ulster story, and has to be left at that.

From prehistoric Celtic times until now, when reading and writing are giving way to instantaneous blips on computer screens, history was oral except among the few scholars. Modern history continually confirms the accuracy of that oral history. Fabricated stories told for whatever reason don't last, but usually pass away with the fabricator. Events that are told about and retold, generation after generation, become stripped of embellishment until only the essential kernel of truth remains and the statement becomes rote, a formula or legend, no longer really understood. The tellers, however, accept the truth of the statement and their obligation to pass it on as the family tradition or, as they would say, the family story.

The lady-in-waiting and the stable-boy have not been named in the many accounts of weddings, masked ball celebrations, and festivities fomented, staged, and costumed by the queen, who, on occasion, even furnished wedding gowns. That she loved to play a part in weddings between members of her household is told and retold by her biographers. Her short reign was one of constant turmoil, and she found relief in the gay festivities of politically inconsequential weddings between members of the palace staff.

Grandma's story has the terse authentic ring of true legend. There is no need to adapt, alter, or explain. It jibes perfectly with published records of the time. Even by twisting, these data could not be made to negate the story she innocently repeated to me, and also to her children and my cousins. I know she knew nothing of a queen, for she had slight education. Her son Ervin, a Master of Science, and a World War I veteran of five battles, who visited Edinburgh with his wife, thought that our name might ultimately have had an Italian derivation. None of the relatives knew more than that the family had come from Glasgow, and were Scottish or Scotch-Irish, which Grandma, a Campbell, was. Many Scots had gone to Ireland, then back to Scotland or the United States during another involved period of turbulent Scottish history. I am sure that the youngest descendants today know virtually nothing of the origins of the family. My lifelong curiosity about this tradition, and our name, had to wait until my children were grown, and I felt I could start to investigate without feeling too guilty about the amount of time that it would take. I found that, in the year that I was born, *The Border Magazine*, published the first "research" that I have seen about the family. I quote both sentences:

> "Can any reader give me information respecting the family of Dippie, who, during the 17th or 18th century appears to have settled in Tweedside? It is said the family came from Dieppe during the Huguenot persecutions."

The following year, in 1909, an article signed "Dieppois," meaning "person from Dieppe," answered the query with what he calls a fragmentary list of the family, the only writing about our family that I have seen:

> "As time went on the family appears to have spread into Berwickshire, and Roxburghshire, and across the borders into Northumberland. The Parish Register of Wooller records the burial, in 1735 of William Deepy, a stranger; a David Dippie of Etal, born 1769, etc. The Northumberland Poll Book 1774 gives the name of Thomas Deepy as a freeholder in Wark-On-Tweed...The family in the early part of the last century were very numerous on Tweedside; there were

Dippies at Wark, Coldstream, Kelso, Berwick, Chirnside, Eyemouth, Sprouston, Ednam, and Edinburgh. They were found in England...etc."

American members of the family with the name so much like Dieppe will be astonished to know that in Scotland and other parts of Great Britain, only the spelling "Dippie," has survived. We who spell our name "Deppa" had it brought from Glasgow in 1850. It came pronounced with the inevitable Scottish diminutive "ie" tacked on. Now the "Deppie" pronunciation is virtually extinct, and the name is pronounced as it is spelled. Unbelieving shock would strike any Deppa of the last couple of generations if the old pronunciation were to be directed at them, yet that is how it was said, and occasionally still is. To say Deppa, incidentally, is beyond the power of that half of the population that always puts an "er" on words that lack "er," and leaves it off of words that do. This is a phenomenon of our "Southeren" brand of American English, but the problem reaches its extreme in Texas. This is, apparently, beyond their control, and we do not count it as a variant. The standardization of the name as "Dippie," apparently occurred in the southeastern Lowlands at the very time when spelling began to be recognized as a cultural objective in the 18th century and people in general gained the ability to read and write, and look with favor on correctness in these matters. Through all the years, at least twenty spellings have been used, even by siblings. The Deppa spelling will be traced later.

The list signed "Dieppois" was certainly written by one of the Borderland Dippies, and he seems to have written from personal knowledge and study. Perhaps no one else made any record at all of the family. His effort should be recognized as the only move ever made, except for public records, to give recognition to this unique family. On close scrutiny of his quoted sources, as contrasted to his personal knowledge, one finds that he fell into the trap of unwarranted attribution.

Most of his article, which I did not quote, but will comment on, was taken from a large and prestigious book published in 1886 for private circulation. This book is now very rare, and is not in the Library of Congress, nor three other large collections I tried.

The book is identified as:

Protestant Exiles from France, chiefly in the reign of Louis XIV, by the Reverend David C. Agnew, University of Edinburgh 3rd edition, Volume I, 1886.

The book is in the Harvard College Library, where Librarian Henri J. Bourneuf very kindly provided me with a copy of the title page and page 259. It had seemed impossible to find this book, but it turned out to be the key of keys to the origin of the fable that our family started as Huguenot refugees. Mr. Bourneuf said, "I found it after much lucky searching." All I had been able to tell him was what the *The Border Magazine* told me: the author's last name, Agnew, and the page number, with not even a hint as to the title of the book.

This is a very fine book, but "Dieppois" jumped to the incorrect belief that it said we were descended from Huguenot refugees. Then, to compound the error, Robert F. Black used the magazine article as the authority for his great work, *The Surnames of Scotland*. No one questions this prestigious book, so the word went out that the family Dippie has a refugee origin. To find this error is not, however, to reflect on any of the three authors whose work ran circles around each other. One has to remember that the best doctors used to bleed patients who would, today, be given, or rather sold, more blood. When these authors wrote, no one had yet dug into the records of the Lord High Treasurer of Scotland to find that Alexander Depo or his son, as we will explain, was slaughtered in Stichel in 1564, which was eight years before the Massacre of St. Bartholomew's Eve. That happened eleven years after our ancestor had landed with the queen's horses. Years or decades must have passed before refugees arrived in Scotland, if, indeed, any went to Scotland, which was distant, and not especially hospitable to strangers.

Agnew's book is mainly concerned with the many, many refugees to England, just a few miles from France by boat. He was specifically tracing this movement during the reign of King Louis XIV. This time-frame is nearly a century later than our non-refugee, man-from-Dieppe.

One excerpt from Agnew concerning a burial is very pertinent to our family history, for I will later link it directly to the first Depo family through Edinburgh records of the marriage of this person. To quote Agnew (page 259):

> "Eupham Deippe, relict of Robert Moreson, burgess of Canongate, was buried in the Abbey of Holyrood on 17th May, 1665."

King Louis reigned in the 17th and 18th centuries, but the first Depo went to Scotland in mid-16th century. This is an exhaustive, scholarly tome, but nowhere does it say or even imply, that our ancestor was a refugee or exile. The fact is that he was employed by the queen's agent in Dieppe to attend her horses being carried in one of two Dutch ships en route to Edinburgh. Although Agnew mentions Dippie, he does not say the name was connected with the refugees:

> "..I might give specimens of other names which are said to be Huguenot, and which date from an earlier period than 1685, for instance - Cousin, and Fish, [both with comments] Dippie. Robert Dippie, or Deippe, or Dippe, upholsterer and trunkmaker in Caldtoune, Edinburgh made a marriage contract October 7, 1663."

Then follows the note about Eupham, given above, and also the fact that a Peter Dippie died at about the same age and year that my great-grandfather departed this mortal coil, which doesn't much prove that we are descended from refugees. So much for the refugee fable. That's all there is.

Also, extraneous but interesting, is a long footnote which followed the above; I have abbreviated it somewhat:

> "A Scot named Thomson bought from the Papal Mint in the Vatican, in 1828, seven medals struck for him from the original die. This medal 'had been denied by the Romanists, and forgotten by the Protestants.' Pope Gregory XIII (de Medici), had it struck in 1572 to glorify the great achievement which he also memorialized by having bonfires lit all over France."

The medal is the *Ugonatorum strages*, which I construe "Massacre of the Huguenots." A specialist in the Smithsonian said they have one in bronze among their 850,000 pieces, 99% of which are not on display. Just before going to Scotland in 1985, I was in the Irish National Museum in Dublin where there were cases of Papal Medals. There, this fascinating medal lay for close inspection. About an inch and a half in diameter, the Latin inscription and date were set off by an angel complete with wings, on the left. In the foreground was a dead *Ugonotus* flat on his back. This Pope, in his first year, was thus misguided by his niece in typical Medici, Italian style. She had been the Queen of France until Mary supplanted her on the death of the old King. Later, and more constructively, Gregory updated the calendar of Julius Caesar which had been losing one day every 128 years for a long time. We now use the Gregorian calendar, but the English and Americans both waited a couple of centuries to make the change. By that time, our calendars were eleven days out of sync with the sun, and we had to drop those days from our history. The tombstones of last century often tell how many years, months and days a person had lived. That is because eleven days were lost to them, if their age were expressed in dates. The tombstone of Thomas Jefferson bears the date: born 1743 o.s. (old style).

Huguenot refugees did not flee to poor, poor Scotland either by the expensive 600 mile passage up the very dangerous North Sea or the much longer, but somewhat calmer Irish Sea to Glasgow. They fled on foot, or however they could, a few miles to the borders of Belgium, Holland, Poland. That first night of horror was signalled at two in the morning by church bells. Townspeople of the old religion, neighbors, murdered the Huguenots as they poured out of their houses at the sound of the bells. Rowboats and all kinds of little craft carried great numbers across the channel to Protestant England. The port city of Dieppe was especially inclined to the new Protestant faith, and it was hit more than many other parts of France.

From the Scottish archives, numerous bits and pieces verify, and name names, to flesh out the tradition preserved in the Deppa line from 1561. It can be traced out by following the queen's horses, and by the court records of her stable-boy throughout his long life in the parish of Melrose Abbey. I am certain it is now being written down for the first time. Although my grandmother told me the story, her oldest child, Sarah Elizabeth Deppa, who was my much loved Aunt Lizzie, repeated it when my relatives got together. She was born in 1867, and must have heard the story from her grandfather, James Deppa, as well as from her mother. He was born in Scotland in 1806 according to his death record. Thus a very numerous family had discussed this cryptic story and kept it alive.

As in the life of all family traditions, a time comes when the last person who knows the background, and the meaning behind the words, dies. Then the story becomes a code without specific meaning, but a ritual to be passed to descendants as a trust not to be neglected. Such an obligation may not be understandable nowadays. Jet travel, electronic gear to bombard our brains, broken families where parents are denigrated to justify breakups, and all the rest of our modern scene, means the end of oral history and traditions. Within the past dozen years since I have been working on my puzzle, I have talked with my Aunt Lilly, who died in 1988 at the age of 96. She was the widow of Uncle Ervin Deppa. I also talked with my older cousin, Florence, a former teacher, (died March 1989, almost 90), whose mother was my Aunt Lizzie, to see what they thought of the records I have found. Their main reaction was that they never had any idea what the story might really mean, except that it was a strange thing for a lady-in-waiting to the queen to marry a stable-boy. They knew nothing of Dieppe, nor did I, until I saw *Surnames of Scotland* in Edinburgh in 1969.

To recapitulate briefly: Our family began when a pleasant girl, probably from a Canongate family, lived in France with another child who was Mary, Queen of Scots. Then in about thirteen years this young woman, still living with the queen, fell in love with one of the many French palace servants, a stable-boy named Hendre Depo, and they were married. Since they all spoke French, but had no occasion to write, none of them knew, perhaps not even the man, that his name was in records as Hendre. That was the non-word the clerk had put in the time book. There was no need for saying any surname, so he was André to all of them, but we don't know the girl's name. It may be recorded somewhere, but we haven't found it.

This new family, named Depo, lived on a farm in the parish of ancient Melrose Abbey. It can be taken for granted that the children visited their mother's parents in the Canongate suburb of the Capital, which is adjacent to the Palace and about forty miles from the farm, which I have visited. A daughter, Katherine, who spelled her name Dippo, is all but recorded as having been brought up in the home of her grandparents. A number of records sustain the belief that two of her brothers also lived with the grandparents. The records also show that at least one grandaughter lived in the Canongate: Eupham Deippe Moreson, who was mentioned earlier. In the nature of things these three city offspring must have long lines of descendants extending to this day, including my own.

These records are laid out in detail in a later tabulation and discussion, but it is worth repeating just to bring out one salient point: The first generation of children initiated two geographical groupings. One was along the River Tweed, and the other was in the city. The larger number of descendants, by far, was near the mouth of the Tweed.

Figure 1. The University of Edinburgh quadrangle covers the site of Kirk O'Field. Darnley was convalescent in the provost's house when he was strangled and the house blown up about 2:00 a.m. on Monday, the 10th of February, 1567. The salt trone (tron) and the butter tron were public scales. Placards were posted on them, as well as on the market cross (croce). The gaol (jail) was in the tolbooth (city hall). Edinburgh tenements were notoriously terrible habitations. Horses could go along the north side of town from palace to castle using the steps and the castle-bank. The city was guarded by 32 men at night.

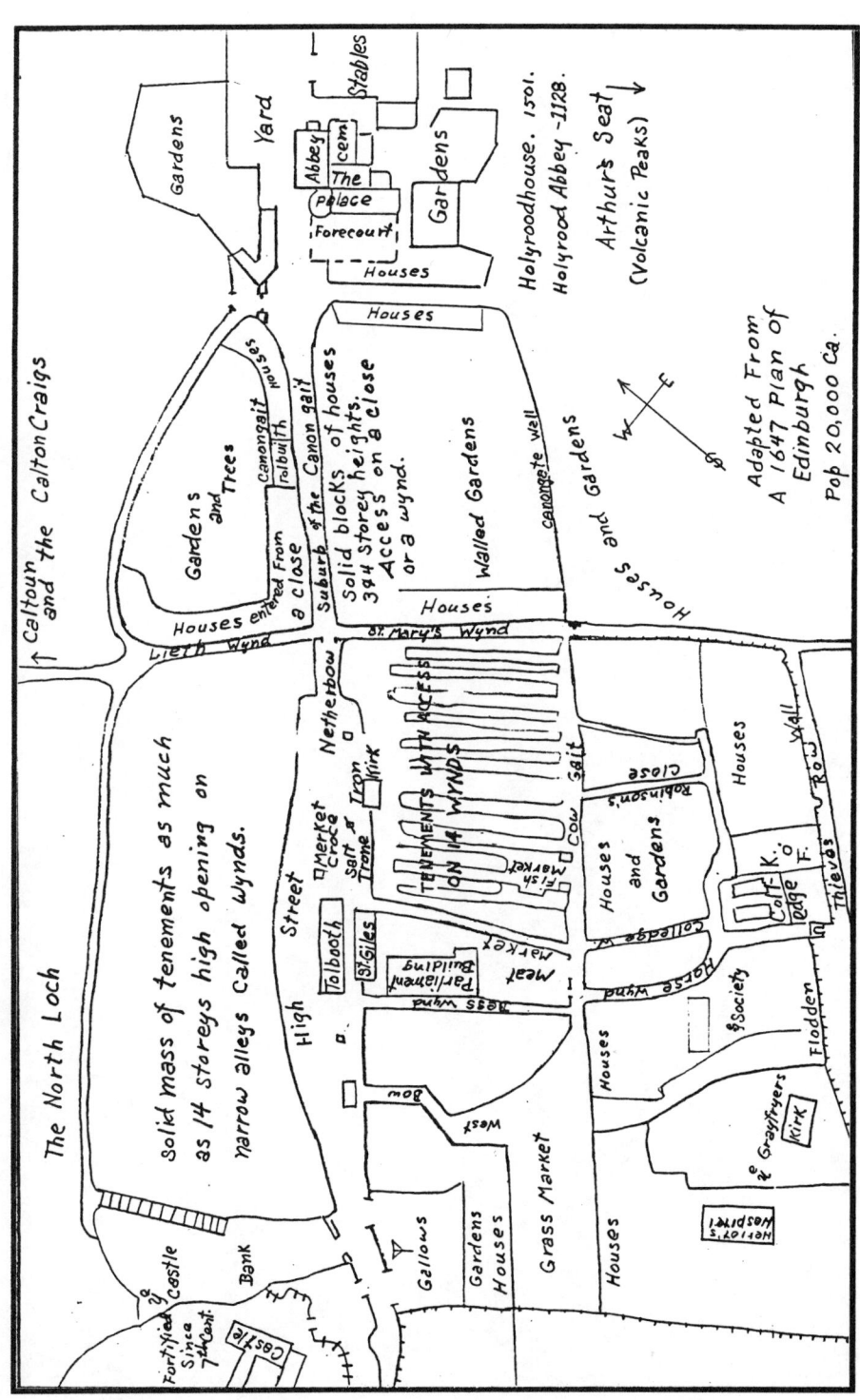

The social, economic, and agricultural picture in those times is so foreign to our experience that a brief note may be useful here: A burgess and tradesman upper-class existed. These astute entrepreneurs often attained social status, and their sons a good education. Well-off burgesses could outshine impoverished noblemen. They often bought landed estates and property, jockeying themselves into a social position ordinarily denied them.
It must be assumed that the lady-in-waiting came from a noble family, for she could not have been chosen from a lower class or tradesman family. How much money they had is immaterial. No matter how little, it would have far exceeded a Melrose tenant's grubstake. If there was considerable wealth, all kinds of advantages could be given to grandchildren. The parents of the daughter who married the queen's stable-boy certainly played a major, if unknown, part in the lives of our first family. The children who were taken to live in the city were helped to enter that world, and the ones who stayed at Melrose would have found their way also smoothed in entering their world. The social discrepancy between the bride and groom can be ignored, for to marry a Frenchman simply mimicked the queen's father. There were many other examples.

Ordinarily, the labor of farm children was important in sustaining a family, but the new tenants at Melrose sent a daughter and two sons to live in the Canongate. This unusual action fits the thesis exactly: parents help their daughter ease her farm-wife burdens, and give city advantages to grandchildren. Even slight financial aid could provide the services of a woman to help in the kitchen and farm-yard. In those days, pay was little besides bed and board for a grown girl. Sending children to live in the same parish as the palace is unexplainable by any Border criteria. No farmer of Melrose could have done it except this one. The wife of this farmer was not a Border woman, nor was the man a local rustic. She had lived intimately with the child-queen and had been educated with the children of French noblemen. Nothing had been spared in nurturing the miniature court of the future Queen of France. The French were little concerned that this little Marie was Queen of

Scotland, although that had been her "union card" for admission to their royal family. Someday her queenship might serve as a lever to pry her country away from England. Secretly the French thought of the Scots as scruffy, if not actually barbaric. For Marie, herself, there was nothing but praise.

Many poor French people had settled in Edinburgh. Often French soldiers brought by Mary's mother, her regent, took their wives with them when they went off to foreign fields. Agnew tells of a Frenchwoman who was granted a warrant to sell pretty pebbles four years after our relative was buried in the Palace Chapel. But our French progenitor fared much better than the migrants from France. Ours were favored people, for the records show over and over that perquisites and status came to them not explainable by ordinary criteria.

Indeed, the lady who was our maternal ancestress spent her whole married life in the Borders, where discretion dictated silence about her former status and good fortune. This silence was a necessity there, but not in Canongate, where some of her children lived and founded genealogical lines, including my own.

At Melrose, the Depo family was certainly known to have been founded by a Frenchman who was a Protestant. Therefore, he was known to be a Huguenot. In time, the massacre news intertwined with the dimly remembered, or forgotten, real facts of Depo's coming to Scotland with the horses, which was eleven years before the massacre. For some two hundred years, the many generations in the Borders reiterated the confusing story: the ancestor was a French Huguenot from Dieppe. A horrible massacre of Huguenots had occurred and thousands of refugees escaped. Very likely, ministers, having an education, explained to our people that, by the grace of God, their ancestor had gotten out in time. By the late 1700s this had been solidified into the accepted origin legend, which was eventually published. Actually, our ancestor had escaped that onslaught by leaving France with an eleven year headstart, but who would remember that, after Huguenot became synonymous with massacre? In the Borders this became "refugee from the St. Bartholomew's Eve Massacre." After this was published, the error became what is euphemistically termed "received opinion," which means we don't really know, but it is now too late to disturb a good-enough story.

CHAPTER VI

THE ACCOUNTS OF THE LORD HIGH TREASURER OF SCOTLAND

Perhaps no official of the realm provided as consistent a record of day to day events as the Lord Treasurer of Scotland. The name of the annual fiscal report is given in our chapter's title. However the official was not originally accorded the title, "Lord." That was added by editors, a fact not discovered for fifty years after the book had been printed. This official was an educated man, for he wrote some sixteen pages in Latin in this volume of 682 pages. They seem to be annual letters of transmittal, since they list the auditors for each year, and the money received from various sources. Even a little understanding of Latin makes it possible to see how people who used this ponderous language short circuited its endless pollysyllables by the use of a great many abbreviations. This was also true of archaic Spanish, and English, so full of abbreviations that only the initiated can cope with the old scripts. Today's acronyms will some day be printer's pi, too.

As simple a matter as writing 1561 became: *anno domini millesimo quingentisimo sexagesimo primo*, all spelled out. Even our treasurer, *computum magistri Roberti Richartsoun*, who knew perfectly well how to write 1561, balked at writing out the whole date, and abbreviated it to: *in anno dominii, etc, Vc sexagesimo primo*. People did think differently in those days, but the use of Latin with its strained circumlocutions would slowly start yielding to more direct expression. Was this simple example a move in that direction, to a time when when Arabic notation would become acceptable?

We would not be able to converse with our first family. The vocabularies are too different, and the accents on each side would be impenetrable to the other. I cannot see that I have an accent, but it is, of course, readily apparent to me that other people have difficult accents which they could improve if they tried! With a written page you can puzzle over what you see, and maybe make out the sense intended. A good many excerpts are included in these pages which show that we can almost read what they wrote. Very likely we could understand almost nothing of what they said. It is a baffling situation to this day, for an American tourist in Great Britain to have to ask twice, what was said, then give up. A German or Mexican native gladly helps you to understand, a Frenchman usually doesn't, but you hesitate asking someone speaking your mother-tongue to repeat more than twice. Stories in this vein could fill a book, and they are often funny. One time I asked a St. Johns Island High School boy what he was saying to his friend in English. I said he talked so fast I couldn't understand him. He told me, "I don't talk too fast, you listen too slow."

The hand-written originals of these twelve volumes are treasured possessions of Scotland. The entries go back many years, for Mary's reign is in volume eleven. It was deciphered and set in modern type in 1916. Fifty years later, after two World Wars had passed, it became possible to publish volume twelve. It covers the last year of her reign, and the four regencies that followed. Nothing in it involves our family, but several items are of general interest. Volume eleven which covers expenditures for Mary, is excerpted at some length, especially in our Chapter IX. The marriage of the lady and the stable-boy becomes a very credible event as one reflects on the day-to-day palace activities that are sidelighted in this book. Mary rode every day if possible, and these two young people would have been next to each other, where their duties placed them, at the mounting pavilion. These excerpts blend with biographical sketches of Mary to make this wedding seem almost a routine incident at the palace. An early spring wedding is entirely compatible with the queen's history in 1562. It was an afternoon's diversion for the whole family of servants presided over by a sentimental monarch who seems to have especially loved this particular form of charity. As I will show, the records of the Regality of Melrose complete the verification. Amazingly, a man who worked with the queen's reserve horses at Stichel, a day's ride south of the palace, is mentioned in Volume XI of the *Accounts*. Thus our surname appeared in print in 1564.

In that long ago time, the year began on the 25th of March. That was Lady Day, exactly nine months before Christmas. Among other ambiguities in reading these books was the old English monetary system which was used in Scotland, although the Scots pound was worth much less than the English. At least the farthing and the obolus were seldom referred to, but the pound, shilling, and pence, were to remain in use for centuries, to baffle the whole non-British world. They are abbreviated: "L" or "l" for *Libra* (pound), "s" for shilling, and "d" for *denarius* (the Roman penny or pence).

The Roman numerals used throughout these records, and in other books, are not quite as we learned them in grade school: the symbol for 1 is a lower case *i* except that *j* indicated the final unit, *viz iiij* (4). One thousand, (one *mille*), appears as *jm*. One hundred (one *centum*), appears as *jc*. Thus, in Scots money, a price of 1,534 pounds, 28 shillings, and 4 pence would be written: *jm Vc xxxiiij£, xxviijs, iiijd*.

Arabic numerals were used in the Lord Treasurer's Account book only for writing the year. Such an avoidance of a superior method of dealing with numbers is hard to understand, even though we know those people stuck with inefficient, laborious methods, and stamped out any budding innovative notions. New ideas and methods offended an ages-old sense of tradition. Overtones of laziness, and unseemly pretentiousness were also read into any deviation from the customary ways of doing anything. It pays to remember that the capacity of the human brain apparently hasn't changed for thousands of years, and a Cro-Magnon could have used a computer if he had had a chance. The difference between using a steel pen versus a quill, or using a pointed shovel instead of a square point, is advanced technology. Brain power couldn't advance faster than the tools of performance would allow. That's why we cannot justly criticize the old time slow-pokes. Right now it may be that our technology has gone out ahead of our human limitations. Those tradition bound Scots had descendants far in the future who became World leaders in innovation.

We can wonder just how the Treasurer's clerks manipulated their Roman numerals to tot up invoices for merchandise they bought, *i.e.*, the sum total or *summa*. The Romans used dust-covered boards, which gives us the word abacus through the Greek. At a later time, pebbles (*calculi*) were moved in grooves to calculate the answers we find today by the four basic processes of arithmetic. The abacus is thousands of years old, and still in widespread use, especially in the Orient, and it is speedy in the hands of experts.

There was undoubtedly a permanent staff of skilled clerks coming up through the ranks under the Lord Treasurer, who seems not to have been a professional accountant himself. These men brought to their work the methods they had learned as young clerks. Tradition was everything, and one can correctly visualize autocratic old head clerks demanding that nothing newer than what they had been taught should creep into the accounting methods, or into the record books. Accounting as an art stretched back through the Middle Ages, the Dark Ages and before Rome began. The Sumerians were good accountants; so were the Incas, but their itemization was sketchy. The Lord Treasurer didn't explain his entries very well either. Perhaps nothing has changed as little as the art of calculating how much is owed to whom. The excerpts I will display indicate a backwardness, a resistance to change, although there are reasons, even for that.

It has bothered me to say we use Arabic numerals ever since I saw on the doors of the Shepheard's Hotel in Cairo that real Arabic numerals have no resemblance to what we call "Arabic numerals." The Arabs gave the western world the concept of zero combined with ten digits, but not the shape of the numerals. The Arabs can't read the Roman numerals that we call Arabic, nor can guests read real Arabic numerals, thus both are posted on hotel doors in Egypt. Arithmetic was being taught all over Europe in the sixteenth century, yet totally archaic computation held fast. We cannot even guess how an "accounting house" was organized, but it would have been an amazing and baffling sight, I am sure. Counting tables had the Roman numerals represented by "counters" which were adroitly shifted as pounds, shillings, and pence were multiplied by repeated adding, or divided by halving. Ells, quarter ells, and half quarter ells were manipulated to produce a *summa*, all without recourse to decimals or fractions.

The average Scot had neither the counting board nor the calculating ability of the clerks. He was largely at the mercy of those who could figure, but he was not stupid. There was also an almost universal Christian morality then. Ambiguous in many ways, but protective too in many matters including common cheating. It was part of the environment, like pure drinking water in mountain burns. An uneducated Scot might have bought things as I saw Navajos do 50 years ago at their trading post, buying and paying for things one by one, counting the change each time without recourse to arithmetic. Decade by decade, Scottish education improved, and small schools appeared, paid for directly by parents. In time Scottish education surpassed even English before levelling off, I have read. The local manufacture of paper and books in the seventeenth century was a great breakthrough. It is too easy to judge the past negatively, for instance about the cumbersome counting tables. Paper had always been scarce, and expensive, and reserved for special uses akin to the use of parchment and vellum. Pencils had to wait for 250 years to be invented in Germany by Faber. Until pencil and paper arrived, Roman numerals did the job, although Arabic notation would have done better even on the counting board or the abacus.

While the Lord Treasurer was fumbling with Roman numerals, there was a man named John Napier a mile away, who was inventing logarithms. This simple concept, but elaborate procedure, could handle very large numbers, and it revolutionized engineering and scientific calculations. New ways were fermenting under the surface, and their advantages being recognized very slowly, but persistently. With the advent of the 1600s, attitudes began to change everywhere, and progress could be seen here and there. But this was 50 years too late for our first family to participate even at the farmer's level, which, of course, was slowest of all to accept change.

An editor's preface of 78 pages precedes the records of the Lord Treasurer. It says that he recites inconsequential expenditures such as the cost of ells of *claith* (cloth) for making dresses and bed hangings. The editor points to an entry:

> "Johnne Morrisone, gardnar of the south yard of Halierrudhous, had bought seidis for the yeir of God, etc. 'prattling on just as if Scotland were not going through the most tremendous turning point in her history.'"

The critical situation that is referred to was that the Lords of the Congregation had recently been twice defeated by the Regent's force of a thousand French troops. According to custom, many had brought their families with them. Some never returned to France. The Regent, be it remembered, was Mary's mother, of a powerful French family. France was intent on swallowing up Scotland, as was England under Elizabeth, who had sent ships and troops to help the Scots. She did not want the French entrenched on what she hoped would be her island from bottom to top.

No one but I would notice that, with all this history being made, and the nation up for grabs, Johnne Morrisone was tending the south garden of the palace. This was located about where my family parked our rented cars in 1985. These *seidis* were entered in the Account book, in preference to momentous events, year after year, in mindless detail. It is not recorded, but it would be strange, if the gardener did not know the French stable-boy, André Depo, who handed the queen her horse when she rode. The stables and riding pavilion were very likely arranged around the garden complex south of the palace, and a bit north of the volcanic peaks called Arthur's Seat.

Depo and Morrisone didn't speak the same language, but they had a common interest. They were only workmen, but uniquely placed to personally provide simple services to the greatest person in the land. A queen, then as now, could take genuine pleasure in her garden, and the stables with her favorite interest, her precious horses. Some would be with foal, kept there for her special pleasure, we can be sure. Her questions and comments directed to her gardener would have been in Scots; to the hostler, in French. The two men would certainly have become well acquainted as the one struggled to pick up what he could of the Scottish language, for he would have had but little contact with the house servants, most of whom spoke his language. His world was changing too fast for comfort, for his French was of no use among the workmen with whom he associated. The brand of broad Scots spoken by almost inarticulate stable hands would be hard to imagine. Even today there are guttural noises from human throats that barely qualify as speech. No matter how their speech came out, these men had to have been his first teachers.

His wife-to-be had received an unusually good education, a contrast worth thought, but not necessarily an obstacle to a good marriage, and they did speak the same language. Her education, and her husband's city experience, were totally new factors in the agricultural world of Border life where they were to be sent. The children they launched into that world were favored with an outlook on life that must have been worlds apart from that of their neighbors. It is tantalizing to visualize the parents, so far removed from their former sophisticated life, dealing with the environment they had entered. Their children would have been outsiders, with almost no chance of gaining a tenancy on land. They would have had little choice but to go to villages and towns where they could work into trades and crafts.

Approximately 34 years after they were married, their daughter, Katherine Dippo, married an Edinburgh man named Alexander Moresome. By riddling out other records I found that her brother had a son whose daughter, Euphemia Deippe, married Robert Moresone, a Burgess of Canongate. At her death she was buried in the cemetery of the palace chapel. There were a lot of Morrisons mixed up with our first four generations, starting with Johnne, the gardener. There is much more to reflect on about the Canongate branch of the family. It is evident that Katherine's brother, or more likely two brothers, grew up here, and that one of them established the line that eventually lived in Glasgow, and then the United States, carrying the legend of our origin with them.

The state of the accounting art in Queen Mary's time is shown in the entries in this and other chapters. They also convey, better than description, a picture of court preoccupations; what was on the mind of the ruler. It is also clear that the record leaves out far more than it tells. For instance, there is no record of buying great quantities of horse feed nor of pantry provisions for the various palaces and castles. As our story develops, it becomes evident that the queen had some of her horses kept at Stitchel in the Merse. Perhaps this establishment is recorded as a royal horse farm only in the one terse entry that a person named Depo was "slaughtered" there. This laconic message is not only of interest in my genealogical search, but it casts a sharp light on the neglected story of Mary's beloved horses, those best friends she ever had. Depo's presence at Stichel is evidence enough that Mary had a horse establishment there. Perhaps the only documented record of them is contained in the excerpts scattered through my pages. Mary may have personally assumed all of the expenses of their care, for there is no entry in the official account book. However, it was the Lord Treasurer who recorded that James Knox "slaughtered" Depo there. This entry has no reason for being in the royal record except in the context of the queen's horses. Nowhere else in the Accounts is it made a matter of national concern that two boys were fighting on a remote crossroads estate, the queen's horse farm I believe. How helpful it would have been if the sometimes loquacious LHT had given us half

The Accounts of the Lord High Treasurer of Scotland

a dozen more words which could easily have been subtracted from his typical inconsequentials such as:

> "...Item, to Katherine Smalloun, remanand in ward within the tolbuith of Edinburgh be the space of this moneth of October ilk day vj d; summa.xv s.vj d. ...
> ...lettres of proclamation to the mercat croces [market crosses] of Jedburght, Hawik, Kelso, Lauder, none sell ony nolt, scheip, or uthir cattell to ony Inglismen ...
> ...Item, to Charlis Burdens, gunnar, for his Witsounday and Martinmes termes 1560, and the Witsounday terme 1561, ilk terme 1 li.;summa...jcl li."

Lengthy payrolls must have been funded and disbursed too, but not a word is said about them. On the other hand, messengers, accounted for one by one, are given their fees for carrying messages all over the country. Others are given stipends for their board, even tips in the form of "drink silver" are recorded. There are hundreds of pages of this.

The brave and able Queen Dowager died June 10, 1560. Her body was wrapped in "ane wobe of leid," and John Weir, pewterer, soldered the lead robe airtight. Burial was at Reims, for there could not be a Catholic burial in Scotland. There had been about a hundred in her household, not at Holyroodhouse, incidentally. They were mostly French. Some stayed in Scotland, but most returned to France. The influence of the French had been very important for at least thirty years. Mary's father, King James V, married a French Princess in 1547. She died within a year, and within a year he married Marie of Guise-Lorraine, who was the mother of Mary. The marriage of our Scottish ancestress to a man from Dieppe differed from this Scottish/French relationship only in that he was from a city with a Norman/Scandinavian history rather than the typical Gallic of Paris, and other places not far away in miles, but very different in ancestry. Also, of course, there was the distinction that he was only an honest working stiff.

Servais de Condie was Queen Mary's valet of the wardrobe, and Seinyeour Francis, master of her household. John Balfour was one of the valets of the chamber of the newly arrived queen. It is probably accurate to visualize over thirty times this many names, and positions, as comprising her household, but the prospective bride and groom we seek are not linked in this book, but to quote: ."..the slaughter of Alexander Depo his sone, duelling (dwelling) in Stichell in the Mers," is however, recorded. This is news that will be studied later in detail.

Every whim of Marie Stuart, the Queen of France, was an order; true also when she became the reigning Queen of Scots, but within limits. Her attire, her retinue, manner of conduct, and her horses, were unquestionably matters where her wishes were obeyed as orders. History books deal with the controversial matters where a ruler's wishes are not so readily obeyed, but often opposed. The tiny facet of the history of the queen that involves our family origin does not even come close to any affair of state. What she did that established our family in Scotland with its French-derived name was no more momentous to her than ordering eggs for breakfast instead of Krispy Krunch and, by the way, she had to cook her own eggs in one desperate situation, but that was after our first couple were safely launched on their life at Melrose.

She made four moves that were inconsequential in terms of her realm, but vital in the establishment of our family:

- As she prepared to leave France, she ordered the shipment of her stable of horses. They were under the care of two men, and apparently a boy, of the city of Dieppe.

- She ordered a farm prepared where one of the Frenchmen could give special attention to certain of the animals.

- She staged a wedding, with one of her ladies marrying André, one of the French stable-boys.

She combined generosity with policy by placing the new couple on the lands of a troubled abbey.

Insignificant as these moves were, it is only because of them that the family with the Scotticized French name exists. Besides what the queen did, the children and grandchildren of our progenitor became responsible people who left enough records that the development of the family could be traced after more than four centuries had elapsed.

The tradition of my family never faltered. It had to have started with one of the sons in the Canongate. He told the story to his wife and children, the whole story as his mother and grandmother had told it to him, and in that first all-Scottish generation, all the marvellous details were known and relished, we can be sure. The romance and the emphasis which he conveyed to his line lasted. The story lost details, but the essence survived. His tale, continuously getting shorter, passed down through his male line to my ears. The women in this line, just like my grandmother, told the story to all who would listen. But it was a story also told by all of the men of the line, to their wives. About thirteen successive husbands told their brides how their name had started, but many more failed to tell. Obviously the story was told with pride even after all knowledge of its real meaning had vanished in the mists of time.

Unless our generous and impulsive young queen stepped entirely out of character, she helped perhaps all of her eleven minor ladies-in-waiting to be married. This queen did not abandon these young women, nor the favored young men who were her pages. Not married was almost literally not alive for a woman, then. Mary's biographers agree that she helped the young people of her retinue to marry within the palace family. Undoubtedly some of the attendants were helped by their families to become acquainted with suitable young people in the city where they were newcomers, and strangers, even to the Scottish accent. The *sine qua non* of source books for virtually all of this is the Lord Treasurer's *Accounts*.

CHAPTER VII

THE STABLE-BOY AND THE LADY-IN-WAITING

On Tuesday, the 19th of August, 1561, at about 10:00 a.m., a girl watched Mary, Queen of Scots, disembark after her voyage from Calais. It was at the port of Leith about an hour's ride north of the Palace, Holyroodhouse. Mary's mother, while regent, had made this port an effective link in the vital traffic between France and Scotland.

The girl, whose name we do not know, was one of eleven minor ladies-in-waiting who were first off the galley. I have never seen the number given as eleven, but information in the *Accounts of The Lord High Treasurer of Scotland* makes it quite certain that the queen had eleven, plus the four Maries, in her immediate train. This total of fifteen is studied in Chapter IX.

Slightly younger than their queen, who would be 19 in December, these young ladies were undoubtedly very attractive in every way, and able to provide a colorful and proper setting, first for the reception of the four Maries of song and story, and then to receive the queen as she stepped on the soil of her native land after 13 years away. Now the Queen Dowager of France, with a stipend of 40,000 livres annually, she was still the Queen of Scotland as she had been since her coronation at the age of 9 months. It was a large group that disembarked that morning. In fact, applying common sense to the problem, there must have been far too many people to have fit in the two speedy galleys. There were many French noblemen in the second galley escorting their queen back to Scotland. As with many other interesting but unrecorded details, I have not seen a specific reference, but I will hazard the guess that many of her household functionaries, chefs, apothecaries, etc., travelled in the -

> "..divers ships laden with the Scottish Queen's provisions that landed at Inchkeith and Dunbar."

The English Earl of Rutland made this observation in a letter to Lord Cecil, who certainly passed it on to his boss, Elizabeth of England. The English lords who reported back to their queen were always condescending, if not contemptuous, of the Scots, so Cecil wrote that the Scottish Queen's "whole train, not exceeding 60 persons of the meaner sort, disembarked from only two galleys."

This is a surprising capacity in addition to the crew and prisoner oarsmen. The "meaner sort" crack simply shows that Mary, very properly, had had no Scottish nobles in her French court. She had French attendants, with just enough Scots in her personal household to keep alive her true nationality, insurance against a day when she might rule her native land in person. That day had now come unexpectedly.

The anonymous lady-in-waiting we seek will never become visible to us in the swirling crowd at the disembarkation, or later. We can be sure all were attractive, vivacious, and beautifully attired in style straight from Paris. Thus the first lady of our family can be described. All of the girls of Mary's train were Scottish, and undoubtedly almost overcome with the emotion of seeing their families. They had really been in a sort of exile since the age of about five, and wouldn't even know their parents or the parents know them, for cameras were about 300 years off in the future. One of the young ladies and her parents appear and reappear in our story. In fact, she has lived on in our family legend. We will learn a surprising amount about this woman, but it will be circumstantial, inferential, and derived from the records and customs of Scotland. For instance, we know there were many ladies in the queen's train, but to learn from the ordering of 15 saddles and cloaks that there were 11 minor ladies may be an inference, but there could scarcely be any other interpretation. Nowhere in the literature have I seen an analysis, as in Chapter Nine, of the Lord Treasurer's record, which certainly can only be understood as meaning that Queen Mary had fifteen ladies-in-waiting. Similarly, as will be evident, our French stable-boy and the French speaking Scottish lady were thrown together by their appointed duties with nothing to do for extended periods of time but to talk. There doesn't need to be a record to foresee that this could lead to a marriage, especially one so freely facilitated by the queen, a fact that is told and retold about so many of her retinue. This, almost by itself, authenticates our legend, but is just the beginning.

On the same August morning that Mary was landing at Leith the ships carrying our stable hands and Mary's horses from Dieppe were wallowing up La Manche through the narrow passage between Dover and Calais. (The people on the opposite shore called it the English Channel). The ships may even have entered the increasingly rough North Sea. Before the hostlers ever encountered the strange, almost English, dialect they would have to master, their immediate problem was to communicate with the Dutchmen who would be their crewmates for 3 or 4 weeks. The Dutch crewmen, for their part, very possibly called the horse-men "Dieppe," or some Dutch equivalent, perhaps something close to "Depo."

Each of the attendants would have had 15 horses on his ship, a fact that was provided by the Lord High Treasurer himself. Perhaps the horses were the best friends the grooms had on shipboard. When the Dutch ship-masters stood into the port of Tynemouth, they would not have been personally apprehensive, for their nations were at peace. Almost certainly the feed and water for the animals had gotten too low to continue on to Leith, about 100 miles away. The ships must have started out looking like floating haystacks, for there were no bales then. The water would have been in awkward barrels which could scarcely have been adequate.

At Tynemouth the shipping agent, James Household, made himself available, and the ship masters presented their bills for payment through international clearing house facilities. Then the ships headed for home, with or without a return cargo. There is not a word in the *Accounts* about the fact that the horses were not delivered to their contracted destination.

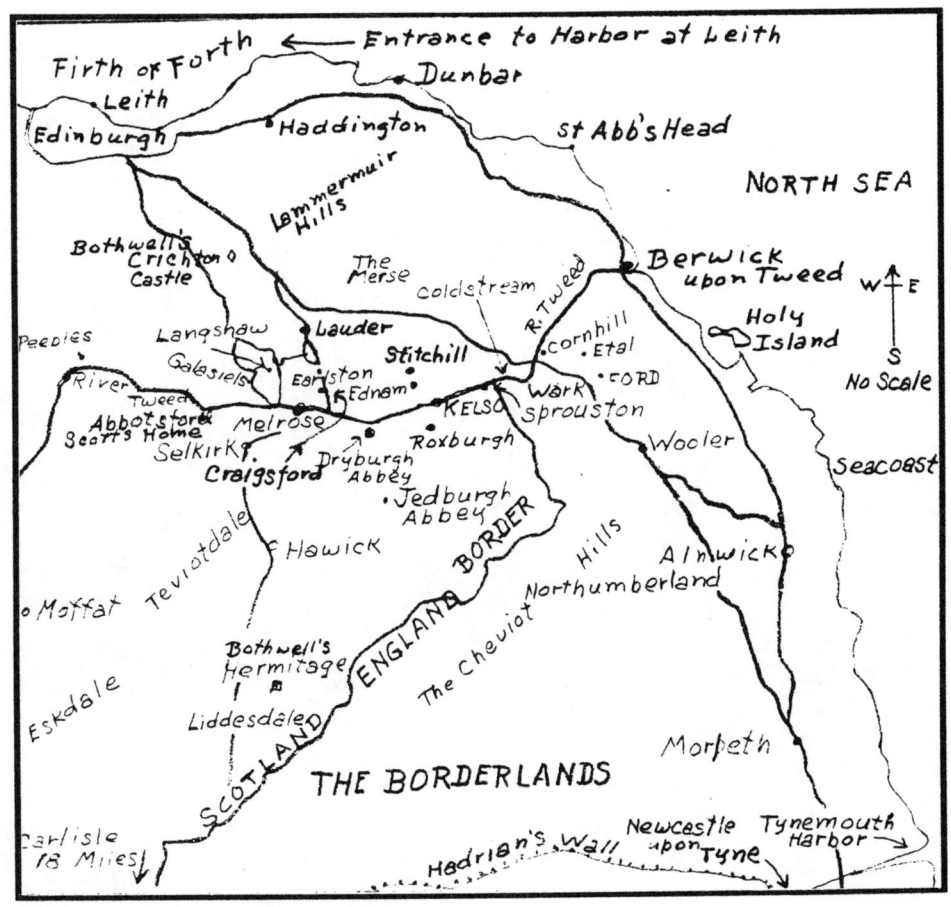

Figure 2: Map of The Borderlands

It has been written that these ships may have been forced into the harbor by Queen Elizabeth's fleet, and that the horses were held by her orders. I think that a shortage of horse feed and water is a much more likely reason. A safe conduct had been sent to Mary, even though too late for her to know she was safe from capture. The port officer wisely decided that these horses, mules and servants were not to be carelessly treated. He could be confident that he would be reimbursed. The ship masters could have assured him that they were not transporting ordinary cargo. They all had to be paid by the Scots - or else. It was a tricky international situation.

This piece of business seems very interesting to me. As I will show in the next chapter, the dramatic story of Mary's horses, stranded in England, was misinterpreted back in 1916 when the *Accounts* were edited. The statement was made in the editor's Preface that the horses had been "bought in the north of England" which we can see was not so. The real story has a fairy-tale-like quality befitting the life of Mary, Queen of Scots. Her whims were gratified and her steadfast equine friends were kept with her. They were better friends than some of her later choices.

I may be the only person who has tried to write the story of the queen's horses, and I have encountered more blanks than records, but I had our legend to start with. Certainly, no one else has ferreted out and collated the many connections between the ships carrying thirty horses, two men and a boy. There was also the special young lady hastening home by galley. Their destiny was to meet at the Palace. Other chapters trace the consequences when Cupid and a queen contrive with Fate.

The LHT tells what color pants the King's *fules* wore, but not a word about how the authorities learned that the two shiploads of horses were being held for ransom in unfriendly England. For the highest fiscal officer to not mention the amount of the impoundment charges would also seem lax. I think that the blanks can be filled by good solid inference: Mr. Household, the agent, sent his bill to

Edinburgh for payment by special messenger, or by a general courier. Men and money did arrive to redeem the horses and, importantly to us, "*the servandis witht thame.*" These were the stable-boys named André and Alexander, and perhaps André's young brother designated as "*sone,*" but we will see later just how very ambiguous that word is. Especially intriguing was the roundabout way we were able to learn there were originally 30 animals, but that one had died. As we have said, clarity and efficiency in those days, even in accounting, was "a tale told by an idiot."

Perhaps for the first time all of these things are being looked at in detail. All through our book an effort is also being made to see things through the eyes of common people in the very short time frame of fifty years, the fifty years after André of Dieppe landed in Scotland. In a way, we are writing the story of the queen's horses, and their keepers, and her lady-in-waiting, from her realm's financial records, a very sound biographical source book. When our story is finished, a mystery will remain. What ultimately happened to the fine breeding stock that came from the royal stables of the castle Saint Germain-en-Laye just northwest of Paris?

Mary's obsession with horseback riding, fortunately for us, created certain records that left a trail that could be followed. Our two horse handlers were necessary workmen every step of the way; they were key personnel. No other interpretation of their situation is possible, for they were there from the beginning of the adventure.
André certainly continued with the horses in closest proximity to the queen, for he had brought the horses safely to her from Dieppe to the Palace, and he spoke French to them and to her Majesty, all uncontrived, but a beautifully congruent scenario. Our story will show, despite the scarcity of specific records, that Her Grace rewarded him in a manner that could not have been more appropriate and lasting. André and his wife lived forever after, at least figuratively through their descendants, to the present time. Even the term "stable-boy" was the colloquial name for André's job. It was still his identification long after his actual name had disappeared from the legend I heard as a boy.

Alexander, or his younger son, was lost to our story, as we shall see, but his contribution to this saga was vital, for it validated the start of our surname in Scotland. The Lord Treasurer didn't ordinarily record where and when boys fought, and hurt each other, but he did on only this one occasion. He knew that one of the queen's French grooms was tending her horses at the royal stables at Stichell, and he recorded the event to be on the safe side if a question ever arose about the killing of a boy who had cared for the horses from the beginning.

Both stable-boys worked for the "maister stabillar," Johnne Levingstoun. We know: the names of the Dutch ship captains, and their home towns; the shipping agent's name and address, and the freight bill; the voyage time of about three weeks; that the ships did not take the horses to Scotland; that 30 animals started out, but one died without much question; that there were fifteen ladies-in-waiting who received new saddles. A clear trail is discernible here. Our three people are visible along the way, and Alexander's older son is eventually named in the *Regality Records of Melrose*, Volumes I and III. From that point on there are birth, baptismal, marriage, and death records by which to follow the family.

The transportation system of Mary Queen of Scots is being scrutinized in all the detail we have been able to muster from the records, and some have probably been missed. If Johnne Levingstoun's diary and time book have been preserved somewhere, many blanks in the history of horseback and mule pack-train transport in the 1500s could be filled. If we ever see these and similar records, we can stop bridging the gaps in the *Accounts of the Lord High Treasurer of Scotland*, who so murkily wrote about clothing, bed hangings, the *clois writtings of hir Quenis grace*, and endless trite phrases, but scarcely a word about the thirty precious horses that were lost to the authorities for weeks while impounded by the English at Tynemouth. Nor had anyone signed to pay for their expense, or was it more likely their ransom?

Our Dieppe stable-boys are all but named in this entry:

> "...two schippis frauchtis [freight] awin to thame [the ship captains] for the fraucht of the Quenis grace horss, mulattis, and servandis witht thame..."

Far more is omitted than made clear in this entry, which is all the record there is about a royal enterprise involving two freighters full of horses, two or three horse handlers and the port-master. A month later, a time clerk gave two of these *servandis* names. There was a third, apparently, but as a young son he was not recorded nor paid. Thus our family received its surname. The story could fill a very interesting book. It would be a horse biography told by these stable-boys. Over forty years later a court clerk at Melrose made records crucial in our search for one of the stable-boys, André. He was our ancestor.

Stabling, feeding, grooming, breeding, and scheduling horses are essential operations that made it possible for the government to function. In the days when wheeled transport was possible only on High Street, and a few wynds in Edinburgh, people were almost exclusively afoot or on horseback. In other towns, and across the countryside, roads were virtual trails. In each town the street billowed out into a market square where goods were bartered around the "market cross." Proclamations were posted there, and other notices, and speeches were sometimes made there.

The palace horse operation was a relatively large facility, but not particularly so by standards of the time. Thirty or so horses were comparatively few, for the queen had 8000 men at her command eight days after Riccio's murder; Bothwell, 800 after Darnley's assassination. Large numbers of these were horsemen, and imagine how many horses were in the logistical backup for the men on horseback. The particular needs of the horses had to be met in a first class manner, but still be meshed into the numerous services required of them and their handlers. The palace required riding horses, perhaps twenty of the new ones ready at all times,

The Stable-boy and the Lady-in-Waiting 103

besides others for messengers, pages, and general use. The advent of these startlingly superior animals must have been a great novelty. Under the Regent's thirteen year tenure, Holyroodhouse had been neglected, for she had used other palaces and castles. After this interlude, the situation was radically altered in the reorganization of the palace, its staff, its stables, and the extensive grounds and parks. The horse accommodations, both for their care and their presentation for use by the queen and court, were undoubtedly upgraded, or rebuilt in more opulent style. The change was not just in the physical expansion. The tenor of the whole royal establishment accelerated. John Knox could hardly contain himself in his denunciations of the queen who shortly turned the dank and dismal, almost abandoned old palace into a buzzing beehive of festive occasions.

Any large horse operation divides into active and reserve management phases. Brood mares, injured or sick animals, sires, and young animals would have been kept at Stichill in the Merse. Alexander was sent there, where he, or his "*sone*," was recorded as a casualty two years and five months after he and André had arrived in Scotland with the horses.

A great deal has been written about the queen's constant riding: "half her life was spent in the saddle," with endless stories to illustrate. Much of this was strictly business, but much was hawking, hunting and pure pleasure. It is realistic to visualize André Depo in the very midst of this. The queen's chosen mount would always be brought to her, and taken away, by the groom favored for that service. It would be naive to think of him as other than good looking, intelligent, and well outfitted. André would suit both Mary and the horses.

Our hero, yclept Hendre Depo by the payroll clerk, as I will explain later, probably never heard that name spoken, and that he did not read or write we can take for granted, certainly not in Scots. There was no need for him to attempt speaking Scots as he approached the queen and her ladies, and in that distinction from the native stable-boys, he would certainly be favorably set apart. His French manner and speech may very well have created waves of nostalgia among them, for they had been transplanted from the most elegant surroundings in the world to, as the French nobles said, "an uncouth place populated by dirty barbarians," a crude remark. Its source remains a sore spot in the minds of some, for eventually that estimate was reversed.

There was a camaraderie completely unique to Mary's court. We have every reason to believe that this monarch drew no lines, except utter respect, between herself and her domestic household. In affairs of state she could assume the imperious, French manner she had learned so well, but her biographers always tell of her almost obsessive concern for her little people.

The necessity for travelling by horseback did not mean that simplicity ruled. Elaborate protocol would have governed when state occasions demanded. Pavilions for sheltering the people and mounts involved in the goings and comings of the queen, must have been suitable for either formal or simple exercises. The contrast between being Queen of France, then of Scotland, was not lost on Mary. Perhaps this incongruity was her license to throw convention to the winds as she often did. The French manners were stultified, and were to become worse. While the Scottish were stiff, and perhaps crude to boorish, Mary was free to steer between the two as she chose.

As we have put this picture together, she didn't just saddle up a plug, and go for a ride. Even the simplest trip would have involved gentlemen, messengers to the stable master, the ladies, pages, costume mistresses, and maids for each and every lady. Equerries, masters of hawks and hounds, perhaps armed outriders, hampers of food, whatever was desired was ordered "through channels." Nor did the queen just walk down to where the horses were tied up. A veritable bevy of her ladies-in-waiting might go to see her off in the lighthearted glow she loved.

In this elaborate setting and swirl of activity there were quiet intervals of great importance to us. While the queen was away, the jolly band of young ladies had nothing whatever to do but wait. Perhaps embroidery bags appeared, and girl talk filled the interval. André had duties in the stables, but his main duty would be to take the queen's horse when she returned, and that was not predictable, so his post would be adjacent to the gossipy young ladies. At least he was within earshot. What was said will never be known, but something essential came about between two people there, and when the queen returned she knew, and picked up the teasing in her own time and discretion. Mary's biographers don't paint these actors on this stage in the detail I do, but they do say repeatedly that Mary rode every day she possibly could. They would also, if asked, have to say that the whole performance was about as we see it, but my description does not begin to convey the sumptuous display of clothing and jewels requisite to a royal scene of the sixteenth century. Mary, in spite of the poverty of her country, wore her splendid clothing and jewels almost obsessively.

In the course of time, in just a few months I think, the queen herself precipitated the wedding. A great deal has been written about how Queen Mary promoted weddings, for she was incurably romantic. They seem to have been an emotional escape valve, and actually her favorite entertainment. Her position in the closed circle that was her domestic household was akin to that of a mother. Her official court of noblemen and lords, in contrast, might be likened to a den of wolves, for many men were against her, but women were for her. The parenthesis must be added that the time was to come when the women of Edinburgh, calling for the traditional penalty, hung out of their windows and screamed "burn the whore" at a bedraggled and frantic Mary accused of complicity in the murder of her husband.

Although it was obvious to everyone that Mary benefitted by her involvement in these weddings, there was another equally visible facet; her attendants needed her help in forging marital ties. As a very human person she may have set herself the goal of helping these nearly lifelong companions find suitable marriages within her household. That is, as a matter of fact, what she accomplished, as her biographers tell. It would have been very peculiar and pitiful if all the young people involved had stayed single. Our two were only two among a number who married, but very few were specifically recorded. Mary was greatly criticized for her informality and person-to-person interactions, especially with her personal attendants and servants. It would be incongruous to look for a story like ours in any other court in Europe. In Mary's, our wedding was almost foreordained.

She made a will, as required by law, before her son was born a few years later, for childbirth was a hazardous time. It inventories her treasure in jewels and specifies their distribution. The list shows how small a matter it would have been for her to give gifts to the newlyweds she sponsored. The 40,000 livres she received every year from France was for her personal use. Scotland was poor, but she was very rich. "Mary was a born matchmaker, and delighted to grace weddings with her presence...Mary was a lavish giver, who never counted the cost." These quotations from *Mary, Queen of Scots*, by Morrison, are matched in Lady Fraser's book of the same title, where we are told that her "attendants formed tight little circles. They were both related to each other and married each other." On the eve of the king's murder, she left him sick in bed to return to the palace by midnight to grace her page's wedding masque. When she was in the Borders "so ill the soul-bell was sounded" she called her nobles to her bedside for her final instructions, including care for her personal servants. Another incident of her pervasive concern for the little people around her was recorded: just before her beheading, she sorted out her remaining money into little packets for her servants, writing each name in her own hand.

Nothing in Scottish or even English court life could equal what Mary had been accustomed to in the extravagances of the French court. Something of this was evident in the furnishings, festivities and diversions that she brought to Scotland to everyone's amazement. Her own wealth made this possible, not the slim purse of

The Stable-boy and the Lady-in-Waiting

the nation. She had a simple sense of fun that fit in with the boisterous and bawdy Scottish sense of humor. There were paid court jesters, or fools, both male and female. Weddings of the nobility might be followed by three days of banqueting, games, and masqued balls, and she loved it all from her first year at Holyroodhouse, giving bridal dresses, feasts, and gifts. The most splendid were fabulous celebrations. The wedding reported by word of mouth, and carried down through four centuries to my ears was more important than any other, to me at least. The record of this wedding lies in the genealogical consequences, some of which are written down in many places. A certain obituary can serve to pinpoint this wedding which left no written record, but which must have occurred:

> "Eupham Deippe, relict of Robert Moreson, Burgess of Canongate was buried in the Abbey of Holyrood on the 17th May, 1665." (Agnew, Vol. I, p. 259).

As our chart will show, Eupham's grandfather was son of the two people married in the palace in one of the celebrations. Only November and December remained of 1561 after André (Hendre) arrived, but during the 12 Months of 1562 the setting was ideal. In the next year Mary's world started falling apart, and a gay wedding was less likely. Her powerful uncle in France, the Duke of Guise, was assassinated, she was profoundly disturbed by the death of her half brother, John Stewart, and by the death of another uncle. Nothing to relieve the deep sense of doom intervened. Even the crops were largely destroyed by too early storms. Mary became desperately ill and remained in bed much of that winter, at least partly as protection against the cold and damp of the squat and dismal palace.

We do not have the wedding date nor the bride's name, but our legend of this wedding is so blunt and positive not a word could be subtracted, nor does one need to be added, to tell how our name started. Janetta Campbell Deppa, my grandmother, and her oldest child, my aunt Lizzie, encompassed all the records we did not have in the story we were all told:

"A lady-in-waiting to the queen married a stable-boy."

CHAPTER VIII

TRACING THE STEPS OF OUR DIEPPOIS

It is a temptation to elaborate on the quantity and magnificence of the palace furnishings from Paris that were unloaded from the queen's two cargo vessels at Leith, the port which her mother, and regent, had built about two miles north of the palace of Holyroodhouse. That can be read in biographies, but we have found almost nothing about her two shiploads of horses except mention of the contrast with the scruffy little broom-tails the Scots had. They, like their masters, were hardy, and adapted to the harsh land and rough forage. The French had bred powerful chargers for their knights, centuries before, and it was their peculiarity that they disdained emasculating their stallions; thus these new animals certainly brought to Scotland much more than merely favorite horses. The infusion of fine bloodlines had to be of inestimable value in the long run, especially after more suitable fodder became available. Our stable-boys did not get to Leith by fast galley in five days. They were in lumbering Dutch ships as planned, but by misadventure they and the animals did not get to Edinburgh for two hectic months.

Tracing the queen's horses in order to find her stable-boys has been a solitary quest, and mine alone, I feel certain, for who but a descendant would be looking for them? Mary's pre-eminent biographer gives the matter a full sentence. Another fine biography disposes of the horses with five words between two commas in one sentence. A distinguished Scottish historian very properly does not mention the horses at all. This makes it incumbent on me to bring together, and interpret, the considerable amount of evidence about these horses. In the process, quite a few men and women are brought to life and action in those interesting times. My specialized search has also uncovered several errors in prestigious books. This is a practically unavoidable hazard besetting those who write nonfiction, including this.

This queen arrived and needed to use her horses on the 19th of August, 1561, but nothing was ready for her. In order to mislead the English, she had left Calais much earlier than planned. Holyrood was being renovated, but was not ready. After years of disuse it had not been restored after its sacking by Hertford. Henry VIII, in his "rough wooing" of the baby Mary for his son, had ordered the burning of Edinburgh, and destruction throughout the land. The palace and abbey were still in deplorable condition. Temporary measures left much to be desired, but she and her retinue needed to be seen by her subjects. They had waited for years to see a reigning monarch, and this one stirred their imagination. In Chapter IX the preparations to have suitable harness and riding cloaks will emphasize the adaptations that must have been put up with while everyone waited for the horse ships to arrive.

Not only inconvenience, but also anxiety, grew intensely as days became weeks. Visualize the absence of communication in this dilemma. Mary had seen a fishing boat capsize, and drown all hands, as her galley was leaving Calais. "Ah, my God, what augury is this," she had exclaimed. She and her train certainly drew the parallel, for all feared the North Sea and its storms. The *Accounts* tell that 18 days after the arrival, replacement horses were being paid for. Action must have been taken almost immediately to strike this bargain.

> "Item, the vj day of September, to Johnne Levingstoun, maister stabillar, to be x horss in Striviling to hir grace houshald agane hir grace ryding of Edinburght, as ane compt [account] subscivit by the said Johnne at mair lenth beris [bears out]...ijc xj li. Item, for expensis maid upoun the saidis horss, in corne, stray, and the boyis for keiping of thame,...-xxxiij s. iij d."

The horses from France were expected on every tide, but the days came and went. Apprehension was building as to their fate, but the queen had to meet with the lords, the Parliament, and be seen by her people. As this excerpt shows, ten horses were bought and paid for on the 6th of September. Stirling Castle lay northeast of Glasgow more than an ordinary day's ride from Edinburgh. "...as the Royal stables were excellently furnished with hors flesh," this source was called upon for the ten horses. Other references indicate the emergency nature of the entire episode, and the hard fact that communication had not been established with the English authority at Tynemouth by this date. Not a word in the Treasurer's *Accounts* indicates the arrival of a messenger from there with the news that the animals were safe, and could be redeemed by the Scots. Instead of such vital information, the Lord Treasurer tells that the oats, straw and boys cost a bit more than 30 shillings. He doesn't even tell how a horse could thrive on a diet of straw, or does he mean hay? We mustn't make comparisons about his acuity, of course. After all, he could write in Latin, and I can't even figure out if it is as murky as his Scots.

> "Item, the xviiij (19th) day of September, to Johnne Levingstoun, maister stabillar, gevin in drink silver for x haiknais [hackneys] brocht in the palice of Halierudehous, xx crounis of the sone...xxvj £i. xiij s. iiij d."

Notice that the drink silver comes first in this record of national expenditures. It seems that to bring these hackneys (ordinary horses) to the palace cost 20 crowns of the *sone*. *Sone* means sun, and also son. In this case the reference is to a French coin - *crown'de soleil*. This coin, crown of the sun, may have been very current in this part of Scotland, for large numbers of French soldiers had been brought here in recent years by Mary's mother, the regent. I won't attempt it, but if anyone wanted to see how much one of these coins was worth, the equation is here, for the total of Scottish money is equal to ten of the French crowns. This total is too little to be the price of these horses. It is more likely the cost of bringing the ten referred to, to the Palace, but the LHT doesn't make that crystal clear. Sterling was quite a distance away, and the hostlers would have had round trip expenses to deal with, but this expense was itemized as "drink silver."

Two months after the queen arrived in Edinburgh the missing horses were found to be in England, and arrangements were made to pay the freighting bill and get them to Edinburgh. Quoting the Lord High Treasurer of Scotland:

> "Item, to Johnne Levingstoun, maister stabillar, for expensis maid be him upoun xxix horss and mulattis convoyit with xxviij men fra Morphet to Annik and Berwik to Edinburght be the space of ij dais, that is to say, fra the xij of September 1561 to the xvj of October instant, as compt subscrivit be the said Johnne at mair lenth proportis iijc, xliij£i." [N.B. -- as account submitted by -- at more length supports].

On the 16th of October the two shiploads of horses and mules were released by the English, who had held them for 31 days. The officer at the port of Tynemouth, either under orders or seeking to avoid blame, had held them. The two ships had taken about three weeks to get to that port. The queen's galleys had travelled about 100 miles farther than that in five days. Shortage of horse feed and water had probably compelled the stop, even though it was in England, not a friendly country.

During my search for any records of these two men, it had intrigued me to think that bills of lading or ship manifests were undoubtedly made in Dieppe for the horse ships. These would give the names of our stable hands, an exciting possibility. With the help of my French-speaking son, Roy, and his friends, we sent a request to the mayor of Dieppe, who referred us to the Regional Archives in Roen. The archivist, Georges Guerif, responded, in effect, that no useful records existed, although he cited various possibilities. He also referred to the "unreadable" 16th century documents involved. It would have been a wonderfully lucky break if I had found that what was hoped for was buried in those archives.

Tracing the Steps of Our Dieppois

I cannot handle French, but shamelessly hounded those who could, so we could peek under that stone for what's-his-name, and the other Depo-to-be.

Perhaps there was a lack of stabling in Tynemouth that necessitated holding the 29 horses and mules in two towns not far from the port: Morpeth and Alnwick, by present day spelling. The account above says that 28 men took the animals to Berwick in England, just short of the Scottish border. From there to Edinburgh required two more days. The expense account submitted by the *maister stabillar* in an itemized statement showed expenses of 344 pounds. Very likely this was the bill submitted by the English commander who had provisioned the animals, but did not intend to absorb any costs. I cannot guess, and the Lord High Treasurer of Scotland does not tell, whether 28 Scots went after the horses, or 28 Englishmen were hired on the spot to ride them into Scotland. In either case, one leg of the trip had to be made without horses to ride.

This interesting problem forces me to guess again: the horses were the special pride of the queen, they were much larger than the men were accustomed to, and they would be unaccustomed to the speech and handling habits of the Scots. The *maister stabillar* knew all of this, and that they would not dare to try driving them as a herd - they had to be ridden, one man for each horse. Then, as now, money was kept at home, not spent abroad, meaning that Scots would do the riding. They were sent by boat from Leith, I believe, with bridles and saddles or at least girths. Johnne Levingstoun may have ridden down a few days early to make arrangements, and probably carried the money to pay the bill. If he did, the amount had been made known to the LHT. The *maister stabillar* must have planned to have the two French hostlers (recorded as *servandis*) each ride an animal, along with the 28 who were going by boat. He discovered, however, that of the 30 horses he had expected, one had died, meaning that two men would have to double up on the way home.

The road they travelled was a very important thoroughfare, not far inland from the North Sea. There were villages, or at least inns, along the way, where the riders could find food. As likely as not each slept on the ground at night, or in any shelter he could find, with his mount picketed or hobbled nearby. Those men knew a trick of sheltering from pelting rain by crouching under a horse's belly, but ordinary rain they laughed at.

This busy highway, (probably two horses could pass in wide spots), had other important traffic: the queen had a great many very important people in attendance upon her arrival. She handed some of them gold chains upon their departure.

> "Item, to Schir Peter Mutus, Inglis Ambassatour, ane chene of gold of iij crounis of the sone,...iiij£ [pounds, Scots money]...

> "Item, deliverit to the Quenis grace ane [one] chene of gold contenand jC [100] crounis of the sone, and two chenis of gold, ilk ane of thame contenand L [50] crounis of the sone, quhilk hir grace deliverit to Monsieur Marques to gif thre Franch [men] that passit with the Grande Priour [of France] and Monsieur Dauweill, iijCxxxiij£i [i.e., Libra or pounds], vjs [shillings], viijd [pence]. This totals 334£, 6s, 8d [denari or pence].

> "Item, to James Mosman, goldsmytht, for the making of the saidis iiij chenyeis, xxix £.x s.

> "Item, to the said James Mosmannis servandis in drink silver, xx s."

On their way home these ambassadors travelled the road to Berwick accompanied by three outriders, named in the *Accounts*, which show they were allowed *iiij* £ for their travel expenses. A numerous company of Lothian Lairds had been summoned to go with them to the English border town. Lothian lairds were frequently called upon for ceremonial appearances, I suspect, for the Lothians were to the east, south and west, a few hour's ride from the palace.

From time to time we moderns need to pull up short and get our time sense synchronized with these people of long ago. It is our shortcoming, not theirs, when we cannot read their writing nor conceive of their way of life. While we concentrate on these roads, inns, and myriad inconveniences, as being ancient and crude, and in need of change-for-the-better, these people had not the slightest perception they would one day appear backward, or whatever other term might be applied to them in the future. Morpeth, 12 miles north of Tynemouth, was, to them, a castle and abbey town. It was old, they knew, but contemporary to their way of thinking. We have moved so far away from the world of feudalism, with castles, abbeys, and serfdom, that it takes a conscious effort to comprehend those times. Sixteen miles farther along the coast was Alnwick, where markets and fairs had been held for centuries. It was well equipped to hold the queen's horses overnight. The Percy family had held the castle there longer than the United States has existed. I am sure our travellers, as they rode past, didn't give its age a passing thought. It is we who have to be wary of our opinions. We probably are not capable of understanding the lack of meaning of time in those centuries. Edinburgh was 60 miles, or two days, away to the north.

Twelve days after the animals were retrieved from the English, the matter of paying for shipping them was settled, as the following excerpt from the LHT account book explains:

> "Item, the xxviij day of October, to James Houshauld, duelland in Newcastle, procuratoure for Williame Williamsone of Tergone and Cornelis Cornlesone of Dorth in Holland, for the rest of twa schippis frauchtis [freight] awin to thame for the fraucht of the Quenis grace horss, mullattis, <u>and servandis</u> [and servants] witht thame, thair furesing and pertinentis [appurtenances] as the charter partie thairupoun

and the said James acquittance [receipt in full] at mair lenth proportis [supports], extending to xlii £ grit in Scottis money, to jClxviij l [168 Scots pounds]."

Up the river Tyne from the docks where the two horse ships had tied up there was a shipping agent named James Household who had international connections to clear accounts and transmit money. This bill was for 168 pounds, to be sent to the Dutch ship masters in Holland. They, undoubtedly, had long since returned, we hope with a cargo, but maybe deadheading home. 168 pounds is 84 per ship, or 105 when the *grit* is added in. Grit, in our language, is called earnest money, the deposit undoubtedly paid in advance in Dieppe by the Earl Bothwell. *Grith* is pure Anglo-Saxon, meaning security agreement. I wish I had the letter *thorn* on my typewriter. It looks a bit like a longhand *y*, and its sound is "th," as in thorn. "Ye Olde Shoppe," of course, gives me a pain, for neither the proprietress nor the sign painter has the faintest idea that their "Ye" is simply "*thorn e*," pronounced "the," but it gets called "yee." The *grit* should be spelled with a *thorn* at the end, not a "t." The word would be pronounced "grith." It was either abbreviated, or the publisher in 1916 did not have the letter *thorn* in his typecase.

This record in the old account book is an ambiguous and inadequate account of an important matter. It, and the preceding quotation of October 16, may, however, be the only basis extant for solving the mystery of how the horses, and André and Alexander, got from Dieppe to the Palace. The Dutch were becoming a great shipping and trading nation on their way to world leadership in the seventeenth century. It was surprising to me to learn from this document that our heroes sailed from Dieppe on Dutch ships, probably with an all Dutch crew. These two men were soon to be thrown into what can only be termed a narrow and utterly hidebound environment, especially, as we shall explain later, in the case of Alexander. When Bothwell contracted for the transport of the horses and mules, 15, apparently, were to be loaded onto each ship.

One "servant," meaning stable-boy, as this excerpt confirms, went with each load.

Thus it is recorded that our progenitor, the first Depo, landed near the Scottish border on September 12, 1561. Alexander, the father, his older son, André, (our ancestor) and a young son whose name we never learn were the hostlers on the two ships.

This information about the Dutch ships re-opened the possibility that had failed with the French authorities. I had new hope that the manifests of the two ships hunting cargoes in Dieppe, were lying in Dutch archives waiting for me to find them. In January of 1986 I sent a letter to the Research Institute Mairim, in Rotterdam, asking if they had the information I hoped for. A reply was received from Dr.A.A.M.Schmidt Ernsthausen, Department of Reference Service. It made extensive references to all the possibilities of indentifying the ships and their officials, but I learned that most records had been destroyed by fire. Rotterdam harbor, one of the world's greatest, was utterly detroyed by the Nazis. (It was a thrill for me to be able to tour it by boat in 1969.) Pointing out that the names of these ship masters are very common Dutch names, he concludes that "the chances of finding the payroll records, regretably, are nil."

While it would have been a fantastic piece of good luck if the names of the two men could have been found in archives, still the Scottish record book was, by itself, a great find. Twenty-nine horses ridden by thirty men is a conundrum easily solved by making the very reasonable assumption that one horse died during the two-month melee after leaving Dieppe. A violent thrashing stallion breaking his neck, or a leg, in a wallowing ship, or while being led down a strange gangway, could be expected. Though they are scanty, the excerpts from the *Accounts* make it possible to reasonably infer how the horses got from Paris to Edinburgh. These horses and our two horsemen have never been traced down before, I suspect, for only a nosey relative would be interested in focusing on two *servandis*. The search has not been easy, but these two men are in the contemporary government records. The two source books giving their names were sufficient to be the corroboration, or verification, that our legend needed. Most people did not rate even a word in the rudimentary records of that long-ago age. The surprising number of facts that were recorded can be fleshed out with general accuracy. A complete biography of each person is not needed. My task was to find the bench-marks, and sketch in the details, just as a surveyor connects his known points to make an accurate topographic map. I hope that in making these people become visible in the queen's household, and among her horses, an interesting and realistic picture of her Lowland Scotland can be seen.

The important people of history books ride the backs of nameless masses who are purportedly just as important in the eyes of God. But this riddle has no answer. Two who were rated as unimportant were André and Alexander. These *servandis* had their hands full with the queen's horses. They spoke only French, in England, which was just barely not at war with Scotland. They had no inkling when, or if, the impasse would be solved. From Dieppe to the queen's palace was an experience that they could tell the rest of their lives, a very dramatic story that has certainly never been told except as I reconstruct it here. It has to have been an element in Mary's later noticing of her two stable-boys, one of whom she saw married to an appropriate young lady. I believe that I am quite proud of my ancestor from Dieppe, France.

To go back to the citation about payment of the shipping agent's bill. I have found one reference to it. It is on page *xxiii* of the Preface to the *Accounts*, where the whole matter of ransoming the queen's French horses is set forth in complete error:

> "John Livingston, the master stabler, was paid 343£ for twenty-nine horses and mules which were bought in the north of England. They were taken from Morpeth to Alnwick and thence to Berwick where, for some unexplained reason, they were delayed a month...."

This misinterpretation is neither surprising, nor significant. It does show, though, that the biography of the horses needed to be written. Their keepers got in the spotlight too, for you can't have horses without men to care for them. Who but a relative of these men would take the pains to uncover every detail of this episode? With just a bit of imagination, one can see these two men, the featured stars in the scenario, as they singlehandedly maneuver the horses for two months. They became involved in an international incident in a foreign land, anonymous laborers in the vineyard of history.

They had no money, spoke only French in England, did not know why they and their horses had been impounded, and the Dutch ships had departed. As prisoners of a sort, they would have been fed, at least. No one gave them medals, of course, but they must have been resourceful and faithful men. One could hope that the queen thanked them for what they had done. We cannot guess what reaction they got from the 28 Scots, and the *maister stabillar* who arrived talking in still another strange language. At times they may have wished they were back in Dieppe.

They were owed back pay when they got to Edinburgh and they needed clothes suitable to enter into the queen's service. A clerk of the Lord High Treasurer needed to enter their names in his time book. This clerk would have been literate, but not able to speak or write French, as is amply proven by the entries he made. It was probably the same clerk who had enrolled all the new French attendants and servants on the queen's payroll. Some of the names he wrote down for them became famous through their very corruption, such as Sebastian, with no surname. Forever after he has been called Bastien. He was a favorite. Another who served the king was tagged "Paris." Our heroes, coming before this clerk, knew they needed to be recorded. If they told him their French surnames, they might as well have been speaking to his table.

One said his name was Alexander. The clerk could spell this universal name, for two Kings of Scotland had borne it. (In time, the name, abbreviated to "Sandy," had become so common that Sandy was often used to mean "Scotchman." The notion that "Scots" should supercede "Scotch" is, of course, quite a recent fancy.) The other man said his name was André, so the clerk wrote Hendre in his book. We have given some samples of spelling which show that this clerk did quite well spelling André as he did: Hendre. Speaking in French, both of the men told the clerk, "we are from Dieppe." In French, that phrase is simply *Dieppois*, so the clerk wrote what he heard, "Depo," in his book, and that is a pretty good rendition of *Dieppois*. In that brief episode, we were given our name. André's descendants spelled Depo in at least twenty ways before they settled down to the present two. The payroll episode proved the men were either brothers or father and son. The clerk gave them the same surname because it was perfectly obvious. The two men permitted him to give them the same surname, which strangers would not have allowed. This is one of the key situations in the search for our name. Perhaps these men were the talk of the week. Even the queen must have demanded to know the whole story of her horses. There was no one else who knew all of the details of the departure, the voyage, the putting-in to Tynemouth, or any of the story prior to arrival of the rescue party from Edinburgh. Mary would have had urgent questions about the death of the one horse we can be sure.

Hendre became the ancestor of our line, for Alexander (or his young son) was lost, as we will tell. There never was such a name as Hendre, and it hurts a little each time I write this jumble of letters, but it doesn't change the essence of our tale, or matter now. Whatever name Hendre answered to after he arrived in Scotland mattered not a bit to him, I expect. He and his wife certainly spoke in French for many years. He must have learned Scots, but I doubt he ever mastered what I have read was the atrociously-mouthed speech of the Border rustics. There are court records showing he was Hendre for 45 years, until he was about 64 in 1608. Then another court clerk, realizing that there was no such name as

Hendre, wrote down Henry Depo. This, again, had no connection with the name André or, in English, Andrew. All of these malapropisms have been very useful 425 years later, as they tie our beginnings firmly into exact times and places in Scottish history, and link both of the Depos into these ancient record books.

Spelling in 1561 was in a chaotic predicament, caught part way between general illiteracy in the native tongue, and the refinement of Shakespearean poetry just around the corner in England. Written words were often formed by a jumble of letters combined with almost no phonic sense as the writers struggled without rules or dictionaries. Also rules were regarded with more or less contempt. The guttural speech they were attempting to reduce to writing contributed to this impasse. The Gaelic of the Highlands had never been corrupted by a deluge of competing tongues as in the mixing bowl that was the Borderlands. I feel privileged to have once attended a Gaelic church service, in Gairloch, not understanding one word, of course except for the warm greetings in English. The Lowland speech, in contrast, was an archaic mixture, based on Anglo-Saxon, with contributions from Pictish, Celtic, Norwegian, and English. No wonder the scribes had trouble writing it down. Any Latin in this dialect the Scots spoke did not come from the Roman legions stationed at Hadrian's wall, for they seem to have left no words behind. Our Latin words came through Norman French 800 years after the Romans had left, a legacy of the Norman Conquest. Part of one sentence will be quoted from page 354 of the *Accounts*, because it is the citation which dates the first written reference to our family name in Scotland:

> "Item,...charging all and sundrie oure Soverane Ladeis liegis duelland withtin the saidis Sherefdomes, alsweill realitie as ryaltie, quhilkis hes obtenit ony new fewis yit unconfermit of kirklandis sett be the prelattis and uthiris beneficit men sen the viij day of Marche jMvCLviij yeris, to compeir befoir the commissionaris appointit in the comptaris challmer in Edinburght the secund day of Aprile nixttocum, thair to exhibit and produce thair infeftmentis quhilkis thai haif

obtenit of kirklandis to tak new confirmatioun and with lettres to serche, seik, and inbring the gudis and geir pertening to Johnie Knox and James Knox his sone, for the slauchter of Alexander Depo, his sone, duelling (dwelling) in Stichell in the Mers...and with lettres of proclamatioun to the saidis mercat croces anent the violatioun of the Sabboth as said is, vij£."

There are 682 pages of sentences as readable as this one, which is not quoted in full. This one sets the limit of exasperation with its murkiness, for it is so important to me, since it does place our name in Scotland in 1564. Dates given in adjoining sentences point to a time in late February of 1564 when this deadly deed was done. Since this preceded March 25 (Lady Day), the year is 1564 by their calendar, and by ours. For over two hundred years a belief has persisted in Scotland that our ancestor was a refugee from the Huguenot persecutions in France. The flight of Protestants did not occur until after the Massacre of Saint Bartholomew's Eve, August 24, 1572. Then the genocide and flight continued, with people escaping as best the could on foot, on horseback, or in small boats, to adjacent nations. This persecution and migration continued for roughly a hundred years. But Alexander Depo, with his son André and a younger son who was later "slaughtered" came to Scotland in September 1561. They were recorded as *servandis* (servants tending the *Quenis grace horss and mulattis*) on two Dutch ships. This was eleven years before the massacre.

The ambiguous writing we have quoted emphasizes once again that "writing must be read in the circumstances of its formulation." Not only I, but also an expert, read the sentence to mean that Alexander had been killed, if that was the meaning of *slauchter*. Alexander was not our ancestor, André was. Were they brothers? That logical assumption fits all the facts, but one. That is the word *sone*. Two men were hired to care for the horses. They had to be skilled and old enough for that responsibility. Two brothers could fit that requirement, but the word *sone* forces us to guess what the sentence was intended to mean.

Neither Jamieson's famous dictionary of the Scottish language, nor several others, really help with the usage of this common word. The definitions cite *sun, sone,* some taxonomic pedantry, and a French coin, but no guidance in the constant use of *sone* in the old writing. The Oxford English Dictionary with its system of actual usage doesn't include Scottish dialect, but this common word needs clarification. The LHT wrote in Latin, and the structure of this excerpt may show that he was thinking in that language with its genitive case, and didn't really know how to show possession without it. I believe that he meant to tell that the son of Alexander Depo had been killed, but was unable to shape his phrase to read "son of A.D." or Alexander's son. He simply repeated the words as he had used them for the other boy, James, where the meaning was clear.

Alexander's son must have been a young boy. He was not referred to in the record of 1561 about recovery of the queen's horses at Tynemouth where the two men were referred to as *servandis*. That word could refer to two or three servants. A young boy would not be paid, but allowed to go along as a helper to pay for his passage. His father, his older brother André, and he were the *servandis*. This suggests that the mother had died; otherwise the husband would not likely have gone away as he did. This excerpt, and all the intervening episodes, can be trusted to the imagination. An interesting novel could be written around the facts that we have unearthed, but our family story would not be altered. It is based on the life of Alexander's other son, André, or Hendre, or Henry, who was the stable-boy to the queen, and our ancestor.

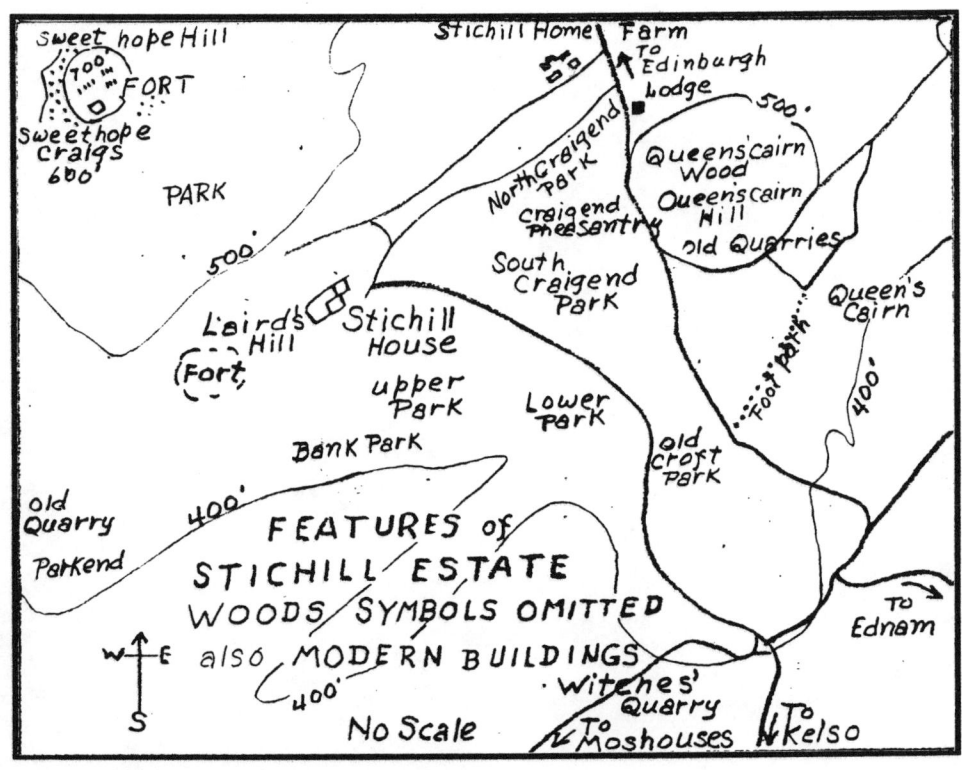

Figure 3: Features of Stichill Estate

Although he never intended it, the LHT of Scotland incorporated in his monster sentence several bits of information useful to me, Alexander's ultimate shirt-tail relative. He told me:

1. That Stichell was a royal horse farm.

2. That it was in a famous stock raising area, the Merse, an extensive agricultural tract northwest of Kelso.

3. That John Knox, through his son, James, would very likely be in lifelong enmity to Hendre Depo. I believe that this man was, perhaps, a nephew of the reformer of the same name, and that he, himself, or a son named John Knox, became a minister in the parish of Melrose where our ancestor's family was enrolled. It would be unproductive research to verify this further, but such a situation would be loaded with hostility for decades for the Depo family.

4. That Alexander Depo worked for the queen, and was paid by the national treasury, a day's ride away in Edinburgh.

All of the evidence of this and previous excerpts answers a question that has been in my mind since first learning of two shiploads of horses. What happened to the horses? Some of them were sent to Stichell. I went there in the fall of 1985, and made what I call a windshield survey. It is good, rolling agricultural land, well elevated, and obviously well developed. A prestigious background is indicated by the presence of an old mansion, monumental gates and a gatehouse. A very old mansion, I was told, preceded the present one. My visit was simply to get a sense or feeling for the place I had become so interested in. I already had precise surveys at six inches to the mile that portrayed this place, and the whole Borderland. A sketch map is included to give an idea of the

Stichill estate. Some of the history of this part of the Borderlands is needed to see how all these events so naturally fit together.

Kelso, down the river Tweed from Melrose Abbey, had been a market town and livestock fair for centuries. Though repeatedly burned by the English from across the nearby border, it had always been a favorite stopping place for royalty. To its northwest there were large tracts of choice agricultural land. This was the Merse, part of the March of Borderland, frontier with England. Stichill is about 37 miles south of the palace, and about that far from the ancestral home of the powerful Hepburn family. The 4th Earl of Bothwell, James Hepburn, who had great influence with the queen, very likely saw to it that her new horses were so stationed that numerous rewarding side effects could flow his way, not the least of them being the breeding up of his own Scottish horses. He had not hesitated to go to Paris the previous year to beg, and receive, cash from Mary. It would have been entirely characteristic of him to deviously provide for her horses, and himself, in his own neighborhood. His castle, Crichton, was just to the north, and his Hermitage was south. The map of Stichill, the modern spelling, shows the features of a magnificent estate: a fort and reservoir, much wooded acreage, six named parks, Stichill Home Farm, Stichill House, Laird's Hill, a playing or training field, kennels, pheasantry, Queenscairn Hill, Queen's cairn Wood, and finally a witch's quarry. These names have persisted down to the present, yet Mary's interest in this estate lasted not much over five years. She reigned about six years, and for much of that time she was in desperate, deteriorating circumstances. Perhaps no better record exists that this estate was her horse establishment than the terse report of her Lord High Treasurer: "Alexander Depo, his sone, was slaughtered at Stichell."

When I first encountered "Stichell in the Merse," the odd gargling sounds of the words were disconcerting to my American ear, like a thump in the basement at night. But I found that in old English, *stighe* meant a foot path. When hill was added, Stichell became a name. The "merse," which came from O.E. *mersc*, meant swamp, or in Scots, "low flat land" thus something like "footpath-through-lower-land-to-a-hill" emerges from the etymology.

This hill, or, as I found, series of gentle hills, was from time out of mind, the site of a fine estate where King James II left his queen and nine year old prince to wait for him. He was besieging Roxburgh Castle, a few miles distant, when one of the first cannon in Scotland exploded and killed him in 1460. This event very plausibly bears out the traditional belief that the numerous references to "Queen's" started at that time. It was exactly a century later that the son of a servant of another queen was "slaughtered" here. Both queens were named Mary, but only the first is reputed to have lived here. The features named for her as well as the tradition of the royal domicile would naturally have led to its use by Mary Stewart. Also leading to its choice was the arable land, the proximity to Kelso with its age-old horse tradition, its relative nearness to the Palace, and the fortress castle of our calculating Earl.

Was the laird of this property peremptorily informed that he was to have the honor of caring for the queen's horses which would be arriving within the year? In those times monarchs progressed around their realms. Sometimes their hosts were bankrupted by the honor. Quartering some horses would be preferable to an extended visit by a monarch and retinue. We will never know the details. Horses and their attendants were always at hand, but not written about with the fortuitous exception which was bad for Alexander, but good for us, in a manner of speaking. He did, at least, get mentioned, which was more than was achieved by a certain lady-in-waiting. She married André, his other son, as the records all but state.

The queen needed her horse farm for very few years, and her baby, Prince James, had no need for it at all. The farm would have been organized to care for the horses and dismantled within six years, the length of Mary's reign. The resident laird probably avoided publicity about the use of his estate by royalty. Records may exist about this episode or a metal-detector search might turn up harness parts or buttons from French clothing that could fill out this interesting mystery. In a brief summation it might be noted that, in quick order, Darnley, the King, was murdered, Bothwell married the queen, she abdicated, she was imprisoned, she escaped, Bothwell ran away, and she fled from her own people, to England. That was her last mistake.

That avalanche of disastrous events provided no opportunity for the wily Bothwell to gain control of the breeding stock on the queen's farm. He must have recognized the superlative horseflesh, and planned on improving his own stable of native horses. He did not have that opportunity, but some one did. How were these animals dispersed? Did they provide basic blood lines in Scotland's horse population, or was the herd dissipated to no lasting advantage? We wonder if the Clydesdale breed has any relationship to these horses? It is not surprising that, in the tumultuous chaos ending the reign of Mary, no attention was paid to her horses or the estate at Stichell. Like a puff of smoke, the episode was past before most people had even heard that horses had been there. Once again, Stichell belonged to the memory of the widowed queen with her little prince whose father had been killed by the exploding cannon.

We don't know what the men from Dieppe looked like, but, as we have said, their likely Northman blood could have made them big and blond. The Angle, Scot, British lineage of their new neighbors may have produced a general similarity in appearance. Certainly the men from Dieppe should not be visualized, out of hand, as typically Gallic in appearance. Bothwell, in choosing the two horse grooms would have favored husky, intelligent men, and if they bore a general resemblance to typical Borderers, and he was one, they would have been favored.

None of the people we are writing about were of docile disposition, whether of Border stock or the Viking stock of Dieppe. It was commonplace, in the Borders, for poker and tongs to be chained to the hearth so family arguments could not be settled by their use.

> "...witht lettres to searche, seik, and inbring the gudis and geir (goods and gear) pertaining to Johnie Knox and James Knox his sone, for the slauchter of Alexander Depo his sone, duelling [dwelling] in Stichell in the Mers..."

It is apparent from the use of the word "slaughter" that "Alexander his sone" got the worst of the encounter with James Knox. Maybe a pitchfork was used in that attack. The history of Scotland is gruesome in the details of homemade jurisprudence, but we have a particular interest in conjecturing the scenario that precipitated this attack. We can visualize the cause of conflict between two men, not old, not young, of firey disposition. Two teenage boys would have similar feelings, but not the necessary restraint of violent impulses. Alexander, and his son, wore French clothes that were undoubtedly better than the natives had. They had come from a seaport city, and must have had a sophisticated flair far removed from the manners and deportment of the locals, very few of whom had ever been out of sight of the reek of his own lum. The Scots were said to speak in guttural tones more from their throats than their lips, far different than the enunciation of a French speaker who must have repeatedly been nonplused, and unable to comprehend or respond, a perfect situation to incite boys to violence. I, myself, have had many such stalemates of comprehension in the United States, and in Great Britain. On one occasion in France, my son Roy, hostelling with Irish and Australian companions, found that they could not understand each other in English, but that they could get along fine in French, a compromise not possible in that conflict at the stables.

At Stichell, the locals would have resented what they took to be supercilious mannerisms of the newcomer. Perhaps James took exception to the way the other boy appeared to be his rival for the attentions of local girls. In addition, John Knox is in the records as something of a local leader. He may have been in charge of the horse operation. If so, James may have felt privileged to lord it over a French boy. We don't know, and it doesn't matter now, just how all this built up to such a drastic end. It must have been known, or the new boy may have been foolish enough to tell, how his brother André and sister-in-law had been favored by the queen.

It is very strange that the Lord High Treasurer of Scotland went beyond his accounting duties to report that two boys got into a fight. He knew that the three French grooms and the horses at Stichell were of great personal interest to the queen. He was an appointed official and his job could be at stake if he failed to anticipate her feelings about them. There is complete agreement that Mary had a teen-age girl's obsession with horses. She had undoubtedly agonized in Paris over selecting only thirty, and having only two transport ships. The two men and the boy, with their familiar French deportment, who fit so well into her personal world, must also have become loved as part of this obsession.

When the boy was attacked by a Border roughneck, it would not have been politic of her officials to simply replace him with a local workman. They knew that the boy was special. There is no possibility that the fight would have been entered in the <u>Accounts</u> if the victim had been just a local lad, nor would the hue and cry have been raised against the guilty boy and his father. They were important local people versus foreigners. This was the killing of a protege' of the queen. There were constant murderous attacks in the Borders, but this seems to be the only one about two boys fighting that was entered in the national journal of accounts.

The terse record of a "slaughter" conveys an amazing amount of collateral information, but we do not know how the crime was resolved. The idea of the state prosecuting a slaughter was new for the times. Like the Greeks of 600 B.C., and on through the ages, relatives could sue or take revenge as they chose, but the state was not ordinarily interested except in treason or heresy. The Hatfields and McCoys of feuding fame in the Appalachian Mountains, were still following the old ideas of equity they had brought from Scotland and they feuded themselves nearly to extinction, just a few decades ago, without invoking either treason or religion.

Grave injuries were certainly inflicted on Alexander's son, but the report does not positively say he died. Hendre was living on Melrose land 10 or 12 miles to the west at this time, and the boy's wounds may have healed under the care of his brother and sister-in-law. In the absence of follow-up records a conjecture has to be considered: If the boy did not die, was he nursed back to health at his brother's home, or could it have been by his mother-in-law? His father may have remarried.

As this book was about to be published I found an answer to a puzzle about this "killing." In the sixteenth century the word "murder" meant that the killer was not known, but if he were, the word "slaughter" was used as in this case where the culprit was James Knox. The Lord Treasurer recorded the slaughter and ordered pursuit as soon as he received the news, for pursuit could not be delayed. However, in the messenger's haste to ride to Edinburgh, the boy's exact condition could have been very uncertain. It is significant that the news was sent at all. Did this boy live to become the founder of a family in the Borders named after him? Or did he found a line in Poland that was named after him? This is a startling possibility.

I chanced on a book published in Scotland in 1915 for the Scottish Historical Society, which tells of the migration of Lowland Scots to Poland, particularly to Cracow and Lublin. Extensive migration was a necessity more than once, as population pressure on scarce arable land beccame so great that desperate poverty left no alternative but migration for many young men. One well-recorded migration started at about the time Alexander's son needed a place to go if, indeed, he lived and left the land he must have come to hate. In Warsaw the Scots were so numerous there was a Scot's tax, and in Lublin a Scottish Brotherhood. As I worked on this, my son, Roy, told me he had an engineer friend who was Polish with the name Aleksander Macander. He, in turn, had a friend whose name, Gordon, was pronounced in Polish.

Dr. Michael Lynch, at the University of Edinburgh, in a letter to me, cited a current Polish researcher estimating the migration of 30,000 Scots to Poland through the years. In tracing my Deppa family, I found about forty of the name, mostly in Minnesota. This seemed totally out of line, for I have a pretty good idea where the Deppas of my lineage are living. I found that these people are Polish, and as surprised as I that there was another, totally separate line. Are those Polish Deppas descendants of Alexander Depo's son who had sought a new, and better life in the eastern land which seemed to be refuge for so many in those years? A further possibility is not at all remote. Within a few years after his son's death, or emigration to Poland, Alexander may have started a new life for himself and not at Stitchell. It seems unrealistic to think that he did not. He must have been about forty years old at that time.

The queen's horse farm began and ended within her six year reign. Beginning in late 1561 the next date we have found is 1564 when the stable-boy was attacked. A famous ride by the queen in the fall of 1566 very likely involved the people and animals on the farm. She, and her court and ministers rode from Holyroodhouse to the town of Jedburgh, famous for ages for its Abbey and castle. There she held assizes and went on to make a complicated bit of history that has been told many times. In Chapter XIV a contemporary news-item about Bothwell's involvement is reproduced. The parade of riders from the palace certainly needed a rest stop on the fifty-mile trip. The route passed not far from Stitchell and by pre-arrangement a full-scale, and sumptuous, bivouac was undoubtedly prepared at a suitable place. Did Alexander see his queen, did the son, did Hendre, and is it possible that the once-upon-a-time lady-in-waiting saw her? Did any of these many people have any idea that in less than a year violent events would sweep Mary off her throne?

Only a distant relative extricating his name from the musty record books of Scotland would have struggled through the many hundreds of pages of strange words and constructions to find just the few significant references. The earliest is reproduced on our page 115; the second is on page 122. These citations from the *Accounts* are separated in time by 29 months, 277 pages apart in the Lord Treasurer's day book. He had watched the Depo men for a long time. There is only one reason that makes sense: he knew the queen was interested in them. The beginning of Hendre's record is in our Chapter XI.

The archaic language of these key citations has presented a problem from the time I first saw them in the *Accounts of the Lord High Treasurer of Scotland*, Volume 11, page 354. Dr. Lynch gave me the reference in February 1983. I found this very rare book, and the rest of the series, at the Library of Congress. The exact date of the "slaughter" is not given, but it works out to be in the last week of February, or the first week of March (before Lady Day), 1564. Shakespeare and Galileo were born, and Michelangelo died in this year.

The presence of Alexander Depo in Scotland in 1564 is really irrefutable, but many facets of our history are tied to this short record. The arrival of the two men and the boy with the horses is beyond reasonable argument. The clincher is that Alexander Depo and Hendre Depo are both recorded. That strange name, in that time-frame, surely makes them the *servandis* on the ships with the *quenis grace horss*. The presence of André at Melrose is recorded in the *Regality Records of Melrose*, Vol. I. This series of books I found at Catholic University in Washington, D.C. The new name links the two men, and the attack on the boy was the key. The first record of our ancestor was on the 12th day of September 1561, about a month after their landing at Tynemouth.

My original interpretation of the Stitchell quotation was the same as that of a researcher of Scottish documents: Alexander had been slaughtered by James Knox. After much further study, however, this idea has been re-interpreted as has been told. Since John Knox was a father, the indication is that the son of Alexander was young, like James Knox his antagonist, both in their teens. André was an older son of Alexander, competent to handle the horses on a ship. Thus it becomes evident that the plural word *servandis* refers to a father from Dieppe and his two sons. André was old enough to be an employee. His brother was just a boy not on the payroll.

At first reading *his sone* seemed a redundancy or slip of the pen. It seemed clear enough that Alexander was the casualty. No matter; the overriding significance of the record is that the fight links the Depo men to the records of Melrose, and the queen's horse-ship episode, three clear-cut citations. After much puzzling over this muddled sentence and other evidence, I had come to the conclusion that two brothers had been hired in Dieppe, and that the younger one had gone with some of the horses to the farm at Stichell. There he became embroiled with another young man named James Knox, with a bad outcome. In November of 1986, an etymologist gave me an answer to my questions about the use of word *sone*. It was clear, he said, that it was the son of Alexander who was the casualty. Thus abruptly Alexander became the father of André, not a brother. By a reasonable supposition he also became a widower. He, and André, had signed on to sail with the queen's horses. The father also took his younger boy with him to work for his ship passage, and found (room and board). What was the boy's name? Nothing will ever be known of this French family's background story, but it must have been sad for the three who chose to leave Dieppe and go to Scotland.

I don't work crossword puzzles anymore, as I find archaic Scottish writing more tantalizing, and it has meaning. For instance, *his sone* is used twice in the sentence. The first usage is perfectly clear. The second might have been one of the very common slips of a copyist, or a messenger error. I had not yet plumbed the depths of obscurity, and did not realize that the apostrophe and *s* combination had not yet been invented. Those people could not write "Alexander's son", or *sone*. Did this disability carry over into their speech? When they wanted to say "John's son" did they say "John, his sone"?

> "The kyng of Spayne is
> a foule paynim...
> The king his sonne of Spayn..."
>
> from *King Estmere*, an
> ancient English ballad

At that time, Scottish was struggling even more ineffectually than English to escape from the completely inflected Latin, into the grammar we now struggle with. They had problems with their solutions, but then, so do we, trying to figure out meanings. I wonder if any of their speech would be understandable to us. For the fun of it, I once had a friend expound to me in broadest Yorkshire, to my total mystification. In the same vein, we have tried to re-enter that world of the long ago Borderlands, not just to find our ancestors, but figuratively to listen to them, read their writing, and watch them make do with what they had. Except for that of the nobility, not much is known about their clothing, but some of our young people would say their clothing was funny. I consider myself an expert about funny clothing, for I have seen some of the passing specimens of punk in the Georgetown section of Washington, D.C., and a bit of it in England, too. Those old timers wouldn't even come close in a funny clothing contest.

CHAPTER IX

QUEEN MARY'S FIFTEEN LADIES-IN-WAITING
As Recorded By The Lord High Treasurer Of Scotland.

There are relatively few contemporary records of the six-year reign of Mary, Queen of Scots. Her many biographers pieced out what there are with information gleaned from every collateral source, such as letters and records of important figures of her time. Thus her life has been portrayed in great detail in many respects. My search has been for two people too obscure to warrant recordation; yet they served the queen, and were close to her in very personal ways. In the mind's eye they can be seen quite distinctly carrying out their duties. One was a Scottish lady-in-waiting, the other a French Huguenot stable-boy. His identity as a servant merged with that of another Dieppois or Depo: the record states ."....the Quenis grace horss, mullattis, and servandis (servants) with thame...." Three years later the same book records one of these servants, Alexander Depo, by name. Another ancient record cites Hendre Depo, the other stable-boy, by name, on five occasions. This amazing official recognition of two servants could not have happened except for the intervention of the queen in their lives.

The name of Hendre Depo's bride has not been found, but some day it might be, if her family left any records, and if they still exist. In the meantime our search has concentrated on finding out more about the ladies as a group. There has never been more than a passing reference to ladies-in-waiting except for the four Maries, and not much about them. They all, according to the custom of the time, moved about the court with great freedom as occasion required. In perfect familiarity with Mary, their task was to anticipate, reflect, and enhance the mood of the queen - to be her alter ego. Appearances were everything, and no court could appear to be sparse, drab and colorless: hence the ladies, gentlemen, pages, fools. Everything was stagecrafted as background for affairs of state or the pleasure of the court.

Most references to the queen's ladies-in-waiting mention the four Maries as though she had no others. When Mary, the queen of fabulous France, returned to meager Scotland as reigning queen, she maintained a splendor that shocked her countrymen. Such luxury was beyond their ken, even though for Mary the shock lay in the penury she found.

Just before Princess Elizabeth acceded to the English throne, she went to hunt the hart with her retinue of twelve ladies in white satin accompanied by twenty yeomen in green. This gives an idea of how things were done then, and also that the Queen of France and Scotland would have at least as many ladies as the English princess. The Lord Treasurer of Scotland could have had no idea that he alone, it seems, recorded the number of Mary's ladies-in-waiting. His over-meticulous recordation of saddles, bridles and cloaks was a very accurate unintentional statement that the queen had fifteen ladies in her train.

His account also shows that eleven of them were distinct from the four Maries. The eleven were anonymous, but the number can hardly be questioned, for the accounts were audited, as is explained in Latin. The Auditing Commission entertained itself very generously on an expense account, as is customary today. Even tips, and 15 shillings worth of string, were entered, and ten horses were hastily bought to replace those that obviously were thought to have been lost at sea with their hostlers.

The queen always occupied center stage, but the two people whose existence in her household I have sought to find served her best by being anonymous. Only a relative with unlimited curiosity would make the effort needed to pry them out of their obscurity. My cue was to find every word the records might contain about the queen's horses, and that idea did bear fruit. The horses, their harness, and the riding clothes made for the ladies, and very importantly, the dates, provided a sequence, and a framework, which was more important than names would have been. But I would have been happy to have had names, too, the name of our lady, that is. The records give the names of our ancestor and his father and refer to his young brother. It has been a sobering thought all through this search to see that no one else has ever been interested in these people, a foretaste of what is in store for us all, with few exceptions.

Perhaps a better title for this chapter would be "Accountancy as Practiced in the Mid 16th Century," with a subtitle: "Sidesaddles and Riding Garments Explained." The books I have worked with are not obtainable for most people unless they live in one of the larger Scottish cities, but they have a cultural interest, it seems to me. Anyone with curiosity about the old Scots tongue can read some of it in these excerpts with the archaic words, and the circumlocutions that reflect ways of thinking which we can hardly follow. Auld lang syne (long ago) can have a fascination that beats what can be seen on the tube most nights, and has led me to include details beyond the bare essentials. Mary, Queen of Scots, has a far greater following today than in 1561, and certainly greater than in 1567, when all the things that went wrong brought about her abdication and worse.

On first reading these excerpts, the general impression is of a strange hodge-podge of archaic English made almost meaningless with words not to be found in a dictionary, and beset with Roman numerals, and obsolete or unknown denominations of money and measure. Ancient writing has always fascinated me, for language is man's greatest invention. Unlike the really ancient, and foreign, this is just an archaic dialect of English, and I have been able to riddle it out, mostly. In England and Scotland, before they got into decimal coinage, I have been reduced to helpless trust in the native honesty of tradespeople as I held out my money for them to take what was owed them. In some countries it is more advisable to learn the language than to hold out your money. The treasurer's clerks produced a *summa* on their counting boards for the purchased items. Sometimes they resorted to the obolus, a coin of Europe that went back to Roman times, and was archaic even then.

This book, the *Accounts*, has 682 pages copied from the original, plus a 78 page Preface written by the Editors. The book is in Scots, except for many pages of Latin. One can literally become dizzy deciphering the meanings, and the words not in current dictionaries. Webster's International of 1864 solved an impasse for me many times. It is particularly frustrating that Jamieson's Scottish Dictionary, 50 miles distant, did not help me with words common in the book, such as *passand, clois, mottat, cussinettis, culvering, sone*. When it was made in the 1700s, words archaic then were not included.

To a layman floundering beyond his depth in the land of linguistics, the scholarship of the editors of these old records is astounding. They transcribed them into modern type early this century, but now the books are very rare. The original Treasurer's ledgers are locked away in vaults where virtually no one may see them. This inaccessibility has led me to quite freely display this 400-year-old writing. A layman could not decipher more than a word here and there of their crabbed goose quill squiggles. Even at that time this old-style script was passe', for a better Italian hand was known to some. A sample of the old script is given in a later chapter. If you look at it long enough, a few words begin to emerge from the tangle.

Perhaps there is no best way to organize the material we wish to present. The original text is given for its philological interest, but the Scots needs some translation. Here I must apologize for presuming to do this 3000 miles from where experts reside, but I have tried. Of all the people who have read the Treasurer's *Accounts*, perhaps no one else has scrutinized every word to discover exactly how many ladies-in-waiting the queen had in her train. I found there were fifteen, the four Maries, and eleven others.

Queen Mary's Fifteen Ladies-in-Waiting 143

Mary landed at the port of Leith on August 19, 1561. She was in mourning for her husband, Francis II, the boy King of France who had died eight months before. She knew that two shiploads of her horses were following her on the North Sea. It was necessary that these mounts be available without delay for her immediate use, but there would be some lapse, she knew, for her galleys had far outrun the horse ships. The first moves she made in this nebulous situation were made almost immediately.

Although under no delusions about the palace she was about to move into, she made no complaint nor comparisons with the magnificence she was accustomed to. If she had ever seen Holyroodhouse, it was through the eyes of a little child, and it had been virtually abandoned all of her life. In France she had chosen enough grand furnishings to fill two ships. These goods arrived soon after she did, and were added to the efforts that had been put forth by her unsophisticated countrymen to upgrade the place. Her horses were coming with only their halters. They would need to be fitted out for service; not exactly caparisoned, but properly saddled and bridled. Her ladies, too, needed attire for riding, and that in black. There is no way to know when the purchase orders went out for these goods. The *Accounts* are a record of payment, so one must conclude that the goods had been delivered by the dates given. If so, the ordering must have commenced almost as soon as the queen had set foot in Scotland. By the second of September, accounts were being settled. Saddles had been made and paid for thirteen days after the arrival.

Imagination can fill in a picture of the hubbub summarized in these few sentences. The shop proprietors, the master craftsmen, tailors, deliverymen, chamberlain, master of the wardrobe, master of horse, were in a frenzy. This rush order exceeded anything they had ever seen. Excerpts that we have taken from the book are indented. Definitions will be in parentheses. The unindented commentary will be an attempt to correlate the many pieces of evidence contained in the excerpts. None of this makes for smooth, fast reading, but insofar as this begins to resemble a textbook on sidesaddles and ladies' riding attire, the charge is admitted.

> "September 1561"
>
> "...The expensis debursit be the Quenis grace preceptis and speciale command in this instant moneth of September 1561.
>
> "...Item, the secund day of September to Anthonie Guido to by him claithis,...xij li.111j s.(j at end =1)
>
> "...Item, the said day, to Arthure Erskin, v elnis ij quarteris half quarter of blak stamyng to be ane fute mantill and harnesing to the Quenis grace, the elne xlvj s. summa...xij li.xviij s.ix d.
>
> "...Item, for xlv elnis ij quarteris of blak to be dule sadillis, and thair fute mantillis and harnesing to hir grace ladeis, the price of the elne xliiij s,; summa j c (the superscribed c signifies 100) li.ij s. (total 100 pounds, 2 shillings)."

This entry showing that Mr. Guido received 12 pounds, 4 shillings to buy clothes, also names Erskin as her majesty's draper. As we proceed, it will be evident that his shop had an inventory of exotic as well as domestic fabrics in quantity. The capital city may have had an exclusive corner on foreign imports. Guilds and other restrictive arrangements were so tight that one must forget any notion that a competitive commercial society existed then.

In this first excerpt, the term *fute mantill* highlights a garment needed in horseback travel, so old that it is crudely illustrated as worn by the wife of Bath, and two nuns, in Chaucer's *Tales of Canterbury*.

Queen Mary's Fifteen Ladies-in-Waiting

> A good WIFE was ther of bisyde BATHE
> upon an amblere esily she sat
> A foot-mantel about her hipes large
> And on hir feet a paire of spores sharpe
>
> - Chaucer

When I was a little boy riding in a cutter, and later in a Model T Ford open touring-car, we fended off the cold with our bear-robe. My father got his bear in the Potter County mountains before I was born. Foot mantles could be wrapped more tightly around one than could a stiff bear-robe. This archaic garment needs investigation, and explanation. The modern reader could have only the foggiest notion of the use of a foot mantle. Other terms also come across as almost meaningless jumbles of words, about the way Latin, or any language can sometimes be pronounced fairly well, by a reader with very little comprehension. When this account book was written over 400 years ago, everyone knew about all of these things. It is not necessary now to know about them, but in the same spirit that archaeologists dig up artifacts from 17th and 18th century sites, so we will "dig up" riding accessories from the 16th century. By studying these passages it is possible to determine exactly how many ladies-in-waiting the queen had in her train. The numbers are repeated several times in several contexts, but always lurking inscrutably behind strange apparel and horse-tack. Prices and quantities are always in Roman numerals to remind us that this is in 1561.

Mary, the queen, rode continually, sometimes violently, we read, but even in a book about the saddles of queens, I found no discussion of her mode of riding, *i.e.*: astride, or side-saddle. Nor have I seen anything about this in her biographies. These particular excerpts may actually be the most definitive evidence there is. She could only have ridden side-saddle when she and her maidens used the equipment listed here, especially the foot-mantles. When one tries to correlate the limitations of the side-saddle of that time with the hunting, hawking, and roaring around the countryside attributed to Mary, it seems that either her riding feats have been exaggerated, or she was riding astride. The side-saddle, then, was little more than a fabric pad.

She made a 60 mile ride, without sleep, to visit the wounded Bothwell in his Liddesdale fortress, the Hermitage. For a lark, young women of today try to retrace her trip, but one could safely bet they don't use side saddles like the ones being paid for in these accounts.

Before 1400, women rode astride whether they were peasants sitting on a donkey, or St. Helena entering Jerusalem in the 4th Century. During the 1400s, women rode astride or sat sidewise as they chose. When Mary was Queen of France, hunting scenes showed ladies riding astride, and aside, in the same tapestry. Mary knew women had always ridden both ways. She was an independent spirit, and an inveterate rider. She lived in the period of transition from the old mode to the new, and increasingly fashionable, notion of sitting sideways on a horse as though in a chair. Ceremonially dressed matrons ensconced as in a chair on a horse's back needed a footman to guide the horse. In a less lumpish style the lady could sit facing partly to the front and hook the right knee around a post or crutch built into the saddle. Then she could handle the reins and have some control if the horse so chose.

Catherine de'Medicis, who became Mary's mother-in-law, was one of the best women riders in France from the time she was a girl until her death. She was too vigorous a rider, and too intelligent, to put up with the one crutch side-saddle that gave so little control. She added a second crutch so the right knee and thigh could be wedged between these two solid posts at the front of the pad-like saddle, instead of against just one. Thus the rider was braced against being thrown off to the right or the left. The left foot in its stirrup added some bracing, but its slipper-like design made it little more than a useless ornament. Apparently the double crutch, or pommel, was actually her own invention. Mary must have been familiar with it as well as the cross saddle for riding astride.

Queen Mary's Fifteen Ladies-in-Waiting

Those who are not accustomed to riding side-saddle might consider the geometry of this posture: the right foot would be pointed more or less to the port side of the horse's ears, for that leg was wedged between two posts at the front of the saddle. At a trot, the foot would wave in erratic arcs. It is said that Catherine rather liked this idea for elaborately embroidered stockings with threads of gold were in vogue, but Elizabeth of England, with knobbier legs, was less enthusiastic. Wind, being unreliable, and vast skirts being flappable, the foot mantle became inevitable for it was a skirt anchor among other attributes. They had been used for centuries to shed rain, snow and mud. One of the last of our excerpts shows that strings for the ladies cloaks were bought. These could be used to tie down the billowing skirts on pleasant days when the more or less ugly-looking foot mantles were not needed, nor even cloaks. The spectacular gowns were not covered if it could be avoided, and the strings were kept handy to tie them down, wind or no wind. Ladies sometimes carried fans or similar devices to shield their faces from vulgar stares as they rode.

For the queen, *blak stamyng* was ordered for "one foot mantle etc." Five ells were needed, plus two quarters (1/2 ell), plus half a quarter (1/8) ell. Almost from the beginning of history an ell was the distance from the elbow to the tip of the middle finger. In these accounts, it may have become as much as 45 inches, but the Scottish ell was probably 37 inches. Equally archaic is the absence of inches and the handling of fractions. 5/8 of an ell seems so much simpler than the breakdown above. But remember these accounts were all done on abacus-like counting boards using pebble-like *calculi*, or counters, that could not deal in fractions as such. Our arithmetic had to wait for paper, pen or pencil, or at least slates and slate-pencils made of soapstone. Chalk for writing on slate is a modern invention.

The *Quenis grace fute mantill, and dule sadillis* stopped me, and I couldn't proceed until these mysterious articles were identified. That turned out to be a difficult assignment. Dictionaries, encyclopedias, and biographies of the queen were of no help. What was finally found will be interesting to those who had no idea that it could be so complicated for a lady to ride a horse. It was my good luck in researching side-saddles to know and be helped by a young lady who is a nationally known expert in riding side saddle. The purchases recorded in these accounts can only mean that the queen and her fifteen ladies were going to use the type of side saddle and gear being made in Scotland, which may not have been like that in France. However, the points that have been raised about Mary's earlier training, and familiarity with the cross saddle, lead me to feel that she had other plans as well. In her two shiploads of furnishings I believe she had included her French riding gear. Saddles, bridles, and apparel for riding in whatever mode, were all stowed away for use as she chose. I can't imagine that she would leave behind equipment she must have been very fond of, even sentimental about. Among other reasons, she had very much loved her young husband, the king, and rode with him often. She knew she would appear before Scottish crowds with her ladies, putting on a good show in conventional trappings, but that would be a very small part of her riding. She certainly did not leave her favorite gear in France.

I see no reason to doubt that Mary rode either way as she chose. As queen, who would argue with her choice, in either country? Children were always taught to ride astride first, so she knew all its advantages. After Catherine's time it took more than 300 years for men to invent half a dozen improvements before the present functional sidesaddle was achieved. Now, at last, in this century, it works, and it has been relegated to exhibition and circus use. The final achievement was within my lifetime. Finishing touches were the "leaping head," or third pommel, first experimented with in 1830. It simply curves down over the left thigh to hold that leg down as a horse leaps, shies, or stumbles.

Ladies could ride pillion, sidewise behind a man, on a cushion attached to his saddle, and this was often the chosen way. Queen Elizabeth rode to St. Paul's, in London, behind her Master of Horse. We mention this to show how variable custom can be. She sometimes was carried in a litter by two horses in tandem led by two grooms. There were many more ways then than now, to be transported by horses.

An interesting distinction is made in the indented excerpt given on a preceding page where Mr. Erskin bills for 5 5/8 ells of a black fabric of wool and linen called *stamyng*. The *Quenis grace* material was priced at 46 shillings per ell. The *blak* for *hir grace ladeis* was priced at 44. It must be that protocol required this tiny distinction in price. *Dule saddillis* means mourning saddles, I believe, however the black would be appropriate for any use.

> "...Item, for ix li.xiij unce iiij grote wecht of philosell silk maid in xj (ELEVEN) bridill reneis to the Quenis ladeis, the li iiij li.viij s.; (the price per pound is 4 pounds, 8 shillings). summa....xliij li. vj s. vij d.obolus.

> "...Item, for ij reneis maid of philosell silk, the price...iij li.xij s.

> "...Item, for xlix elnis j quarter of bukrame to lyne the sadillis, fute mantillis, and uthir furnesing, the elne v s,; summa...xij li. vj s. iij d."

Here we find that eleven of the queen's ladies are having bridle reins made of silk specified as *4 grote wecht*. This sounds like pretty good stuff. Nine pounds and thirteen ounces of it were needed, almost one pound for each set of reins. This much silk for a set of reins hardly seems reasonable, yet leather reins would weigh more than a pound. Whatever *philosell silk* was, it must have been both strong and heavy. *Li.* comes from Latin *libra* or pound, still used in several monetary systems. It is abbreviated *li*, or *L*, or in a special script £, or an *l* with a slash through it. More than one old symbol simply has to be omitted from modern transcriptions, for we don't have the letters in our machines. A Scottish pound then was in the neighborhood of 1/4 the value of an English pound sterling.

This order for eleven reins cannot reasonably be interpreted any way except that there were eleven ladies, especially since eleven is specified in other places. Two sets of reins are then listed, but no indication who they were for. This is a significant separation that shows the eleven were recognized as a specific group. Spare reins were needed, for silk could break at any time. A groom, possibly our ancestor, could carry the spares as he attended the mounts in a procession.

Glue-filled linen is probably what is meant by *buckram*. Forty-nine and a quarter ells of it, almost sixty-two yards, must have stiffened everything up quite uncomfortably. We find equipment for 11 ladies, then 12, and 15 as will be noted, but there were considerations we cannot even guess at in all of this. The queen regent, Mary's mother, had died in June. She and her ladies must have left very fine French saddles that could be used to set apart the four Maries of Mary's train from the 11 lesser ladies-in-waiting. It could be that the Maries had each brought favorite, elegant tack, in the ships from France, but that space could not be spared for all the equipment. There is a pattern visible throughout, that a status difference was maintained between the four Maries, and the eleven other ladies.

1. "...Item, to Robert Abercrumbie, saidlar, for making of the Quenis grace awin sadill, fute mantill, and furnesing thairto,...x li.

2. "...Item, for the making and furnesing of xij sadillis, fute mantillis, and uthir furnesing thairto, concerning the Quenis gracis ladeis, sadill vj li. xiij s. iiij d. .....summa lxxx li. (80 pounds).

3. "...Item, for xj heidstaillis to thame witht staikis to the hors, ilk heidstaill vj s,.   ...summa...iij li.vj s.

Queen Mary's Fifteen Ladies-in-Waiting 151

4. "...Item, to Nicholas Ramsay for the werkmanschip of xj bridill reneis of philosale silk to the Quenis grace and hir ladeis, ilk pece xxvj s.; summa xiiij li. xiij s. iiij d. (14 pounds, 13 shillings, 4 pence.).

5. "...Item, to Nicholas Purvis for xij mollat bittis to the saidis horss, ilk pece xv s.; summa...ix li.

6. "...Item, for ane mollat bit to the Quenis haiknay, ...xviij s.

7. "...Item, for iij ringis to hir gracis harnesing,...xviij d.

8. "...Item, to the foirsaidis werkmen servandis in drink silver, ...xs."

It cost 10 pounds to have the queen's saddle made, but 12 more saddles were made for 6 pounds, 13 shillings, 4 dinari (pence) each. More was charged for making the royal equipment, as we have noted before. Saddles, as we have traced their story, were very simple affairs. No iron, wood, or leather is mentioned, for they were essentially pads, although some sort of a pommel must have been part of the design. Some elevation at the back of the saddle, now called the cantle, must also have been provided. This, and the pommel, or crutch, would seem essential, to give some security, fore and aft. The twelfth saddle could well have been a spare to avoid the embarrassment of a torn or dirtied one at a last minute.

Eleven headstalls were made. These are for the same eleven minor ladies who had bridle reins and saddles made. A bridle has a bit, and reins. The bit must be held properly in the horse's mouth, and this is done by the straps that run up the cheeks to the ears, and around them, also under the jaw. This is the headstall. The "staikis to the hors" part of the headstall I will guess at as being what is now called a checkrein. This strap running from under the horse's jaw between his forelegs to the girth, keeps him from throwing his head up, and making his rider look foolish in front of the crowd. The term *staikis to the hors* means that more than one of something called a stake, is attached to the horse, and that is about all I can be sure of, for the *-is* indicates plural.   Perhaps these "stakes" refer to a cockade sort of ornament above the ears of the horse. Such decorations have always been known, but their proper name eludes me just now. Since each headstall cost only 15 shillings they were not elaborate.

A different craftsman, Nicholas Purvis, made 12 *mollatt* bits. Again there is a spare. What *mollat* means is a secret none of the half dozen dictionaries I looked in could tell. Perhaps it was a very gentle sort of snaffle bit if the root of *mollat* derives from the Latin *mollis*, or soft. The bits cost nearly three times the price of the headstalls which may indicate the difficulty of fine metal working, then.

The eleven reins cost over 44 pounds for the silk alone, while the headstalls, *witht staikis to the hors*, cost a little over 3 pounds, total, for material and workmanship. A special craftsman, Nicholas Ramsay, made the eleven bridle reins for the queen's ladies at a unit cost more than four times as great as was paid for the headstalls, complete. These eleven silken reins cost more than 58 pounds or over 5 pounds a pair. These super luxurious reins come close to equalling the price of all the rest of the harnessing. These figures show that conspicuous consumption at that time could be flaunted in one's bridle reins, the last place a modern might put his money. Western "cowboys" on parade put their big money in a saddle and bridle, up to 30 or 40 thousand dollars - the same motivation.

The queen's *hackney* implies a hired horse, but the word has acquired so many meanings through time that it might as well be interpreted, plain horse. Her own horses were expected momentarily. It is hard to resist wondering why she didn't send a helicopter to find the ships or at least radio the captains. The outfitting recorded in these accounts shows how certain they were that the horses would arrive. They did arrive, but much later, and it is recorded that such beautiful horses had never before been seen in Scotland. I hope that the bridles, and especially the bits, were made either large, or adjustable, not sized to the wirey native ponies. I'll leave it to a grammarian to unravel *to the foirsaidis werkmen servandis in drink silver*, but with their job well done they probably spent the ten shillings with an itinerant ale-woman outside the Purvis workshop.

> "...Item, for vij elnis ij quarteris of blak to be vj cussinettis to the Quenis gracis ladeis, the price of the elne xl s.; summa xv li.
>
> "...Item, for vij elnis iij quarteris and half quarter of blak bukrame to lyne thame witht, the elne v s.; summa xxxix s.v d. obolus.
>
> "...Item, for making of the saidis vj cussinettis, ilk cussinat haifand ane stirrope girth stuffit witht downis, ilk pece iij li.; summa...xviij li."

A sidesaddle was an iffy thing to ride on, each lady having to find her own best position. A pillow could be tucked under the right thigh to lessen the chances that an arthritic hip joint might be permanently crippled by the jolting twists, as the horse bounced the rider up and down. How did those women survive a few hours at a "jolly round trot" with one faulty stirrup, and one foot sticking out front? When I thoughtlessly sit with one foot under me as young people can do for hours on end, I nearly fall down when I stand up, and slowly ease my joints back together. The six little cushions (*cussinettis*) were for the ladies who thought to mitigate the pain. Each was made with about 4 feet of stiff buckram covered with about the same amount of black. *Ilk* (each) cushion had *ane* (pure Anglo-Saxon for a, an or one) girth to the stirrup. The cushion would quickly have been pushed off the horse to the right except for a cord tying it to the one stirrup where the left foot could hold it tight. They used a thick, stuffed cylindrical cord as I interpret it, for that would not only hold the cushion, but also provide a little extra padding. Only six of the ladies were expected to want this device. I would have wanted two of them.

Now that the side-saddle has been developed to the ultimate, and is almost abandoned, it is not padded with down nor made to be soft. It is of very firm leather designed to perform as functionally as possible. Comfort is built into the design. Here, as always, the rule applies: don't judge the past by the present. They had the leather, wood, metal, and good workmen, but we have the will to experiment. Innovation was a bad idea in Scotland, more so than in Italy, or France, not welcomed by either the craft guilds or the public, in Scotland.

> "...Item, the thrid day of September, to Serwaice Duncondie, virlat of the Quenis gracis chalmer, for xxvj elnis ij quarteris of Pareis grene, deliverit to the tapeschar to be ane cabinnet to the Quenis chalmer in Halierudehous, the elne xxxvj s.; summa xlvij li. xiiij.
>
> "...Item, for xxiiij elnis iij quarteris of Inglis grene to the said Dow servace, the elne xxvj s. viij d.; summa xxxiij li."

Here begins the refurbishing of the queen's suite of several rooms. The palace had been worked on before she arrived, but I can visualize her dismay at what she found. Without being critical, she said she would like to have her personal chambers hung with green cloth, which I have read was her favorite color. The effect would certainly be better than the dungeon-like stone. I don't recall what the walls looked like when I visited the *Quenis gracis chalmer* long before I had any inkling that my ancestral mother had seen these wall-hangings being installed. My attention was on the story the guide was telling of the savage stabbing of Riccio in these rooms. A young girl in our group asked the guide why the men had killed Riccio. Non-plussed for a moment, the man stammered out, "because he was there, I guess," and that is a brief, and accurate response well sanitized for a tourist group.

"...Item, to Arthure Erskin, iij elnis and ane quarter of blak serge of Florence to be ane dule riding cloik and skirth to the Quenis grace, the elne iij li. v s.; summa x li. vj s. iiij d.

"...Item, for 1 elnis of Franche blak stamyng to be xv (fifteen) cloikis and skirttis to hir gracis ladeis, the elne xlij s.; summa jcv li."

Much profitless research could be expended on mourning traditions so stringent as to require "one mourning riding cloak, and skirt to the Queen's grace," and for each of her fifteen ladies-in-waiting. This was more than nine months after her husband had died. Mary had been widowed on the fifth of the preceding December. Four years later, in the worst mistake she had yet made, she married Darnley, wearing a great black mourning gown with a wide black hood. Immediately after the ceremony, according to custom, she changed into festive clothing. This episode seems ritualistic, for she always had great quantities of luxurious clothing which she wore before that first year was up, I believe. However, as this excerpt and the next two show, much money was spent on black cloaks soon to be discarded if they were only for mourning. More likely these riding garments were judged to be suitable outerwear for the severe Scottish winters, and the autumn mud.

No clearer statement could be made that the queen had fifteen ladies-in-waiting. Money was spent to outfit them all alike, and like the queen herself. When they were all mounted on beautiful horses, these riders would make a startling procession. It was necessary for the queen to be seen in town, and throughout her realm as often as possible. If it is recalled that the Princess Elizabeth hunted deer with twenty outriders, one could scarcely exaggerate the procession that a reigning queen of Mary's experience would order up. There would be lords and ladies, heralds, drummers, soldiers, horses, and banners. Coins would be thrown, and the sixteen beautiful women would be at the very center. We could hope that on most occasions the cloaks and foot mantles tallied in these accounts, would not be needed, but that the ladies would be seen in all the overstuffed glory of their sixteenth century costumes, under skies as blue as Scotland can muster.

> "...Item, for xxiiij elnis iij quarteris of blak bukrame to the saidis cloikis, the elne v s,; summa...vj li. iijs. ix d.

> "...Item, for v elnis ij quarteris of reid bukrame to stuffe the nekis of the saidis cloikis, the elne iij s. iiij d. summa...xviij s. ij d.

> "...Item, for ij unce of blak steiking silk thairto, xvjs.

> "...Item, v (xx is superscribed after this v, but I can neither write this on my Apple, nor read what this symbol means): that is v??ij elnis of pasmentis of irsatt to the saidis cloikis, the elne iiij d.; summa...xxxiiij s.

> "...Item, for xlviij elnis of silkin ribbynnis to thame, iij li. iiij s.

> "...Item, for xij elnis of braid ribbene silk to the Quenis gracis cloik,...xxxvj s."

From the quantities of buckram sewed into the sixteen cloaks one can conclude that these were outstanding garments. Even the collars stood out, as portraits of the queen show. In this one case, Mary's cloak was not listed separately. The tailors sewed it with two ounces of stitching silk, all by hand, and undoubtedly sitting cross legged on tables, a posture I saw our Selkirk friend, James Chisholm, use when I was a boy, for he was a tailor. It is obvious that a lady would want some *pasmentis of wirsatt* sewn into her cloak, especially at only 4 pence per ell. Silken ribbons cost 3 pounds, 4 shillings, but were probably much more visible, for there were 6 yards of them. The queen's cloak was distinguished by being ornamented with 15 yards of braided silk ribbon, a subtle difference in these almost identical costumes. The uniformity of these processional garments may illustrate the compassionate character of this queen, so different from the almost predatory nature of monarchs throughout history. Queen Elizabeth would not have taken pains to blend in with her troop, but just the opposite.

> "...Item, for ane pair of stringis to the Quenis grace cloik and sating (stitching) to the samyn,...xv s.

> "...Item, for xv (fifteen) pair of blak stringis to the ladeis cloikis, ilk pair v s. summa..iij li. xv s.

> "..Item, for making of the saidis xvj (sixteen) cloikis, skirtis, and thair furnesing, ilk pece xv s.; summa...xij li.

> "..Item,to the taleouris boyis in drink silver,v s."

The queen's fifteen ladies-in-waiting are accounted for repeatedly in these tabulations. We wish they had also been named, and our ancestress underlined. The names of all but four will apparently remain forever unknown. What happened to the queen's Maries was recorded, and there are portraits of them in fabulous finery. What happened to the eleven has never been revealed that I know of, but my grandmother knew what happened to one; so now only ten remain in limbo.

On November 12, 1561, in less than three months after arrival, one lady-in-waiting had left the queen's train. Then only fourteen cloaks were made. Two things are interesting in the following wordy record which could so readily have given ladies' names instead of so many generic classifications of women. Simpartew is included here with the four celebrated Maries: Fleming, Beaton, Livingston and Seton. The LHT specifies these five at one price, then adds Wardlaw at a higher price. Perhaps she had special dimensions at so much per ell. At any rate, the fifteen *madynnis* have dwindled to fourteen, perhaps by marriage. A significant matter is implied. The Scottish nation was not billed for a wedding dress, which leads us to guess that Mary picked up the tab for weddings. Nowhere in this book is payment recorded for wedding expenses, but we know there were many.

> "...Item, to Jacques de Soulis, talliour to hir grace, to gif the madynnis eftir following, viz., to ...Flemyng...Betoun- ...Simpartw...Levingstoun...Seitoun...Wardlaw, to by thair secund dule, ilk ane of the saidis fyve ix li., and to the said....Wardlaw x £i.vij s.; summa lv £.vij s."

> "...Item, for lxiij elnis of blak stamyng to xiiij (14) dammiis, dammosellis, and madynnis to be thair cloikis, ilk ane takand iiij elnis ij quarteris, price of the elne xlvj s.; summa...jC xliiij £i.xviij s."

> "...Item, for xxiij elnis iij quarteris of blak weluot to the saidis dammes, dammosallis, and madynnis to be thair secund dule, price of the elne iiij £i. xv s.; summa...jC xij £i. xvj s. iij d."

If one were to visualize these riding garments as worn by this particular group of women, in the capital city, going from Holyroodhouse to the castle a mile up the Royal Road, a picture would have to be conjured up equal to a movie scenario. The street is still narrow, but clean. Then it was not only narrow, but pinched down by the Nether-bow gate which closed the City of Edinburgh securely behind its wall. Then there were impediments; the Merkat Croce, the Salt tron (salt scales), St. Giles Cathedral, the tolbooth and gaol. The whole way was lined by tall tenements.

These saddles, cloaks, bridles, and *staikis to the hors*, were undoubtedly soon in use, for horses had been bought locally. About a month later, the horses from France replaced them. During that winter, and the first months of 1562, an attraction developed between one of the queen's ladies and the stable-boy from Dieppe. It is not in any public record, but can be believed with no qualms. These girls are recorded, the stable-boy is recorded, Alexander

Depo is recorded, all as being in the queen's service. No record cites 1562, in the spring, as the wedding date, but events in Mary's story make this a likely time. No queen has a more colorful life story than this one. The details are dizzyingly complicated but a simple marriage of two people doesn't upset anything. The oral record of our family authenticates the conjectures of biographers who tell that the queen helped her companions to marry each other. Lady Fraser refers to the queen's "endless string of ladies-in-waiting" and "attendants - a tight little circle, who married each other."

Mary and retainers rode everywhere a queen should be seen, and everywhere she had to go on business. She also rode for recreation, continually. But when she rode between the Palace and the Castle, or even just to a Tolbooth meeting or election, she was undoubtedly watched. A certain family in the Canongate must have stepped out to the road from their home, joining many others to watch the queen's cavalcade pass by. Actually nothing there was far from the Palace. They would join hundreds of others lining the route of the queen's procession. When a certain one of the ladies passed by this family called out to the daughter who had been gone so long over-seas. More than one family in the Canongate and Edinburgh would try to see sons and daughters in processions. It is recorded that during her short reign Mary would go to eat with residents in the city. So much more is unknown than known about that long ago time one can only conjecture what might have transpired to enliven day to day life, especially during that first winter in the dreary palace when dullness could have made any diversion welcome.

A fine line separated our queen and her servants. She had the initiative and often used it, to cross the formal barriers of status. She also had male attendants such as pages, and equerries to do her bidding. There is every reason to believe she may have had a special affinity for the young man from Dieppe who could speak to her and to her beloved horses in their familiar language. A kind of poetic justice excused this use of French, which otherwise displeased many Scots. Who could argue if horses and their stable-boy understood only their native language, which, of course, forced the queen, again, to avoid Scots. That none of the other outdoor workers spoke French can be assumed. Besides the language of the young man, he had to have had other familiar characteristics and manners reminiscent of pleasant past times, even the by-gone glory-days in the French Court. Only conjecture can tell us how the void was filled, the gulf between being Queen of France and of Scotland. Mary's entire entourage was certainly caught up in the rough transition. All this emotion and uncertainty about the future registered in the consciousness of a young lady in the queen's train. In her black cloak that winter, she noticed the young groom as he handed the queen her saddled horse. When she heard him respond to questions in French, the language itself moved her, for she probably had scant ability in the rough Scots of local workers. This lady-in-waiting and the groom discovered in that first winter a mutual attraction whenever their duties brought them together. Their queen picked up the cue, for she considered it her duty and a pleasure to promote the marriage of her bevy of young companions, an unusually appropriate term in the case of this queen.

CHAPTER X

MELROSE ABBEY, THE HOME BASE

Melrose Abbey is now in ruins, but it is still impressive and beautiful. It is owned and maintained by the government, having been given by Anne, Duchess of Bucleuch, in 1919. She had purchased it from the last of the private owners. I have never seen mentioned the amount of land the Abbey owned in its heyday, but, using the maps of the British Land Survey of 1924, I calculated 26,000 acres more or less. The many villages, or *farmtouns*, and the gristmill, were once owned by the Abbott, under the Pope. About two miles down the River Tweed from the present site, monks under St. Columba built the first Abbey in the 7th Century. It was burned in 879 in wars between Scots and Saxons. Rebuilt, it was deserted before the year 1000. In 1136 a Cistercian settlement was founded by King David I at the present site. Monks were recruited from Yorkshire, and they brought skilled masons, and a talented master mason. Singing masses for the souls of the founder and benefactors and their families, was the first obligation of the abbott and the monks.

The Cistercians were famous as sheep farmers, and for their expertise in bringing the roughest land into cultivation and grazing use. Their Abbeys were rallying points for the peasants for miles around, as they learned husbandry, and paid their dues. A medal or medallion came to be made at Melrose that was a rebus on the name. Cast in lead, it had a six-pointed rose in relief set in a mason's mel or mallet, with a circular lattice background. This interpretation of the word Melrose was a lapse in memory, for the monks had forgotten in only a quarter of the Christian era, that the name in Celtic meant bare moor, not rose.

A booklet which one can buy at the entrance gate contains text, photographs, and diagrams showing the present condition, and the very large establishment that it once was. Even the remnants are awe-inspiring to contemplate as one envisions the piety and monumental labor involved in the centuries of quarrying, hauling and laying stone toward an unvarying end. Later, moral decay set in, then destruction. In recent times, skillful masonry repair and protection against weathering have stabilized the remaining walls, the vaulted stone roofs, and the passages. Restoration of a functioning Abbey is not possible without the universal religious fervor of past ages. Only the masonry remnants can be restored today, not the piety.

The original Melrose, which was relatively unpretentious, evolved through these ages. The church structure itself became a glorious edifice, probably the greatest and richest in Scotland, but it was badly damaged in 1385 by the English. After it was restored to even greater magnificence, the English Earl of Hertford did his best to utterly destroy the Church and the other buildings, in 1544 and 1545.

The Borderlands were ravaged in three invasions on orders of Henry VIII. He was infuriated that the Scots repudiated his proposal for the future marriage of baby Mary, already the Queen of Scots, and his son, Edward. Hertford's orders were to inflict all the misery he could, lay waste the country, seize Edinburgh, and put to fire and sword man, woman, and child. As a religious institution, this was the Abbey's end. The Reformation, 15 years later (1560), gave the signal, if any were needed, that local people could carry off stone for cot, byre, wall, and pavement. The massive church, being dangerous to quarry, tended to be left to the last, but the transept tower fell, in time, damaging many vaulted ceilings and walls. Of the many ranges of cloisters and accessory buildings, only lines of stones now show where foundations once carried the walls. What is left cannot be seen in a hurry, for the acres of grounds, stubs of foundations, and the cemetery, create a feeling of awe as one transports his thinking to the past centuries. The stones may be lifeless, but they are symbols of an endless line of monastic laborers literally pouring their lives into this vanished world of religious endeavor. No such expression of sustained religious ecstasy exists in the world today.

There is an element, though, in the present day consciousness that was virtually unknown in the cloistered world of the monks. Responsibility now rests hard on some to heal disabilities of man and nature. This new stuggle will not leave behind such massive monuments of stone, but, as Melrose is appreciated for what it was, the present must not be disparaged. Today is built on yesterday as surely as walls stand on foundations. Our world is built on theirs. For now, it has to be sufficient to see the past as it was.

Shifting once again into the present, an Abbey visitor steps outside the tall security walls of the Royal Commission on the Ancient Monuments of Scotland to admire the greenhouses and beautiful gardens and to explore the busy little town of Melrose.

Figure 4: The Seal of Melrose: The Cistercian rose set in a mason's mel, or mallet.

Figure 5: The vaulted stone ceiling of Melrose Abbey, which still survives. The one central boss, the Trinity Stone, receives the thrust transmitted by the upward curving stone ribs passing through eight major bosses named after Apostles. Sixteen lesser keystones collect and pass on the weight which ultimately presses down against four huge interior columns and the buttresses into the walls. The ribs rise upward in arch-action curves which give the force of gravity perpetual domination over the stones-resting-on-stones far overhead.

Melrose Abbey, the Home Base

Quick judgments must not be made about the later incredible dissolution and inequities of the church. That degradation arose in the centuries after the dark ages had given way to the ecstasies of the middle ages. Knowledge of this era does not lessen the powerful impact, as one walks in the ruins, ignoring thoughts of the shameful times. The delicate stone lacework of the full-height east window, even without its glass, is a beautiful alternative to the rose windows of gothic cathedrals. This structure stands because of the intricate resolution of forces carried through the arches, vaulting, ceiling ribs, buttresses, and walls, to the foundations. This is true of all gravity structures, but, unlike cathedrals, with plastered ceilings, even the membrane between the ribs is clearly visible as long slender stones lying on edge side by side to close in the ceiling arching far above.

These long stones lie on the ceiling ribs that vault from the walls to the apex, where the keystone or boss keeps this skeleton of converging ribs from falling. While the ribs were being built across the open space, scaffolding held the stones up. The keystone or boss was finally dropped into the final gap as all the ribs met in the exact middle. Then, locked by gravity, the rib cage could support everything above including the long stones standing on edge, side by side, that make the solid ceiling of stone. The narrow edges of stone show from wall to peak. Only the slender, graceful ribs support the tremendous weight. Plaster on these edges would conceal the spectacular power of arch-action to defeat the urge of heavy things to fall down. High above all this stone is the Achilles heel, the wooden structure of the gable roof with its lead covering. Vandals could burn whatever was not stone, and they did. Even lead erodes in about 150 years, but the stone was safe until we invented our corrosive atmosphere. From the outside, only the sloping roof is visible. Looking up at the curves of the stone ceiling from the floor inside, one marvels that the space can be filled from wall to wall apparently unsupported. The idea of stones, thousands of tons of stones, leaping across the open air without any support but the law of gravity fighting the incompressibility of stone could keep my mind occupied no matter how bad a sermon might be.

The real meaning of the word static is the force that keeps the stone roof up in the air, not the noise coming from a loud speaker. I can believe that the monks who carried these plans in their heads until they had laid the stones, were religious in a way we, perhaps, cannot understand until we understand that it was an act of worship for them to lay up arches, walls, and buttresses of perfect integrity that could not fall. When the structure was complete their piety began to crumble.

Long after the monks had placed the millions of stones, destroyers burned, broke, and stole, but the most vile desecrators never touched a stone of Melrose. One of the worst was Mary's father, King James V. He wrote to Pope Clement VII asking that three of his host of illegitimate children might be granted benefices (made bishops). The Pope, in fear of losing Scotland to the new religion as England had been lost, acceded to the request. Melrose was granted to the king's eldest natural son, James Stewart, an infant. Mary, his half-sister, was ten years younger than he. This contemptuous expedient was part of the religious climate of the times. Throughout Scotland, the king's illegitimate babies were appointed as bishops over the monks. James IV had led the way, but James V had five of his nine chance bairns made abbots, including Holyrood. The one named James, Mary's half brother and ten years her senior, was her strong supporter, and undoubtedly a factor in our family's start.

When Hendre Depo and his bride were provided a tenure at Melrose, this account should make it obvious they were performing a great service to Mary, not that they understood this at all clearly. From the dates we have given, it can be seen that in their lifetimes they never saw the Abbey except in ruins being used as a quarry, but it was too far away for them to carry any stones home. At that juncture this Abbey, like all the others, was purely a land-holding corporation with no religious function. Nor was there an Abbott, for the Catholic Church had been outlawed, and all the clerics either were converted, and made into ministers, or dispersed into secular occupations. Melrose families made an enclosure within the

Melrose Abbey, the Home Base

ruins which served as their church for many years. There was a commendator, literally "protector of the lands", a gristmill, and other property. The Latin *dare* (pronounced da're) *in commendam* means given in trust, and the layman so entrusted was called a commendator. As a favor, or by purchase, he had gained the right to collect all the rents, milling fees, or *multure*, from the tenants. His *baille* (bailey) court had legal powers to hear his complaints, and those between tenants. These former abbeys were set up as virtual little kingdoms called regalities. They were independent to a degree, but always subject to the monarch, and could be rescinded at will. The Regality of Melrose was the key to our first family's success.

A wry twist of history makes it very unlikely that our family would have come into existence if the conversion of the Catholic monasteries into secular regalities had never occurred. The queen needed responsible new tenants to replace what were called kindly tenants. They had lived on the land for generations, paying slight rent under earlier feudal arrangements, but they were evicted as more profitable tenants were found. Our newly-weds were more profitable to the commendator, not to belittle the queen's gracious wedding gift to them. The Reformation was given effect in three acts of Parliament. This action was taken in August of 1560, exactly one year before Mary returned to be queen in person. One third of the revenue of Melrose and the other abbeys, and title to their lands, reverted to the crown as Mary took up her powers. When I started this study, the idea of the queen giving a tenancy to her two little people gave me pause. As I learned more it became obvious that giving a life tenancy to a man, perhaps with subtenants to work under him, would be a trivial gift. She, after all, would have a loyal family on the land, and ncidentally recoup a certain portion of the annual rent that Depo had to pay to the commendator.

Moshouses, the community where the new family settled, was, perhaps, entirely spared from the reivers or "riding families," and also from much of the English border strife. It was inconveniently far from the strongholds of the raiders. They had hiding places and secret spots where they could hold cattle and sheep in the impenetrable moors, which were called *mosses* in the Borders. Animals too distant from these collecting points were relatively safe, and a map will show that Moshouses may have been just outside the main activity zone of the robbers.

The Earl Bothwell's ancestral home was a 13th century castle situated about 30 miles south of Melrose. It was an immense fortress equipped to quarter 200 cavalry and 1000 men at arms. This was Hermitage, a forbidding place still standing, though damaged. Liddesdale, where it stands, was a notoriously lawless part of the Borders. The ancient castle itself had been the center of cruel and treacherous dealings of four great families in its history. Our Bothwell, and James Stewart, knew how much responsible men were needed on Melrose lands. Bothwell, with his castle nearby, had very special interest in manpower. All the better if their loyalty had cost him nothing more than a word spoken to the queen in their behalf.

The presence of Hendre Depo at Melrose had roots stretching to far-away Dieppe. One need look no farther than the wily Earl to find half the explanation for Hendre's good luck. It needs to be remembered that André of Dieppe got his name spelled Hendre and Henry by the Scots. Bothwell's dominating personality and fluency in French had gained him a task to his liking, with opportunities for personal gain and prestige. As Lord High Admiral of Scotland, he had negotiated the difficult and expensive chartering of ships in Dieppe, with a hostler for each, to carry the queen's horses to Leith. This voyage was to be beset with more troubles than anyone expected. Both Alexander and André knew that it was Bothwell who was their patron, and the queen, too, but it would be the man they would look to first. The gesture of putting the newlyweds on a tract of Melrose Land was pure expediency to the Earl Bothwell. "Beastly" was about the kindest word spoken of this contemptible and foul-mouthed character, who was feared by all, and who mesmerized the too-pliant Mary to her destruction. For our purposes, it is important to know that he did nothing that was not calculated to his advantage. One year before he married the queen, so that he could be king, as he thought, she gave the regality of Melrose to Francis Hepburn, a sometime Earl of Bothwell, a notoriously dissolute relative, but he forfeited the gift. Hendre's fortunes were surely linked to James Hepburn, the 4th Earl of Bothwell.

The Lowlanders were never serfs in the near-slave sense (with some exceptions where they were as bound as slaves, and locked in, especially as miners, in the 1700s). Often they could properly be called peasants, in the 16th century. The Border people lived in near-chaos with the constant threat of unpredictable destruction and theft of everything they had accumulated. Many lived with virtually no possessions in the merest hut of a shelter. At this time most Indians of North America undoubtedly lived with better food, shelter, and clothing, and could well bemoan arrival of the white savages from Europe who took their homeland and destroyed them with strange new weapons and diseases. There were vast discrepancies in Scotland, of course, between the worst and the best conditions. Much could be blamed on frequent warfare, but ingrained habits of common thievery led to a lawless era when the reivers were uncontrollable. The soil had lost its climax vegetation, especially forest and palatable grass, and thus was practically devoid of useful native plants for either man or beast. This tough land, though, produced tough people. In time they moved up with the best there were. The bitter life, endured for centuries, taught the inhabitants dogged persistance. Habitations and possessions improved, but very slowly, in the Lowlands.

Cottages and byres in 1561 were basically stone walls roofed over with thatch. The walls could survive a fire. The principal log, the rooftree, was very valuable since the best trees, the pines, had long since been cut, and not replaced, because sheep love to eat pine seedlings. Smaller rafters and thatch might more easily be replaced, but the ridgepole had to be strong, and straight, and saved. Even the thatch might be taken away by the family, and hidden to avoid its being burned if a raid warning came soon enough. When the house had no window hole or chimney, the interior was not up to present code standards for particulate emissions, or foot candles of illumination, but then the food to be cooked was very simple, and didn't need much fire. Some people were fortunate enough to have pieces of rough cast glass, or broken pieces, to put in their window hole. They might even have a *lum*, so the smoke did not have to drift out through the thatch. This brief resume' does not begin to tell about the hard life of the people, the women, the children, and the men, but it is put down to show that not all Scots dressed in fine regalia, and danced the Highland Fling in front of castles, as pictures might lead one to believe.

The great hall at Holyroodhouse accommodated many weddings. The one that could only be called the worst was between Mary and Bothwell in 1567. Five years earlier, we think, the wedding recorded in our family legend created no stir, but the queen would not have chosen any other place. Before it was solemnized, there must have been plans, not only for it, but for the future of the newlyweds. The bridegroom's father, Alexander Depo, had certainly ridden up from his work with the horses at Stichell. This man, who provides the unarguable date for our name's presence in Scotland, has to remain a tantalizing mystery. He was the bridegroom's father, and *his sone*, who was killed, was the brother of André'. This is the reasonable surmise, just as is the surmise that they both went to the wedding. There is no reason to suppose otherwise, nor does the precise relationship of these three people affect the family that was soon to sprout from the soil of Melrose. Forever forgotten, even beyond conjecture, were the impossibly remote relatives that had been abandoned in Dieppe. Both they and Adam are direct ancestors, but enough is enough: requiescat in pace.

Only the two, and well-wishers among the servants, could have sat with André. There must have been many relatives, and friends on the bride's side of the aisle. All would have brought gifts, and certainly the queen would not have failed with gifts. The greatest was a place to live; a tenancy at Melrose. This has been mentioned, but if we could know all the details, this would be a dramatic, almost fairy-tale-like story. The Earl Bothwell and Mary had another collaborator in this gift that turned out so well for us. We have only a hypothesis to go on, but it is surrounded by facts.

Mary's older half-brother, Lord James Stewart, led perhaps all others, in guarding and guiding his sister. He was her special supporter. The days of his boyhood must have instilled in him a knowledge and love for Melrose that was superior to that of anyone else. Therein hangs a tale beyond the fact that he was installed as boy bishop of Melrose. During his growing-up years he undoubtedly rode and explored every nook and corner of his domain. The mill at Langshaw supplied much of his income, and the little cluster of cottages at Moshouses, less than a mile away, was on one of the roads back to his quarters in the Abbey. The new couple was settled at Moshouses where they lived the rest of their lives. Probably they paid rent on a life-tenancy basis, but to get situated there at all was a master stroke of fortune for them. Lord James Stewart was thirty years old, knew all about the Depos and the wedding and advised and promoted the whole episode. His sister and Bothwell concurred. No other assumption could so well explain the lifelong presence of our ancestors in that place at that time.

Of the queen's two influential advisers, Lord James Stewart, and the Earl Bothwell, we can be glad that both knew Melrose intimately. They knew how much the estate would benefit from the infusion of new strength, ideas, and intelligence. Both may have cooperated on having needed repairs made at the farm, and on arranging for a pack train of ponies to be sent there carrying furnishings for the new family's home. Cash was scarcely used in the back country, but city people with any resources at all had better access to money and goods. Very little would be needed to supply the new family with such things as cooking utensils, a bed, table, stools and some linens. A hammer, saw, a few outdoor tools, and a *kisk* (chest) full of oatmeal would be so little in the city, but a world of wealth at Moshouses.

The activities of the 4th Earl of Bothwell and Queen Mary intersected, however accidentally, the lives of our André and his intended. James, too, was always nearby, a steadying influence that his sister relied on. The earl and the queen were like the warp and the woof of one fabric, for although he manipulated her, she depended on him, and put a disastrous amount of trust in him. These three, and our two, knew each other well, no matter how great their social distance may have been. There was one exception that we can neither prove, nor dismiss: André's bride must have come from a family with a title, as did the four Maries, and it would have been an affront to the queen, and most certainly to the Court of the King of France if Mary had a single commoner in her train. Matters of title, and rank, were fluid, however. A Monarch, like a fairy-godmother, could wave a magic wand, in a manner of speaking: Mary's half brothers, James, John, and Robert, and their sister, Janet Fleming, were the natural children of King James V, but were accepted in the French Court, with appropriate titles, of course.

One of André's daughters was named Katherine. By the workings of the old Scottish naming formula she was named after one of her grandmothers, or her mother. Some day, if we get lucky, the name Katherine might be the key to identifying our lady-in-waiting. At this time we don't know her name. What we do know is that if the queen saw an opportunity to provide a festive wedding for two of her people she could provide everything from the ceremony to the homestead they would urgently need. As easily as waving her hand she could say to Bothwell, "James, please find a place for these two nice people to live after they are married, and fix it up for them, too."

I have always been interested in old things, but never expected to study the lives of people so far back that nothing today gives a basis for comparison, and they my ancestors. Their querns, distaffs, looms, cooking methods, and attitude toward work, I have discovered, were not too strange to me. The Athapascan Indians called Navajos that I worked with in the 1930s were not much different. They were emerging from a primitive state comparable in many ways to Scotland 400 years earlier. The analogy should not be pursued too far, but both tribes knew about squatting on dirt

Melrose Abbey, the Home Base

floors around a small fire in the middle of a shelter without a chimney, as I have done when in need of food and rest. Both knew that words and memory best preserved knowledge, experience, and wisdom. The Indian language, undoubtedly derived from the speech of Mongolia, had sounds I could never learn to make. The Scots speech was about to leave its very special blend of ancient languages to gradually join the language of England.

Washed, undyed wool, spun at home, was made into a coarse cloth called hodden grey, by mixing black and white fleeces. This is just the way the Indians made their gray after they had acquired sheep from the Spanish padres just after Mary was born. Simple garments of this cloth served for work clothes, but Lowlanders had always attired themselves on Sundays to the limit of their resources, no matter how they had to get along during the rest of the week. Parliament, the church, and even James II (1437-1460) tried in vain to restrain the tendency of the commoners to dress beyond their rank. As always, there were rules, and fines for violations of what we might think were petty regulations.

To repeat briefly how our ancestor came to live on Melrose land: André, or Hendre, and Alexander each sailed in a Dutch ship loaded with the queen's *horss and mullattis*. They landed at Tynemouth, England, September 12, 1561. They acquired the surname, Depo, as a Scottish spelling of Dieppois, meaning citizen of Dieppe, France. Luckily for us, all of this cost money, and the Lord High Treasurer held the purse strings, and the expenditures were recorded with dates. Later, his clerk registered the name of Alexander Depo at Stichell in the Merse in 1564. In 1606, forty-two years later, Hendre Depo appears in Melrose court records. There are no intervening records that we have found, but Hendre was at Melrose in 1586 as will be shown. When these two men left Dieppe for a job caring for the royal horses I don't know what pay they were promised, but their ship passage was paid. Not many of us have had our immigrant passage paid by a queen.

The Marriage That Did Succeed

A palace is a busy place with a great deal going on, whether fully functional, as in Queen Mary's time, or as at present, when Queen Elizabeth II may make a rare visit that somewhat stems the tide of tourists trooping through. Holyroodhouse has seen countless individuals come and go, get married, be buried, be recorded, and go unrecorded. We will refer to the time when records commenced, for this genealogy antedates the palace records except for those of the High Treasurer. It is clear that when Mary arrived she found there was no proper secretarial work being done aside from the financial records. Hoping to find that weddings performed in the Palace chapel had been recorded at least as well as a country pastor would do, I wrote to Mr. D. J. C. Wickes, the Superintendent of Holyroodhouse for that information. He acknowledged my letter, and forwarded it to Dr. Ian Grant, the Keeper, Scottish Record Office, Edinburgh. Typical of the invaluable help I have received from experts in Scotland is the reply I received from Dr. Grant:

> "The Register of Marriages for the parish of Holyroodhouse or Canongate commenced only on 20 August, 1564. An alphabetical index of the contents own to 1800 was published by the Scottish Record Society in 1915 edited by Francis J. Grant."

> "...This records the marriages of: John Deippa and Isobell Walker 24 December 1626. Euphemia Deippe in Edinburgh and Robert Morisone in Canongate 6 April, 1647."

I do not have records bridging the gap from the John Deippa who married Isobell Walker in 1626, but this name spelling is by far the closest to my own, and it is in Canongate. Only in the most sophisticated place in Scotland, the Canongate, I believe, could our legend have survived as has been discussed. It seems highly probable that somewhere in this man's line a descendant dropped the *i* which is unpronounceable, resulting in the spelling my people have used at least since 1806 when my great-grandfather Deppa was born. Until recently they used the pronunciation "Deppie" just as the other current pronunciation is "Dippie." I suspect that no matter what spelling was used through all these generations, the word always came out in one of these two ways, but probably with an accent that I can't even guess at. Although the records started a few months too late to catch the marriage of "our first couple," I have found the preacher who very likely performed the ceremony.

Mary's harshest critic, the Reverend John Knox, had his Presbyterian colleague, the Reverend John Craig, ordained Palace Minister just before Mary came back from France. Craig had been a Dominican Friar at one time, and was even condemned to be burnt in Bologna, Italy, for the heresy of Calvinism, but he escaped when the Inquisition prison was burst. It could have been he who married our couple, as well as the many others who came under the wing of the queen's charity. It was he who formalized the marriage of Bothwell and Mary in the great hall of Holyroodhouse not long before he abandoned her, and she went into English captivity.

John Craig died in December, 1600. It could very well have been Craig who officiated when Hendre Dippo's daughter, Katherine, married Alexander Moresome in 1595. That her marriage was not entered in the Edinburgh Marriage Register until 1600 could be accounted for if Craig's personal records were unavailable until after his death. I have investigated and found that none of his personal records are extant. This hiatus in recording Katherine's wedding indicates there was such a record, but that it was lost after 1600.

When our young couple from the palace appeared on one of the Melrose farms or allotments, it would have been a very extraordinary event. This was an ancient and closed community of people derived from Angle, Saxon, and Scottish stock. Perhaps their folklore even "remembered" that Pictish women and children had been stolen in ages past, raised more or less as slaves, then been absorbed in the general blood lines of the Borderlands until the Pictish peoples were considered extinct. The Scots had thus absorbed the Picts, or killed them, and the Romans were gone too. These two new outlanders presented an entirely different situation.

There was implicit caution in the fact that the sudden arrivals came from Holyroodhouse with powerful sponsors.

The queen knew the Borders were rough, and Bothwell knew even better, for his fortress, the Hermitage, was in Liddesdale, notorious for its robber hordes. To quote her Majesty's Stationery Office publication: "Despite their inveterate treachery the Hepburns managed to maintain their grip on this remote stronghold." This was known, but the two innocent young outlanders were probably only warned to keep a low profile; in what words I cannot guess, but a kindly warning nevertheless, for friendliness was usually found only within your own extended family. Our family consisted of two people with no person in whom they could confide in safely. No other reason need be looked for if one wonders why the story of the queen's maid marrying a stable-boy was never known nor repeated outside Edinburgh and the Canongate. In the Borders in those days the new family would have been at risk if they had bragged, or even admitted, the favoritism that had been shown them. The gift they were given was quid pro quo, but that would not be understood by neighbors. One can reflect on the fate of the other Frenchman, Alexander Depo's, son who was "slaughtered" within three years of his arrival.

No French name can be found among the scores of Borderers named in the records. The name Depo sticks out like a sore thumb. Grope as one might, arguments can't be found against the story of these two people being married and established by the favor of the kind and romantic monarch. It wasn't just that she no longer needed them. The girl had been her close companion for 13 years, and a great personal attachment must have existed between the two. The queen, herself, had just turned twenty. Her fondness for her French servants is well known, and she would have favored André as custodian of her beloved horses. He and Alexander had brought them through great difficulties, and it fitted her character that both would be well rewarded. Although there were plenty of local stable-boys they would have meant nothing to her nor could they have spoken her natural language. She had an objective much more pressing than keeping a favorite stable-boy at hand though she must have preferred taking her saddled horse from the comely boy who spoke her natural language.

She had a better role for André. He was needed as a bridegroom for her protegee, and dear companion. A wedding was needed. It would solve Mary's worrisome problem of the approaching spinsterhood of all her young women. Not least, the entire court would join in festivities that would brighten a whole day, and night. It was the queen's touch that could foster such a romance, and bring it to pass. That was something she could contrive for others, but never for herself, even in three tries: This was the marriage that did succeed for Mary, Queen of Scots.

A life tenancy on payment of annual rent is implied in the *Regality Records of Melrose*, which show that Hendre lived in the Moshouses community until he was in his sixties, presumably the rest of his life. His son's descendants carried the name mostly to the east, toward Kelso, but later even into the English Borders of Northumberland. One son is recorded as staying in the Melrose community of Craigsfuird. Very likely the Depo daughters married into local families. We will study this in detail, but those who are mathematically inclined could work on the dilution inherent in a Norman-French father's children marrying into the Borderland mixture of nationalities. I hazard the guess that after only a few generations the French fraction in our ancestry might be on the order of not very much, maybe less. One daughter, and perhaps two sons, grew up in the Canongate. Many bits of evidence show that this is true.

Bothwell and Mary were key people in the lives of Hendre and his wife, but we can be happy for them that their paths never again crossed once they parted. Almost immediately after Bothwell married the queen, he left her to save his own life, and tried pirating in the North Sea. He was put in a dungeon by the King of Denmark for a very good reason that can be found in biographies of Mary. Tradition says that he was chained to a post half his height for ten years, finally dying insane. As everyone knows, after Mary abdicated on July 24, 1567, she was imprisoned for nineteen years, then beheaded by order of her cousin Queen Elizabeth. She died at Fotheringhay Castle, but truly, as her motto said: "In My End Is My Beginning."

CHAPTER XI

THE REGALITY RECORDS OF MELROSE - VOLUME I

This chapter reproduces parts of the court records of Melrose Abbey for the years 1606, 1607 and 1608. There are twenty volumes of this series transcribed verbatim in 1914 by the Scottish History Society. Volume I was copied from the hand written original by Charles S. Romanes, C.A. Because of the remarkable historical interest of this material, considerably more has been excerpted here than would be necessary to authenticate the presence of André, and his wife and family. That, of course, was originally the objective of studies which occupied much of my time from 1977 into 1989. Sufficient proof of the origin of our family name in Scotland was found rather quickly in several old records. The lure of Scottish history, and the study of the lives of ordinary people during the period, 1561 into the early 1600's, became my objective long after my family search was satisfied. The critical years of our first generation were also the years of Mary, Queen of Scots (1542-87), and her son, James VI and I, King of Scotland, and England (1567-1625).

Hendre Depo, the mispelling we alternate with his correct French Christian name of André, appears in the *Regality Records of Melrose*, Volume I, on pages 7, 22, 29, 38 and 68. His name appears in Volume III, which is an index of Volume I. These citations prove his presence, and our name, in Scotland. Alexander Depo, as has been shown, provided a specific first date, and both men are linked as caretakers of the queen's horses in 1561. Throughout this story we have tried to tell how things were in their day. It is a remote age, hard to visualize, for very little was comparable to the present. It could almost be said that they neither thought nor acted as we do.

The 1500's appear to be a dividing century: modern compared to earlier centuries, yet archaic even by midpoint 1600's. For instance, no one knew in Mary's time that the heart was for pumping blood. Every nation experienced its renaissance on its own time scale. I found myself searching for bits of historical information that would reveal the kind of life that was lived by the ordinary people who were the neighbors of our first generation. There is very little information of that sort to be found. Not much is known about the clothing, bedding, utensils and food of farm tenants in those years. Court and aristocratic life is much better documented.

In this chapter particularly, rather extensive excerpts of the writing of those times are given. These are fifty years closer to us than our previously given excerpts of 1561. Those are noticeably more ambiguous, but a point of interest is how gradual the change is towards less obscure modes of expression. By the mid-1600's greater change occurred, for education, commerce, and manufacturing were quickening. It has been difficult to avoid using information too "modern" to apply to the first Depo family. Most of what is to be found was written a century later by travelers repeating what they had heard about the old ways.

Until I got into this project I had rarely seen samples of the writing of old. It was very interesting to me to study the convoluted phrasing, and to see some bits of the handwriting, and the Scottish words that I did not know. Also fascinating was the opportunity to look in on the court sessions. While I had some hope of reading what they wrote, I realized there was no possibility that I could have understood more than a few words of what they were saying. I have had the privilege a few times, to listen to proficient demonstrations of broad Irish, Yorkshire, and Scottish speech, all presumed to be English. None of this approached the obscurity of the Scots speech of 1561. Even in Maryland and Texas I have had workmen and students that I could not understand. Also, I learned that they could not understand me.

My excerpts go beyond my interest in the Depo family. They are intended to make some of the old writing available to those who are interested. The books I have used are set in modern type faces, but they are verbatim copies of original books which are treasures, hand written and indecipherable, except to specialists. Even the 1914 volumes are now rare. If the excerpts seem difficult to read, imagine facing up to the handwritten originals. I will acknowledge before being told, that I am only an interested novice without credentials. Still I have done the best I could to supply definitions for some of the words. It is either that or nothing. If this writing remains a puzzlement, that is really sufficient - a glimpse into the Scot's world of long-ago for those who are curious, but not able to go to distant libraries to study the old books.

A regality was a little fiefdom, almost a kingdom, but subject to recall by the monarch. It could be given to a royal favorite complete with judicial powers except in cases of treason. Given in trust (*dare in commendam*), to a commendator, a portion of the revenues went to the monarch. Queen Mary could, and did, bestow the entire secularized abbey as she chose. For Mary to give Hendre and his bride, her nearly life-long companion, a life-rent tenancy was as simple as sending instructions to Michael Balfour, the Commendator at that time. He would not likely choose a poor 100-or-so acre homestead for the queen to give as a wedding gift. She had provided him with a high position and the income of the whole establishment including rents from the new tenants. The dates we have show that our progenitors, and their family, lived at Moshouses the rest of their lives, a total of perhaps 45 years. At the end of a life-rent tenancy, a property reverted to the commendator, for it was not heritable.

In Chapter X it is told how James Stewart, Earl of Moray, the Lord James Stewart, very likely was influential in having his half sister, Queen Mary, give a life-rent tenancy to her stable-boy and his bride, a former lady-in-waiting. It has also been told how Queen Mary, disastrously obsessed with James Hepburn, the Earl Bothwell, was also foolishly moved to give Melrose to Francis Hepburn. When that worthless character, who was to become Earl Bothwell, forfeited the gift, it went to James Douglas, as cited above.

The dozen or so years of James' eventful life as boy abbott of Melrose had prepared him to suggest this ideal wedding gift, a life-rent tenancy on a farmstead, for his half-sister's proteges'. The Lady Douglas was his mother. His father was the king. She was also the mother of James Douglas, the second son of Sir William Douglas. These half-brothers were born at the island fortress of Lochleven, a hard-day's ride across the river Forth from the palace of Linlithgow. There the king's French wife, Marie of Guise, learned that her husband's illegitimate son, James Stewart, had been born to the mistress of Lochleven.

Although James Stewart was installed as a baby abbott at Melrose, his half-brother, James Douglas, very likely also spent much of his boyhood there as a companion to the king's other son who could not be a true prince but was always treated as one. That the huge extent of Melrose had been an ideal and compatible home for the two boys is indicated by the fact that almost as soon as Lord James became regent in 1569, on his sister's abdication, he bestowed the title of Commendator, and the income, on his half-brother.

In the context of those times, monarchs used this "regality" mode of governing kingdoms which were too unwieldy to control personally. Spanish kings granted immense tracts in the Americas to favorites in a system called *encomienda* (*circa* 1503). The Indios were "commended" to the care of the *encomendero*. He, in effect, owned them as slaves. Four hundred years later in the United States a policy of extermination was followed without benefit of a Latin name.

Even the politically naive tenants were able to perceive that royal shenanigans had once again come to Melrose. A rank

Frenchman who couldn't be understood, and his elegant wife, who had never worked, were placed on one of the best steadings, an obvious signal that powerful people were behind the newcomers. Very likely, too, a hind and his wife were placed there to help them, for they knew nothing about the farm life they had to work into. What happened will never be known, but this was the marriage that did succeed for Mary, Queen of Scots. As has been said before, there were many reasons why both the natives and the newcomers kept their own council. They all knew how suddenly disfavor could flare into disaster from an indiscreet word.

MELROSE REGALITY RECORDS
Volume I, page 7

"...The baille court of the regalite of Melrose haldin thairat be Dene Jhone Watsone, baille deput of the said regalite, the xvj of Aprile 1606.

> "...The quhilk day Jhone Pringle in Langshaw is decerneit to pay to HENDRE DEPO for sevin firlotis aitis of the crop 1605 and that for corne eitin be his guidis, price of the boll,_____ and that in respect of the persewars aith..."

[Gloss: "Quh" substitutes for "wh" in words such as "which." *Decerneit*: judged. *Firlotis aitis* (plural): whole oats in this case, but also a measure of oatmeal. Families stored oatmeal in large quantities, for it was their main food source. A *firlot* was 1/4 of a *boll*, or *bow*, which weighed 140 pounds. Thus a *firlot* was 35 pounds, and seven would weigh 245. "Corn (oats), eaten by his cattle." "In respect of the plaintiff's oath."]

COMMENTS: Dean Watson was the only surviving monk of Melrose in 1606. The Pringle name occurs throughout the hundreds of pages of the records of Melrose, and in other records for they were landowners, and judges, as well as farmers. Robert Pringle was judge of the Baron's Court of Stitchill, and the family may have owned that fine estate at a later time.

A tricky bit of appraising went into the calculation that a certain area of damaged oat seedlings would be equivalent to seven *firlots* of whole oats, grown, harvested, and threshed. The judge forestalled arguments about whether Depo would have to wait until harvest to be recompensed. He was to be paid in oats in storage from the previous year. The clerk left a blank for inserting the price per *boll*, but obviously was told that a unit price was not needed since payment was to be in-kind. This record on page 7 was a thrill for an ancestor-hunter. My man is mentioned four more times, but this entry provides several leads of great interest to me: my ultimate ancestor was positively identified in the records of a court proceeding. He was an old man in 1606 for I think he was born in about the year 1542. At any rate, here was the Deppa/Dippie progenitor in a court record.

From this record it can be deduced that Hendre Depo's run-rig field extended west from Moshouses to adjoin Pringle's farmyard, as we will show in a later chapter. This could have been as little as an eighth of a mile. There were no field fences, but if Pringle's cows, that had fed on the roughest of fodder all winter, smelled the lush oat plants only five or six weeks old, they would do just what this case explains. They were in an enclosed farmyard, but the people were all asleep, and the enclosure could be breached by cows ravenous for something green. Since oats were raised in the rig farthest from the farmyard, the outfield, it is safe to assume that Depo's oat rig abutted Pringle's barnyard wall, or near enough that the cattle could smell the young plants. In early April the barley (*bear*, in Scots, or *bere* in Anglo Saxon, which they still used) that was planted in Pringle's infield, would not be up yet. It is likely that Depo's *aitis* adjoined Pringle's infield, and the cows streamed across it to get at the young oats. I have maps of 1924, that show the stone walls that were built all across this landscape about a century after run-rig was made obsolete by good iron plows. This run-rig layout has to remain a mystery. Depo was lucky that the newly-planted oats were destroyed before the court was convened on April 16th, or he would have had to wait until the fall session to make his claim.

> "Compeirit Thome Trotter and Sande Andersone anent the clame acclameit be Jhon Waichtman and James Moss agane thame for Jhon Cairncross, and because this day is assigneit thai compeirit nocht, the saids parte protestit for expenses.
>
> "The quhilk day beand assignit to James Hall to pruif the mairche stane liftit wrangouslie be Edward Derling fra betuix the roum pertaining to him and Jhone Hall his brother sone, quhilk sufficientle he hes done, and ordanis the same to put in agane, and the cairn of stanes to be removit, under the pane of x£i (10 pounds) within xlviij hours."

[Gloss: A *march stone* was a boundary marker. *Sone* in this case means son, but I leave it to the reader to untangle the attempted trespass.]

The same court reconvened the *xxiij of Aprile 1606.*

"...WILLIAM MEINS RETOUR

> The quhilk day compeirit Jhone Hunter, procurator in name and behalf of William Mein, oeye and aire of umquhile David Mein in Newsteid, and produceit ane breif raiseit at the instance of the said William dewlie execut and indorseit to be serweit as aire to his said guidschir to all landis quherintill he deit vest and seasit lawfull tym being bidin and laufullie proclameit in jugement, na pairte compeirit to object, dessyrit ane inqueist to be choisein to serve him in maner foirsaid, and for instruction produceit ane boundand charter of the lands of Newsteid quherintill the said David his

name is speciall expressit, conteinand sax acres toun land and sax acres of coit yard land, and desyrit proces, quhilk the juge grantit, quherupon the said William requyreit instrumentis, and electit an inqueist, to wit, Jhone Notman in Moshouses..."

[Gloss: A probate hearing. Attorney - *umquhile* (the late) - a *brief* - grandfather - died *vested* (died in full ownership) - since lawful time has passed - no party appeared to object - bounds and deed - Jhone Notman was a neighbor of Hendre Depo since both lived in the cluster of farmsteads called Moshouses.

MELROSE REGALITY RECORDS
Volume I, page 22
Absent Vassals at Court
xv October, 1606

...James Boustoun, Jhon Cairnecroce, Sande Barre, Androw Mar, James Thomsone, Robert Halewell, Quaintein Scot, Androw Clerk. (all deleted, i.e., present).

WESTHOUSES: Robert Prunstoun, Mark Mertone, Gawen Cesfuird, Gawen Mertoune.

DERNIK: Jhon Neilsone, Wille Chisholme, Quhintein (Quentin) Boustoune. (All deleted.)

BRIGEND: Androw Howme, elder, Jhon Wschear, Thomas Merser, George Kate. (All deleted.)

APILTRELEVES: Philp Darling, Andrew Darling, Jhon Pringle of Bukholme.

THREIPWOID: Jhone Spottiswoid in Quhytle, James Hunter in Halkburne.

BLAINSLIE: George Pringle of Blindle, William Hunter, James Hunter, Thom Fogow (deleted), Thom Lyall (deleted).

MOSHOUSES: Jhone Carter Wester, Robert Mitchell, Jhon Broune, William Notman, <u>Hendre Depo</u>, Gawen Woid.

John Home of Coldenknowis, Androw Home (deleted), George Pringle of Pharnielea, Jhon Rogear, Jhon Cairncroce there, Thome Lythgow."

COMMENTARY: The men called to attend the fall court session held on *xv* October, 1606 were to be empaneled on a jury as needed, and perhaps for other reasons. They were listed as "absent vassals," and fined unless their names were crossed out by the clerk as they arrived; marked "deleted," by the modern editors. This date is in the midst of harvest, and could mean a serious loss of crop to the farmers as the rains threatened. Perhaps the fine was preferable to the loss of crop, or some of the absentees may have been registering a protest at the summons to be forced witnesses.

Only one name in this list is conspicuously outlandish - Hendre Depo. As we have told, a payroll clerk who spoke no French made up the name on the spot back in 1561 at Holyroodhouse. I will never cease to wonder how our Frenchman's staccato speech was eventually modulated toward the Scottish speech he had certainly learned to deal with 45 years after he first heard it. Like a person's shadow on a sunny day, one's accent sticks with him, and can't be shaken. Even though this chapter may appear to be a legal or even a linguistic study, what I am watching for is a trace of my earliest family. There were children in their house and they were half French and half Scottish. None of the names we find here are French except one. Perhaps all of the Depo children, except the three living in the capital city, married into these neighbor's families.

On and on through the generations the French blood was halved. I suppose that the children spoke broadest Scot.

WESTHOUSES: Mark and Gawen Mertone, probably brothers, were here given two spellings side by side. Gawain, from the Round Table, was a favorite name.

DERNIK: Neilsone shows a Scandinavian derivation transplanted to Scotland. Quentin shows a phonetic use of the "qu" sound, but in *quhytle*, see below, the "qu" is pronounced "wh."

APILTRELEVES: The Darlings and the Pringles were prominent names in this locality. This is the only reference to apples that I have seen. Perhaps they had apples and other farming areas did not, for the Cistercians very likely brought them to Melrose, perhaps choice grafted varieties from France. One or two of these ancient varieties are still available in nurseries.

THREIPWOID: *Quhytle* = Whittle. Apparently "wh" was not known. One wonders what pronunciation came forth as these men spoke up in their language, and their accents, which show so little connection with the spellings the clerks made up as they went along. Speech, not writing, was the communication skill common to all. I have worked with Mexican college students using surveying and forestry text books, written in English, who were unable to recognizably pronounce the words which they nevertheless understood. Presumably they understood each other, but to the complete mystification of an English speaker. Navajo speakers, even orators, like the illiterate Scots, had no writing to record their fluency. Scots who could write were in the position of having almost no guide lines when they committed speech to paper.

BLAINSLIE: In 1682 a George Pringle of Blindlie was the regality baille who fined dozens of "irregular persons, and delinquents" who were named with their occupations listed, including these neighbors of his grandfather's generation. This wholesale fining, in 1682, was a fore-runner of the Killing Time, for these people may have been fined for being absent from the established church, on orders from England. You were fined if you missed church on three consecutive Sundays.

MOSHOUSES: Since Depo was the "stable-boy" of my grandmother's legend, I am interested in the names, and number of people who were his neighbors in Moshouses. Five are named here. The Notman family, in this and later references, seems most numerous.

John Home of Coldenowis, who appears a little later as the Laird of Coldenknowis, has his name spelled John, the first time that spelling is used. The laird can be presumed to have been educated, perhaps in London, or France, and he probably told the clerk not to use the customary "Jhon." Where did this unpronounceable spelling come from? Perhaps, like "John," it is a relic of Johannes of ancient derivation, with good phonetic credentials so long as it is all written out. Our clerks trying to get the meaningless "h" into the word, "John," transposed it with the "o" which produced the usual botch, "Jhon." What they wrote down was like a hieroglyph, or pictograph, signifying "John," or whatever word it was that they were struggling with. They had no idea that there could be a phonetic rendering of speech. In 1988, we are creeping out from under a pall of ignorance created by educationists who, like the clerks four hundred years ago, did not realize that words are created and read phonetically, by having certain symbols represent the specific sounds heard in speech.

Part of the interest in reading these old records is to note which words they did spell with phonetic understanding. George, James, money, lands, and many others were spelled consistently right. Jhon, Philp, Androw, and our Hendre(André) contained slight tonal shadings that were lost in the typical throaty growl of those times. Without clear articulation, phonetic spelling would have to wait for the time when both parts of the act were cleaned up.

It can be seen by comparing this page (22), with page 68 of the *Records*, that a new court clerk had been installed whose spelling was more consistent with correctly pronounced words. Even he used "Qu" instead "Wh" in Whitley. It intrigues me to reflect on the numbers of college students from the earliest times, who flunked out because they did not correctly answer that the world was flat, that the moon was made of green cheese, that the blood and the heart had no particular function, etc. In Scotland the scene tightened up in the 18th Century. There was an educational turnaround then with attention given to the finer points of literacy and knowledge.

MELROSE REGALITY RECORDS
Volume I, page 29
Absent Vassals at Court
xv October, 1606

"The baillie court of the regalite of Melrose haldin thairat be Walter Chisholme of that Ilk the xvij of Junii 1607.

Absentes

"LESSUDDANE: All bot James Stoddert and James Couchrane, to wit, Jhone Brydin, James Uneis, David Jamesone, Thomas Uncs, Mongow Riddell (deleted), Jhone Riddell, Robert Cunra, Robert Hunter, Thomas Hunter, Androw Stoddert, Thomas Haiste, Mungow Purves, William Riddell, James Lethen, James Jamesone (deleted), Androw Richesone."

NEWTOUNE: Thomas Coit (deleted), Androw Hetoune.

NEWSTEID: William Fischear.

GALTOUNSYD: Thomas Hoye (deleted), William Boustoune (deleted), Jhone Broune (deleted), Jhone Boustoune (deleted), Androw Clerk, Quhintein

(Thomson) (deleted), Quhintein Scot, Androw Mar (deleted), Gawen Mertaune, Mark Mertaune (deleted).

DAINZELTOUN: Jhon (?Thom) Scot, saudler (deleted), William Ker, vicar.

MELROSE: Robert Wallace, Alexander Rogear.

DERNIK: Jhone Walker (deleted), Andrew Merser, "puile." [N.B. for the first time Andrew is given a modern spelling, likely at Merser's request, for the other spelling is on later pages except for pages 67 and 68, where improved spelling suddenly starts.]

BLAINSLIE: Edward Romanis (deleted), George Romanis (deleted), Michaell Diksone, Jhone Stirling (deleted), George Pringle of Blindlie, Wille Scheill, William Hunter of Williamlaw, James Hunter of Halkburne. <u>Hendre Depo</u>.

LANGHAUGH: Jhone Frater, officer (deleted), Androw Derling, elder, and younger (deleted), Philp Derling, younger (?) (deleted).

REDPATH: The Laird of Coldenknowis, Androw Hom (?) in Bassindane.

COMMENTARY: This court session records for the third time that Hendre Depo was a resident at Melrose. It is interesting to me that Walter Chisholme was the judge over my ancestor. Two of the finest people that I have ever known were James Chisholm and his wife. They were the best friends of my family as long as they lived, and even after I had gone to college in Michigan. Most of these years they had lived in Jamestown, New York, but they were natives of Selkirk, not far from Melrose. The SELKIRK REPORTER of June 18, 1925 has an article and photograph of this man in his uniform as he returned to play his drum in the Common Riding where he had played fifty years before. He had probably wondered along with all of us how we could be so unquestionably Scottish, and have the name Deppa, for we had no idea of a connection with the city of our patronymic.

The roll call above uses the term "Absent Vassals" with interesting connotations. This medieval term, with its requirements of pledged fealty, performance of military service, and other subservient duties in return for the overlord's protection, was obsolete in the time of Queen Mary. Peel towers across the countryside, including three near the Langshaw Mill, were remnants of the laird's protective function, but in Scotland the full-blown feudal system had never been instituted as in other lands. These towers were really for the families that built them, and they could be fatally turned into chimneys by clever marauders. Nor were these "vassals" servile semi-slaves. They considered themselves tenants with obligations, but their minds were beginning to move toward more independent relationships. Contention between tenant and commendator was constant as these records show. The overlord demanded, and the tenant resisted, payment of the *multure*, or grinding fee, which was the main income of the proprietor. It was important to him that the power and the prestige of his court be maintained. The tenants walked the thin ice of defiance so far as they dared risk dispossession. Most had legal life-rent tenancy, but those hanging on by virtue of ancient "kindly-tenant" status were endangered, for the changing times and the greed of a landlord could turn them out with nowhere to go.

Hendre Depo did not go to any of these court sessions except the first one, where he was awarded damages as we have shown. Was he recalcitrant, or ill, for he was in his sixties? Did he have a perquisite registered with the commentator that made him confident he would not be held to account? He knew that there was a paper lodged somewhere, that recorded the queen's wish that he be provided with a tenancy. Two more items of this court session are brief and interesting:

"The quhilk day Hobe Kyle in Lessuddane is decerneit to pay to Patrik Riddell thair for ane yow slane be him the soume of v merkis money in respact of his nocht compeirance.

"The quhilk day Jhone Broune in Galtounsyd is absolved of the xxL. acclameit be Wille Andersone in Redpath in respect of the confessioune of the said William."

MELROSE REGALITY RECORDS
Volume I, pages 38 and 39
Absent Vassals at Court
xv October, 1606

These pages of the court records are relevant in our search for André Depo, but tid-bits of historical interest lie hidden in these paragraphs, too. The almost understandable words, mixed with words not to be found in a modern dictionary, the occasional Latin words, and the legalities, entice one toward philology, but we don't need to be that serious about it. These books are nearly 400 years old, and it is a fair guess that this writing follows a style one or two centuries older than that. This may be as close to reading ancient writing as we, who are laymen, are likely to get; always excepting interlinear Chaucer which isn't quite fair. The writing here is emerging from the Latin of church and law into a hybrid vernacular. Still it is a fascinating jungle of spelling, grammar, and ambiguity. It is done in a crabbed handwriting, which the editors spared us, but with paper and pens cruder than the steel pens and the ink of my grade school days. Our paper self-destructs after a few years, we are told, and our literacy rate is racing downward; theirs was the opposite. Nearly every week, reports tell that our children have so lost their native powers of concentration and verbal expression, that a disastrous number perform on the verge of illiteracy. To rest their brains, we have the children live with T.V., video, and vicarious sports. The jargon-ridden, often meaningless writing of bureaucratic and corporate technicians and scientists is today's education scandal, nor is there any real excuse that facilities for learning are inadequate. Centuries ago, only a few people could receive instruction, and the curriculum was narrow beyond belief. Today, editors are routinely placed at the elbows of technical personnel to help them turn out writing that is not embarrassing to the organization.

The story of Melrose could be told in a small pamphlet, but much interesting detail would be missed. Within the history of this almost ageless institution there are nuggets of buried lore. It is not necessary to absorb it all but, like a walk in the woods, there are things to see in odd corners.

This particular court session exemplifies the endless struggle, through centuries of time, as peasants contested their overlord's sovereignty. There was always a *quid pro quo*. Each had to have a livelihood, but it was the little fellow who did the hard work, so they wrangled. In these paragraphs we see the overlord, Sir Jedeane Murray, bring a legal document to the *baille* court. It asserts his right to the *multure* (milling fee) of all the tenants named in it. That is, they had to take their grain to the grist mill at Langshaw for grinding.

The past tense in this writing is not indicated by "ed" as in granted, but by "it" as in *grantit*. *Landis* is sometimes written *lands*, showing that new forms were creeping in, for these were "modern" times. Scotland was coming out of the Middle Ages. Pages 38 and 39 are quoted verbatim, but in numbered paragraphs so that each may be followed by comments. To a degree, the record seems meaningless on casual reading, but the contention between landlord and tenant is visible, as well as some hidden politics. By presenting the court record one paragraph at a time, followed by an interpretation, I hope to have made this jumble of strange terminology understandable. I can only hope that I have fathomed the actions correctly. The original book, of course, runs the text together in a maze of strange words.

MELROSE REGALITY RECORDS
Volume I, page 38

Sessioun, be Walter Chisholme and Dene
Jhone Watson, the xvj of September 1607

1. "...Compeirit Sir Jedeane [Gideon] Murray and produceit ane precept execuit and indorseit aganes the persones thairintill conteinit, and for instructing thairof produceit his seasing of the landis of Langschaw and Langschaw mylne togidder with ane act of court of this bailliere in favouris of the Abbay mylne of Melrose for the astrictit multeris of the samein, daitit the xvij of Januar 1556 [1586?], and conforme thairto desyrit proces."

The following may help with some of the above words, as we understand them:

> Appeared...a writ...therin...his seising [taking legal possession]...strict payment...for conformance to this writ he desires a court decree.

Looking behind all of this, one finds that the tenants, or vassals to be named, had agreed to, and signed such multure obligations, most likely with an "x" mark.

2. "...Compeirit William Cirncroce of Colmeslie, personallie summodit, grantit the desire of the sumonds, thairfoire decerneis."

William Cairncroce of Colmeslie, was the proprietor of the lands of Colmeslie, and the tower standing just across the burn from the mill. The mill's foundation stones can still be seen. He had reasons which we don't know for helping Sir Jedeane get all of these tenants to once again affirm their obligation to use this mill. Other mills, or the hand *quern*, were preferred, but illegal. Very possibly he was Jedeane's *sub rosa* agent, or tacksman, as is indicated by the fact that he alone, was personally summoned. The apparent purpose of this court session was to build a case against recalcitrants. With Cairncroce's admission of obligation, the other tenants merely had to say yes, and be recorded as *similiter*, similarly agreeing. If any were absent, they were marked as agreeing by their non-*compeirance*.

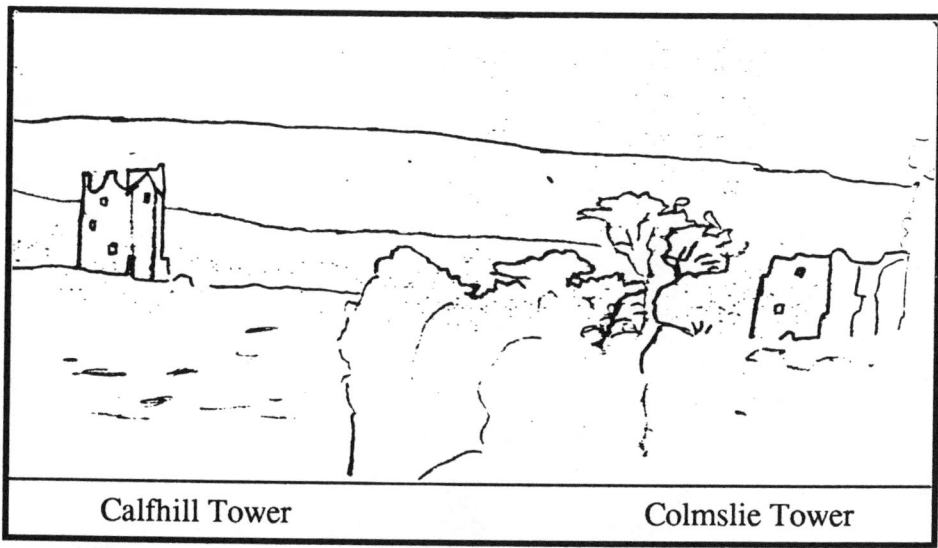

Calfhill Tower   Colmslie Tower

Figure 6. The present-day ruins of the peel-towers are visible from the place where the Depo family lived at Moshouses. These towers were a phenomenon of the 1500s, when reiver anarchy was at its worst. They were often turned into chimneys when the roof thatch was set on fire by a raider who had climbed the wall. The owners had tricks, too. Before fleeing their tower, they might plug the entrance with a mass of damp, smouldering peat, which raiders could neither penetrate nor put out.

William Cairncroce was the proprietor of Colmslie, and Nicholl Cairncroce, elder, held Calfhill and Hilslop in 1607. Adam Hislope was witness at the baptism of the infant James Depo on April 12, 1656. The baby's father was also James, as the charts in Chapter XV show. The mother was probably a Hislope, sister of Adam, and related to the builder of the Calfhill tower.

The dates of 1556 and 1586 which the editors marked with a question mark as illegible, can be resolved: Hendre Depo was not at Melrose until 1562, as his story has been riddled out. No other tenant except this one Frenchman can be dated as to his beginning, but he alone positively shows that the date, 1556 is not the correct date. There are other reasons for deciding that the year 1586 was the year of the original pledge of *thirlage*, or feudal obligation. The year 1556 has no connection with Melrose history that I can find, but 1586 was when the lands were being put under the complete power of the crown in the "Act of Annexation of 1587." In 1556 the Church was in full ownership and there was no need to compel the renters to reaffirm their thirlage. After the Reformation their obligation needed renewal. Also, the span of 51 years is too great for any of these portioners to have signed such an early document.

3. "...Nicholl Cairncroce, elder, similitar for the landis of Calfhill, and Hilslop."

These lands and the tower adjoined his relative's, as our map shows. Calfhill, a half mile south, shows that these families were strong forces at Melrose, the only ones with towers, it appears. Calfhill was built on a site called Pict's Hill, which indicates there had been people on this choice piece of land, with a clear stream, and probably plenty of salmon and other fish to provide scarce but necessary protein. They were there before there was a Scotland with its laws controlling fishing.

4. "...Jhone Notman, officer, and Hendre Depo similiter, portionaris of Moshouses, Jhone Broune thair."

Notman and Depo are listed next, apparently as men also able to help authenticate and promote Murray's claims. He and Hendre Depo are referred to as portioners of Moshouses. Jhone Broune is also cited as living there. William Notman is listed later as a portioner there. These inhabitants practically encircle the mill. It looks as though they were bell-wethers leading the rest of the flock into Murray's fold. They really had no alternative except open rebellion, and there is no hint of that. The episode does indicate that Depo was an influence toward stability and order in the community.

8. "...Jhone Frater, maltman in Langhaugh, grantit thairto."

9. "...Jhone Hoye of Colmeslihill in lik maner."

10. "..Jhone Spotiswoid of Quhitlie for his lands of Quhitlie and Quhitlie Dykis grantit in lik maner."

11. "...Robert Hall, James Moffet, Jhone Moffet, portionaris of Threipwoid, grantit in lik maner."

12. "...Androw Smythe in Langhaugh grantit to the actioun in maner foirsaid."

13. "...William Notman, portionar of Moshouses, grantit in lik maner."

14. "...The juge decerneis aganes all the parteis particularlie aboue specefeit with thair awin consent, quherupon the said Sir Jediane requireit instruments."

This is not the end of the session of September 16, 1607, but our man, Depo, is found to be alive, and active in the litigation. All the defendants are judged, and found to be legally obligated to use the mill at Langshaw, and pay the multure.

This obligation of tenants was so significant a feature of living that a few lines will be quoted in explanation. Things changed so slowly that there is probably no discrepancy between the actions above, and the situation fifty years later. We quote from:

Records of the Baron Court of Stichell
Taken from the Publications of the Scottish History Society, 1905.

VOLUME L

"...The burden of payment in kind occurs most commonly in that ... rent called *kain*, or *kayne*, when the tenant contributed to the laird's pantry annually one or more fowls or hens as part of his rent."

The burden most grievous of all, and one fruitful of constant irritation to every one within the barony, was that of *thirlage* to a particular mill. This was called the *service of the sucken*. Every thirteenth peck of meal ground at the mill was claimed by the miller under the name of multure. In addition to multure, dues had to be paid to the baron. Lesser dues went to the miller's helper, under the name of *knaveship*. So great was the profit from those multures to the baron and to the miller, that act after act was passed ordaining the tenants to confine all their grinding to the mill of the barony. The illegal handmill (*quern*) of the *cottar* versus the water-mill of the landlord contended for centuries. The struggle went back before the days when the monks of St. Albans sallied forth and, after capturing the handmills of their vassals, paved the floors of their rooms with the stones from the handmills.

15. "...Compeirit Jhone Romainis in Blainslie, Adame Derling thair, George Romainis thair, George Greig thair, Jhone Thin thair, Thomas Lyall thair, Charles Pringle thair, William Jhonstoun thair, Edward Romainis thair, Jhone Stirling thair, James Hall thair, Edward Hall thair, portionaris of Blainslie, personallie, quha constituit Frances Wilkesoun procurator for thame, desyrit the inspectioun of the summoundis and peces produceit and ane day to use thair deffences."

In paragraph 14, Sir Jedeane won, for all of the men agreed that they owed him multure. There are two sides to this case.

Paragraphs 15 through 20 show the opposition. We know now that in the course of time multure disappeared, and leases with set prices took their place. However, huge modern shopping malls with their rents pegged to the gross income of a store, give off an odor of modern multure. Perhaps the more things change, the more they stay alike after all.

The tenants who acceded to thirlage were mostly clustered nearest to the mill. As in the case of Depo, probably they had actually signed the document of 1586. Twenty years had elapsed. Considering the life expectancy then, many signatories had died, without much doubt. Their sons, sons-in-law, and incomers had not signed, nor had they been legally challenged in the interval. Kindly tenants were vulnerable too, though their tenure had existed since before the memory of man without any kind of writing. Now this group hired Frances Wilkesoun to represent them in resisting the thirlage. He asked to study the summons, and the evidence, and have one day in court.

The men in this second group had put themselves at serious risk. They were tenants without leases. On their farmsteads at the sufferance of the landlord, each time the annual rent came due he could refuse to accept it, and order them off the land. Peremptory eviction is one of the saddest of Scotland's stories, and it was ruthlessly carried out in the next century and a half by Lowland investors against pitiful Highlanders. Evicted families lost the accumulated farm improvements made by generations of their forbears laboring from dawn to dark. The father could become a "broken-man," and the family scattered as beggars. Emigration to Canada and the United States became a tidal wave, as Highlanders were driven from their homes between 1782 and 1820, and again from 1840 to 1854. This was the Great Eviction, the Clearances.

16.   "...The persewar present compeirit be Mr. Thomas Houp, procurator, quha tuik instruments upoun the compeirance of the saidis deffenderis and Frances Wilkesone thair procurator, and ansuerit that the saidis

deffenders "ante onmia" man [may] gif thair aith "de calumnia" gif thai have ane just cause to deny the contentis of the summoundis, and ane day can nocht be gevein to thame to deffend bot to deffend presentlie, seing thai have gottin ane sufficient tyme of deliberatioun be the space of xv dayis betuix the dait of the sitatioune and the day of compeirance, and thairupoun desirit the juge his interloqutor."

The complainant, or plaintiff, Sir J. Murray, through his attorney, Mr. Houp, took testimony from the defendants, and their attorney, Mr. Wilkesone. Mr. Houp answered the defendants that before all they may give their oath under "penalty" of malicious slander if they have a just cause to deny the claim against them. One day cannot be given them, but they must defend themselves at once, since they had a sufficient time of deliberation by the space of fifteen days between the date of the citation, and the day of appearance. The plaintiff desires the pronouncement (verdict) of the judge.

17. "...Secundlie, it is allegeit be the said Frances that na proces aucht to be grantit in respect of the feriot and close tyme, and na dispensatioune had be the juge."

Secondly, the defense attorney argued that a judgement should not be made since the judge made no allowance for the hurried and short time of the action.

18. "...It is ansuerit thai can nocht be hard to object the feriot and close tyme in respect of the deffenders compeirance, and dessyrit to have ane day assignit to thame, quhairupoun the persewar requireit instruments."

19. "...And forther the juge hes ane dispensatioune for sitting this present tyme in all causes noctwithstanding of this feriot tyme."

20. "...Thirdlie it is allegeit be the saidis deffenders that na proces can be grantit againest thame conforme to the sumoundis unto the tym thai have inspectioune of the persewaris rycht to the thirle multeris lybellit and ane day assignit to thame to ansuer to, quhairupoun thair haile deffence man result [may depend], because we deny the astrictione [restriction] to the said mylne utherwayis nor voluntarlie, [voluntarily or not] and protestis gif your Lordship proceid and assigne us na day to produce our deffences and to have inspectioun of the persewaris tytillis "titles," for remcid [remedy] of law and nullity..."

MELROSE REGALITY RECORDS
pages 66, 67 and 68
Session 18 May 1608

Henry Depo appears in this volume for the fifth, and last, time on page 68. This entry is important in my ancestor search, but in looking for him I have become acquainted with his neighbors. Many of their names have become very familiar to me, and I have learned enough about their way of life to sympathize in the sense of being able to understand their concerns, and activities. This is academic, of course, but if I could drop in on them, what they were doing would not much surprise or astonish me. Yet I wouldn't offer to change places with them, for we have a better deal. Some of the things they do and don't do remind me of Scottish relatives, and friends I knew as a child. My children and grandchildren live in an era far removed from the "old" ways of the early 20th Century. Even in Scotland, the old old ways are a fading memory, but even yet, in some remote dingle there, as in the most inaccessible "hollers" of Appalachia, people will be found making-do in the old old ways. It would be well if everyone knew someone who had lived in the preceding century, and learned in that way about what had gone before. Young folks need to know that they are not just a dot in the present tense, but part of a continuity that needs them alive, and aware, ready to handle whatever comes.

The population on Melrose land was large, dense almost, for farming was labor-intensive; one child herding one goose, for instance, with little interference by school or play. The number of men mentioned in this big book gives an idea of the density, for each name represents a family back on the land. With my wife and sons and daughters I drove over the roads from Melrose town, to Langshaw in the fall of 1985. We saw no houses until we got to the cluster of half a dozen near the old mill site. At Moshouses there was a large barn, and a house, and in a large nearby field one man was operating a tractor with no one else in sight.

Four hundred years ago this landscape would have been alive with men and women especially in the harvest season. Boys and girls would be everywhere, herding, gathering brushy wood for fuel, carrying water. Paths and trails largely took the place of roads, even the narrow dirt roads that are now rare. People afoot, on horseback, or leading pack horses and ponies, could be moving between the dozens of primitive houses and barns. These dismal little structures clustered together behind the walls and fences that made cot and byre into accommodations for man and beast.

Outside each community, beyond a brush-topped dike that served as a wall, was an uncultivated scrub-covered commons for grazing. Boston has a commons that started out this way not long after Depo appeared in this book. The scrub-land commons were often wet "mosses," and sticks for fuel could be gathered there. Boys herding sheep, mainly, but also cattle, horses, draft-oxen, and few geese, would be visible in all directions. After harvest, in the winter, the stubble would all be eaten in the fields, and in the weedy areas between the cultivated rigs. What a scene of activity. What a contrast with anything to be seen today, except in places such as Egypt, where muscles still perform ancient tasks, and aerobic classes aren't well attended. How much interesting history there is in this picture, not due to change much for a hundred years. My book about just my own family changed directions when I tried to see our ancestors as real live people among their 16th century neighbors. The second half of that century became the focus of my work, and I found that my own people blended into the general picture very naturally.

These pages are given in full because Hendre Depo is there. Also because writing such as this is not available to the general reader, and it should be for those who are interested. There are only a few libraries, mostly in the United Kingdom, where such old material can be studied. It is hoped that this glimpse into the distant past will satisfy the curiosity of many who do not have access to such old records. It seems to me, too, that without some context or focus, such as tracing my man, the passages would be too dry, even incomprehensible. These were real people with terrible problems almost as bad as each of us has, but it should cheer us up to know that we don't have to eat brose with neither coffee nor oranges for breakfast every day, as they did.

New spelling appeared in the latest court sessions. Between pages 39, and 67, some words jumped from archaic to modern, and within the same time-frame politics were seething. Power politics in Edinburgh were without doubt the motive force, but there were repercussions in the Melrose farmtouns. These few notes give an idea of the pressures that were brought to bear on the tenants: On December 9, 1606, the commendator had resigned the estate into the hands of the king, that it might be erected into a temporal lordship in favor of the Earl of Morton. In 1609, he resigned in favor of John Ramsay. Presumably the feuars worked their lands oblivious to political machinations between lords they never saw who lived in the far off city. They learned through court summons that old requirements were to be re-activated and enforced as many a poor tenant learned to his sorrow. Sir Gideon Murray, (Jedeane) who brought the action, was probably not a principal, but a delegated enforcer.

The new spelling in these last pages must mean that a new court clerk had been installed. The change is too radical for the old clerk to have turned over a new leaf. The new clerk must have had teachers with new learning. Perhaps he had been brought from the city to guard against his having any local sympathies. At any rate, the record has a changed tone. We first noticed this when our hero, André Depo, had his misnomer, Hendre, upgraded to Henry - still incorrect. There are many spelling improvements throughout, but Sir Gideon led the list, followed by John, Andrew, Philip, and Henry. It remained for the future to discover "wh" so that "quh" would become obsolete, and Whitley would no longer be Quhitlie. Long after this time, the letter "thorn" was still used instead of our quite modern use of "th," in words such as "the." Presuming that this writing bears some resemblance to the sound of their speech, there is no way to imagine how the testimony of these men sounded in their broad, Lowland dialect. It would certainly be Greek to most of us. The following extract, which is a guide to sanctimony, may serve as a final exercise in reading old Scots:

MELROSE REGALITY RECORDS
Volume III
xvj of November 1608

"The quilk day it is statuit and ordaineit that na persone induellar in the Heland in Melroseland byd fra the kirk of Melrose on Sonday or bapteissis any bairns or bureis any deid or makis mariages out of Melrose, under the pane of xls. toties quoties."

CHAPTER XII

GRIST FOR MY MILL

Perhaps thirteen generations separate the newlyweds at Melrose and their descendants 427 years later, in 1989. Mathematical guesswork could make a reasonable estimate of the number of family members who have lived in that length of time. Many more than a hundred have descended from the four children who came to the U.S. in 1850, I believe, although I do not have the youngest ones on charts. There are fairly large numbers of individuals cited in Scottish records, especially after 1700. Sadly, these are records of individuals. Few or no connective relationships between all these people have been traced, that I know of.

Historical records will be used to construct an outline of the first three generations of Hendre's descendants. Thus, when a child's baptismal date is found, the linkage to the father and grandfather is possible, as is shown in a later chart. Marriage, burial, and witness records all help in this tracing of the child, grandchild relationships. Oddly, the erratic spelling of the name has tremendous value in keeping the first three generations in order, and best of all, our name is never confused in the way the Smiths, for instance, could be mixed up. Eventually, of course, conformity homogenized the whole tribe until now only the Dippie and Deppa spellings survive.

As I have worked on this family history, the thought has never been absent: could Grandma, and all of the ancestors who carried the story for more than 300 years down to her ears, have been wrong? Neither she, nor more than the first few of those people, knew what the story meant. They told it because that had always been the accepted obligation in a Scottish family. I am perfectly aware of the old saw - you work backwards, never forwards, in tracing a line. However, I also know that Schliemann did not doubt Homer's Iliad, the epic of Troy, (*A History of the Western World*, L. J. Cheney). By digging where the legend said Troy had been, Schliemann found the city, even though most scholars agreed that the legend was just a romantic story.

Recently, a great deal of further research into Homer's Iliad has been carried on at Cambridge University, and elsewhere. Storytellers in the tradition of Homer still exist. The television presentation based on the book *In Search of the Trojan War*, focuses on an Irish storyteller, and also one in Turkey, not far from where Homer told his tales. They display "bardic memory" in professional recitations of book-length stories. Thus history has been preserved through ages of time, without writing.

The long-ago inability to read and write was very distinct from ignorance. They were far from being synonymes even though they can be bedmates. Illiteracy has always been compensated by adaptations of memory, association, alliteration, even jingles just short of poetry. Mother Goose rhymes were often sly political commentary masquerading as nursery rhymes. When the ability to read and write did not exist in the general population events were recorded in formalized statements to be passed on without alteration. This responsibility was as old as the Celtic race, and not forgotten when the Celts became Scots. Literacy is a fragile flower, easily lost, as is being discovered in the United States where so many are slipping down a treacherously greased slide into ignorance in a high-tech world.

Alongside the epic stories have been family traditions too obscure to live outside the family. These were probably safer carried by word of mouth than by writing, which so readily is lost or burned as attics are cleaned or estates closed. The clincher about Troy is the question, why would such an improbable sounding event be conjured up, and passed down, if it were not true? I wouldn't tell my children a made-up story about their ancestors, would you? Besides, relatives would kill a made-up story before it could get off the ground.

When I started digging where our tradition said our name had begun, I found the two people whose marriage started our family name in Scotland. As my work progressed our name became so enmeshed with the events surrounding Queen Mary's horses that my curiosity almost led to the writing of their biography. Perhaps I have put together their story as based on all the records that there are. This needed to be done, for this very interesting part of the history of Mary, Queen of Scots, has not been told before. I am quite sure of this, for a very prestigious book misinterprets the original Scottish record about the animals, even stating that they were "bought in the north of England and....for some unexplained reason.....were delayed a month." The fact that this unconcerned and careless interpretation is in perhaps the only commentary on the original records shows why this dramatic overseas delivery has to be cleared up. Our sentimental queen had selected from the royal French stables the thirty animals she could not part with, and she gave orders that ships be chartered, and men hired to care for them as they were conveyed to her Scottish palace. This was a very personal episode in her life. Affairs of state were her duty, but her obsession, as with any horse-obsessed teenager today, was her horses. Everyone agrees that she was an imperious character when she chose to be, and besides, fine horses and skill with them was vastly important then.

After I had studied Scottish history enough to appreciate the hectic times the people had endured, I quit wondering why it was that the descendants in the Borders had no legend to preserve the origin of their family name. At the time this family knew the story, but they didn't go around telling it; self preservation was the reason. Only harm could come from telling how the mother had lived for years in the French court with Mary, the Queen of both countries. Possibly the children were never told the story. The father, too, had a tight-rope to walk. He was a foreigner, and a member of his family had been "slaughtered" a few miles away. As best I can learn, John Knox, whose son, James, had done the deed, was a nephew of John Knox, the reformer. A John Knox was a minister at or near Melrose. Hendre could only nurse such a grievous situation in silence. He may even have been compelled to attend services held by this Knox. Hendre had been given position and possessions ahead of the local people. He had to keep quiet and not fan any smoldering animosities. The *Brittanica* says: "to the ordinary man jealousies arose from no profounder source than the instinctive distrust of strangers." These people today are good-hearted, and friendly. There is a fair chance, however, that an outlander won't understand much of what they say, for they have a special way with the sound of words.

One daughter, Katherine Dippo, grew up in the Canongate suburb of Edinburgh and married Alexander Moresom, of the city. She could talk freely about her parents' romantic story, especially to her grandmother, who had sent Katherine's mother off to France as a child. This never-ending tale could be told whenever friends and relatives got together. Through the ensuing 25 years or so, everyone concerned would know the story, for they could remember the people. After that, just one son passed along the story, and then a grandson did. Such a chain reaction almost has to be propagated by sons, for they carry the name, but the continuity inevitably required the wives, mothers, and grandmothers. They preserve the family stories, even the stories of their husbands' people, but the linkage requires the interest of a son. He has to tell his wife, and show his interest, or the story will stop. It is a fragile connection that seldom holds together. Just one uninterested connector, or the lack of a son, and the tale never becomes a legend in which details have vanished in the haze of years, leaving just a nugget of truth.

This research and writing project that has sometimes seemed too big to carry through, has an urgency, for time is now slipping by, for me. The realization was slow to come, but there is no doubt that I am the end of the line. I either put the tradition on paper, or it dies. It is a strange feeling to be in that position. How could

I default on all those people who had carried our story down to my grandmother, and she to me? My father was born in our country's centennial year. At the present moment I have one grandson who probably is the sole custodian of my father's name, though he had three sons. This surname disappearing act cannot be forecast, but it is irrevocable. My mother's father, who had six children, has his Northrup name pegged to one grandson, and he is not interested. Alfred Northrup's wife saw her Wadsworth name vanish in her lifetime.

Just as Katherine seems to have been brought up in the home of her grandparents, I think that, as my chart shows, two brothers were also raised there. A woman named Eupham Deippe appears in later records. She fits the dates to have been a daughter of one of the sons we speak of. She married Robert Morsome; there were many variations in the spelling of that family name. It may be recalled that the gardener at the palace was named Morrison, but we don't know of any connection with him, except that the two places are only a few hundred yards apart. Almost in the shadow of the palace, the story did not need to be hidden. It could even be bragged about with impunity there.

Women can often disappear into their husband's families without leaving a trace. However, it was the practice in Scotland for a married woman to use her maiden name with the appendage, "wife of." Eupham Deippe Moresom is an invaluable instance, for this links the two surnames, and ties up connections otherwise lost. It is frustrating that in the Regality Records of Melrose Hendre Depo's wife was never haled into court, for then her maiden name would have been revealed, as "wife of." We can read Margaret Ker, widow of James Cairncroce of Calfhill; Barbara Cairncroce, wife of Mr. William Duguid, minister, etc. What we have not found is: Christian name, surname, wife of Hendre Depo of Moshouses.

John Deippa, who is mentioned in chapters ten and fifteen, lived in the Palace/Canongate Parish and married Isobell Walker. This couple seems most likely to have begun the line that led to the Deppas of the United States. The confusion these first few generations had with the "ei," and the "ie" when they tried to write their last name is understanable. It seems plain that these people knew that their name came from Dieppe. The clerk who wrote "Depo" was trying to enter "Dieppois" in his timebook and he succeeded well enough. Hendre's wife, though, was well educated in French, and she may have influenced her daughter, Katherine, to spell her name "Dippo." In French, the "ie" of Dieppe is not a diphthong; each letter is pronounced. The spelling "Dippo" indicates a degree of education not found in the many who kept the "ie" and "ei" letters, not as diphthongs, but as baggage left over from recognition that the name had come from Dieppe. The English dialect they spoke had no place for either of these pseudo-diphthongs, but they put both vowels in their names, even though they couldn't pronounce them.

I think that tricky "ie" can be blamed for the twenty variant spellings we have found in records. More than a dozen stabs were made at arranging these two letters even though there was no way to pronounce what they wrote down. I would bet that they used only two pronunciations through all of this: Dippie, and Deppie. As a bit of education crept in, in the early 1700s, these people, sheepishly or not, simply dropped one or the other of the two vowels. My line put an "a" at the end, but continued to say "Deppie." In 1904, when my mother married a Deppa, she refused to pronounce it Deppie. At first she thought there were two families in town, the one she read about, and the one she heard about. To this day, the old pronunciation is known especially in Sullivan County, N.Y. Mother staged her rebellion in Costello, Pennsylvania, where the change she promoted took hold much sooner. The old pronunciation is still known there, but no one of that name lives there now.

I have a clock about 35 inches tall of a very unusual style known as Connecticut Banjo, and there are very few in existence. Its gears and cogs are made of wood, and it runs about 26 hours on one winding. It has kept very good time for 170 years, and the only thing wrong with it is the people who wind it. They quit their jobs every few decades. Its ticks and tocks have no meaning, and no one remembers each one, yet they measure the passage of time. So it was with the days of the family at Moshouses. There was turmoil before, after, and all around them as history records, and we do not know how they fit in, but we do know they survived. We have surmised that their cottage and furnishings were better than average, but our curiosity has to be limited to a few conjectures about their lives.

The book - *A History of the Scottish People*, by T. C. Smout, is a gold mine of information about the times and the people we are investigating. He points out though, that the sixteenth century has very little source material, especially about the common people. Much of what there is consists of comments by a few travelers in the next two centuries when conditions had improved, but were still shockingly crude. I have tried to give some idea of life in those times, but imagination fails to conjure up with even remote accuracy the way things really were. We wish we could look in on the Depo establishment, but have to settle for reasonable conjecture based on the records we have seen.

In the fall of 1985, my wife and I, with our two sons and two daughters, went to Langshaw where the ancient mill foundations are visible at the sod line. Then we went the scant mile to where the cottages of Moshouses had stood. Car rental agencies won't rent even to excellent drivers if they are over 65, but all my children drove us on the "wrong" side of the road in two cars, and they carried our luggage, too, or we could not have seen the places our first family knew so well.

The countryside seemed very familiar to me, for topographic maps on a scale of six inches to the mile had shown me every facet of the landscape before I had left home. I believe the road locations have not changed at all, for even in remote times men walked in the easiest terrain. What a careless, and typical denigration! They, not we, were the masters of the outdoors environment.

The fields are now as large as possible, for tractors do the work, and only one large farmstead with a sign, "Mosshouses," marks the site of our ancestor's home. In his day there were a number of neighboring farmsteads with clustered cots, and byres. Each had a few stone walled enclosures for the milk cow, a horse or two, and some ewes at lambing time. Grazing animals were herded, seldom fenced. The fall of '85 had been very wet in Scotland, but in western Ireland, the rain was a national disaster. What we saw made one realize that in the olden times, cold, wet houses, sickness and famine could follow, for there was no trucking in of relief supplies of food, fuel or medical help, as was contemplated for the winter, especially in Ireland.

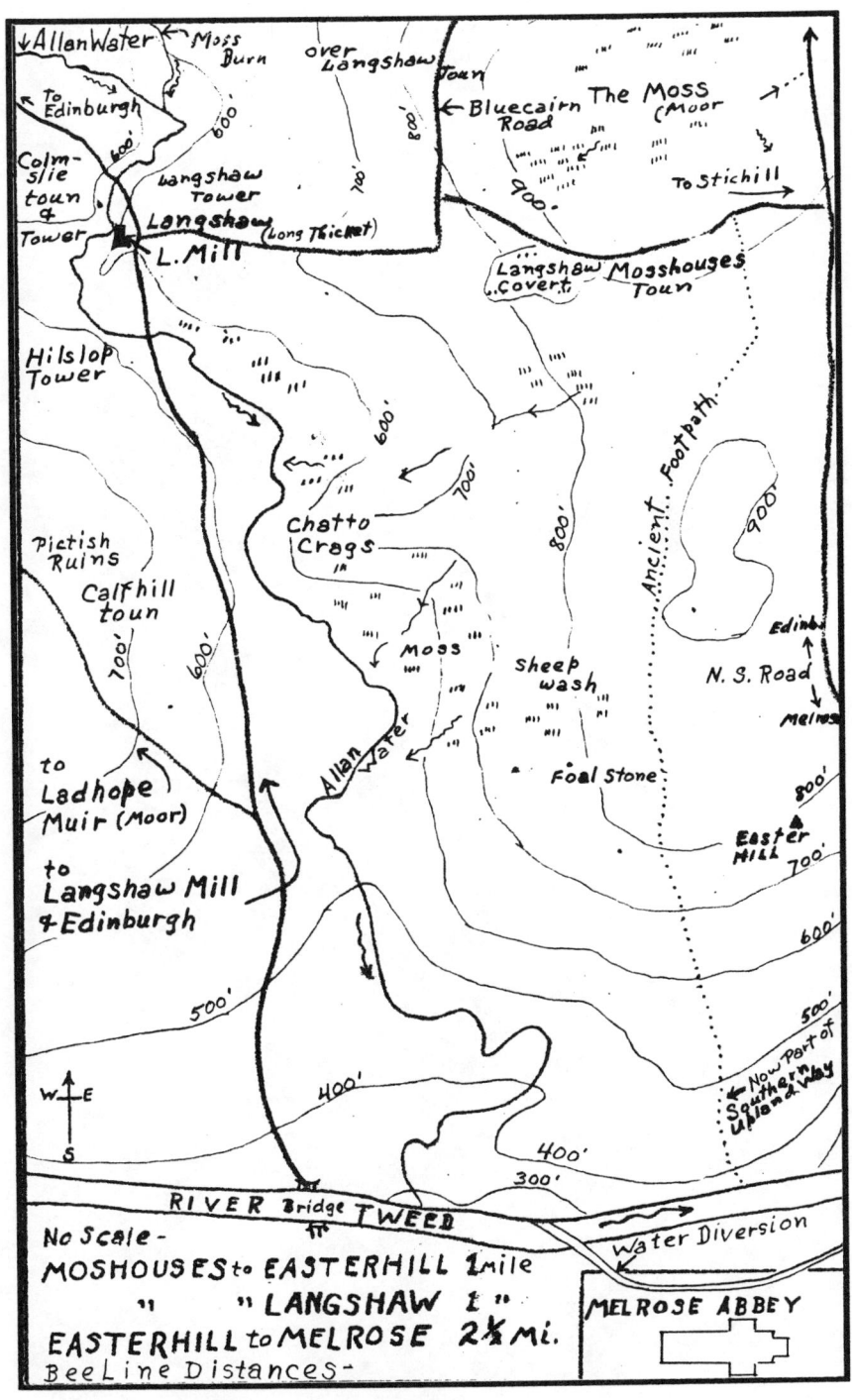

Figure 7: Melrose Abbey Lands

As I walked in the fields, and into a copse of alder and scrub, I could not keep my feet dry. This was close to the highest elevation around, some 550 feet above the River Tweed only four miles away. Thus a "moss" is a hill-top swamp, with any number of variations, not too unlike a Yorkshire moor or a northern bog. The typical vegetation may not be the most tangled in the world, and what thorns there are, are not the worst, which are in desert and tropical lands. As potential cropland though, this would be discouraging. In the sixteenth century only the prospect of starvation would move a man to break this land to the plow. From eight to twelve oxen were needed to pull a massive wooden plow, with an iron coulter, through this tangle, usually in the wet of winter, for oats were planted in the spring.

This kind of a place, plus the political situation we have described, made the queen's gift of a tenancy a little less than munificent, for she had urgent need for loyal and responsible people at chaotic Melrose. Her gift of a run-down place where our ancestors had a chance to fend for themselves and pay the rent was, nevertheless, a gift beyond compare, for a farmstead was out of the reach of common people. At that time, there were tenants whose virtual free-rent had been running on for generations with no kind of a lease. Inflation had come in, partly due to the Spanish gold and silver stolen in the Americas, and these "kindly tenants" were being evicted for more profitable arrangements. Very possibly, Depo was entrusted with more than one plot or ploughgate of this land, with several men working for him. The records of Melrose show that for over forty years our family never failed, or forfeited their gift.

There were half a dozen, or more, gradations in the status of farm worker. Strange to our way of thinking, only the most menial worked for a wage. Depo may have been set up as a *gudeman* or *husbandman*, a tenant who would provide either huts for his workmen to live in, or a common *bothy* for single men. A key worker might live in the gudeman's *but*, that half of his house where some workmen, and those seeking shelter, might cook and sleep, including grown sons of the family. Shelter, food, a very few animals, and a kail-yard, not money, were the preferred terms of employment.

Men did back-breaking field labor, and so did women, whose special lot was to carry things. They carried the manure out to the field, and the harvest to the barn, for example. In the later industrial era they did the work of mine mules literally, just to keep in perspective what manual labor meant in those times. Children, too, worked at cruelly hard tasks. Labor extended from dawn to dark without benefit of timepieces. The universal breakfast was brose. Lunch was also brose and often supper too. Brose was made by pouring a boiling liquid over oats ground at the mill, or illegally in a quern at home. Porridge, like brose, was a basic food, but required longer cooking. *Sowans* was a variation from the monotony of brose and porridge. It was made by soaking raw oats for a week or so until sour, when further steps produced a popular food with many variations. Men, at work or war, could moisten oats with water from a burn. Oats, either ground or whole, could also be chewed up dry. Scottish mercenaries in the Middle Ages were observed in Europe baking oat cakes on small sheets of metal they carried under their saddle flaps. No other grain equals oats for nutrition, and Scots were ingenious in the ways they ate their oats.

As a Pennsylvania-type Scotch boy, I learned to love buckwheat cakes baked on my mother's fine, round, 16-inch, cast iron griddle. I know now that it was just like a Scot's *girdle*, for it had a bail. I still bake many kinds of pancakes on my fine cast iron rectangular number, better for its 50 years of steady use over campfires in Navajo land, and on kitchen ranges since then.

In the XVI century, the very poorest people may have had no kettle in which to boil oat porridge or barley soup, leaving little alternative but to bake those grains in cakes on a stone next to the fire. Meat would have to be roasted. Some utensil for boiling was, of course, desperately needed, and it can be assumed that in a century when soldiers, as well as bands of brigands, had metal helmets and breastplates, a family would at least have a pot. But one cannot take refinements for granted, for sometimes habitations had no table, stools or fireplace. I have seen American/Scottish women prepare vegetables in a dish on the ground while sitting on a low stool or even leaning over to do their work from a chair. In Navajo fashion, one sat on the ground beside a fire in the middle of the hogan. A Scottish family ate, table or not, and a rock could serve as a stool, though a whale vertebra was better and not uncommonly used, especially near the western coast. The *girdle*, made to hang over a fire by its bail, was not invented until 1599. Before that, flat pieces of iron were owned by lucky people. Others still baked on a stone by the fire. When our young couple began their tenure at Melrose, there is quite a likelihood they fared better than average country people. They probably were given basic metal utensils for boiling and baking, for those could be bought in the city - perhaps by the palace chamberlain, if he were so instructed. Wooden trenchers, common bowls, horn spoons, and drinking cups were the usual eating utensils.

An insight into the lives of the border people may be gained by studying the settlers of Scottish ancestry in the Appalachian mountains. They were too poor to get beyond the hills and hollows that stopped them from reaching the deep soils of Ohio and Kentucky. With a few tools and their native ingenuity they survived in those mountains. To this day, old-timers retain many skills and remember traditions that undoubtedly hark back to the Border Scots. By painstakingly interviewing the present day descendants of the pioneers, students of the area have recorded a fantastic array of the subsistence skills by which these people lived in isolation from the flat-land outlanders to the east and west. In the *Foxfire* books one can catch the essence of Border life of the 16th century. These eight books show how marvelous was the Scottish spirit in coping with adversity in the old homeland and in the new.

Bannock is a Gaelic word for a flat, often triangular cake, made of oatmeal, and baked on a stone or an iron plate. Barley meal could be baked as a sourdough, but it was hard, rough emergency fare indeed. I enjoy bannocks with applesauce and mild cheese, and in other combinations. My receipt (recipe to moderns) is given here, but if you want to go back 400 years for the sake of authenticity, leave out the wheat-flour, baking powder and sugar, and the modern oven with its thermostat. King Alfred got in trouble with the Saxon woman because he had no thermostat, and burned her cakes. For shortening, the Scots used whichever they had of butter, chicken-fat or tallow. Cholesterol didn't bother them, for they didn't sit around much accumulating arterial plaque, nor did they live too long. Part of their rent was often paid as *carriage*, for wheeled carts were as rare as roads. They didn't need to jog evenings after their landlord's loads had been delivered and their own work was done for the day.

BANNOCKS

Stir together a rounded 3/4 cup quick oatmeal, one cup of flour, 2 t. baking powder, and 1/2 cup firmly packed brown sugar. Warmed shortening the size of 1 brown hen egg, or 5 T, is then thoroughly creamed into the mixed, dry ingredients.

From 4 to 6 T. of hot water are used to produce a dough. A very moist dough gives a better product, as oatmeal requires water and time for soaking and swelling. This moist sticky dough is harder to handle, but it can be stirred well in the bowl and then dumped onto an ungreased baking sheet. Form into a 1/2 inch thick round cake, and then remove a 2-inch circle at the center to avoid fragile points on the dozen or so triangles that can be cut. This is a very sticky procedure, but the pieces must be pulled well apart so they can rise as they bake. Wait at least half an hour before baking, although I have read that in the old old times, the dough might sit around in a box for days before baking, or even be stuck on a rope and hung up until it was baked. I always double this recipe; otherwise, the bannocks are too soon gone. It is a well-known fact that bannocks will protect you against witches.

Have your oven about 390 degrees F. In Scotland bake the bannocks on an ungreased baking-pan, and bake about 20 minutes. North American types should bake them on cookie-sheets, a term unknown in Scotland. Note: *koekje* is a word the English in Nieuw Amsterdam heard their Dutch neighbors use in reference to a multitude of delicious "little cakes." The English couldn't pronounce *koekje*, but they liked them so much they bought the town, renamed it New York, and called the little cakes, cookies. Eating cookies now supports a major industry in the United States, one occupation where we definitely lead the world.

WARNING: If you should burn your bannocks, under no circumstances should you cry out "Bannockburn." That word is reserved for the greatest Scottish victory over the English, at Stirling Castle, on June 23, 1314.

There was food beyond the brose, the oatcakes or bannocks, and the barley, and it was eagerly sought from every possible source. It was broth to flavor, and add substance to the brose. The merest scrap of meat, a sparrow, a fish or fish head, chicken heads or feet are all good food, or a marrow bone, butchering scraps, sometimes a rabbit. Anything in the meat line would do, including a fat hen, a grey goose, or a fine salmon from the Tweed. Sometimes people ate "higher on the hog," as on the diplomatic and social circuits in Edinburgh and Washington. At butchering time, when animals had to be sold or killed to avoid starvation in winter, there was too much fresh meat, so October was a great time for gluttony. At any rate, it could look that way to well-fed and fastidious travellers passing through. When a robin or a bear gorges itself against the winter, we are very understanding, but when people in a subsistence culture gorge themselves, pejorative adjectives seem to come readily to mind, with little thought as to why they stuff themselves rather than let the meat spoil.

A thriving occupation in Lebanon today is the making of lime sticks to catch song birds for food. I doubt if my boyhood chum, Roger T. Peterson, finds much sale for his bird guides in the Near

East, for sticky bird-lime is to entangle song birds there, for eating, not identifying. The Scots undoubtedly were handy with snares, but I do not know if they had the holly, mistletoe, or elder which can produce bird-lime, an extremely sticky substance made through fermentation procedures. Hunger and poverty are urgent teachers that set aside the niceties of cuisine, yet famine or just incidents of bad luck overtook many. Actual starvation was too common a reality in the 16th Century. Its antithesis, *anorexia nervosa*, is an American perversion which seems obscene in a world where other children starve.

The protein and fat of unsalable parts of an animal added these important nutrients to the brose. The real cuts of meat could be sold, but what the family kept for the winter had to be salted to save it. No part went to waste, and one method in Scotland became famous. Various organs that could scarcely be faced without the dilution of plenty of oatmeal were stuffed into the mutton stomach. The whole package was boiled up and called *haggis*. It is a national symbol, and not half bad as food, I have found. People everywhere have been hungry enough to concoct life-giving protein-rich sustenance from butchering offal. Local names such as souse, pudding and scrapple can be ranged alongside sausage, and headcheese. *Blatwurst, jaternice*, and endless ethnic names for ways to eat the variety meats and blood can be found all over the world, for hunger knows no boundaries. As a fellow engineer told my son, Roy, speaking of "chitlings": "If anything needs to be washed that much, I'm not going to eat it."

Every family had a cow if possible, for its important contributions of milk, cheese, and butter. In the end, its horns might make buttons, spoons, and cups, but its hide was very important after it was tanned. For many rawhide uses, such as thongs, reins, tethers and shields, tanning was skipped. Both the gudeman and specialists used the leather to make caps, jerkins, shoes or buskins, hinges, buckets, belts, armor. Chickens were always kept for their eggs, feathers, and meat. They were used for paying the rent, and for trading. There were sometimes geese, pigs, and goats. Sheep (*scheip*) were the *sine qua non* of the family resources, but horses loomed very importantly in the whole picture.

Sheep could subsist on barely edible browse. Navajo sheep and goats can graze poisonous plant species to death, and the animals usually not die, as I saw in the 1930s. The Scots also raised sheep and goats on what could fairly be called inedible forage. Through the centuries, such destructive husbandry, by grazing the seedlings, all but wiped out tree species, especially *Pinus sylvestris*, the Scots Pine, which, incidentally, grows clear across all the northern lands, including Siberia, under a multitude of names. It provided sorely needed logs and lumber that became very scarce as the trees were cut without reproducing when grazing had destroyed every seedling. Nothing is so destructive as grazing horses, cattle, sheep and goats over the same range. Each class of stock will graze its favorite species to extinction leaving the few totally useless plants to take over the formerly good grazing land. When mature seed trees are cut the destructive forces become fatal and pine forests are finally degraded into scrubby growth worthless to man and beast. Since trees live so much longer than man, this sequence, that stretches out through several human life-spans, is imperceptible and not noticed by the thrifty herdsmen as they complain about having to go so far to find timber.

Domestic animals were very basic food to be used, but frugally. In Great Britain, the word cattle can include horses, and I don't know what else. Americans need a little coaching on this, so we'll quote William Shakespeare: "the steer, the heifer and the calf are all called neat" (*The Winter's Tale*, Act I, Sc 11, line 124).

The Scots added *nolt*, meaning neat. From the pulpit and from Genesis 41 they learned about kine, that seven ill-favored kine ate seven fat kine yet remained thin. Now that some of the words for cow are explained, we pass on. Bovine, or neat meat, and mutton, were used only after the last possible calf or lamb had been wrung from a beast. The meat was usually as tough as leather, inedible by present standards. Cash from what was sold could buy cloth or pay the weaver. Utensils, cloth, salt, and tools could be bought from the itinerant chapman who would also barter.

It is hard to visualize the scarcity of plants that could be used for food for either man or beast, but there was virtually nothing left for the grazing animals to eat after the shoots of sedges, reeds, and browse had hardened in early winter. Any good native grasses that had ever existed had been grazed to extinction through the ages so that almost no hay or fodder could be put up for winter feed. The only solution was to butcher all but a basic number of animals that had to be kept through the winter somehow. Many families survived the usual late winter food shortage by drawing some blood from the cattle to mix with the oatmeal, but the creatures were so weakened that as soon as green growth appeared in the fields the weekest were carried there to regain strength. Particularly in the Highlands a "lifting day" was a necessary event in the spring. No matter what the exigency, grain had to be hoarded for *teind and seid* (tithe and seed).

A very rough form of barley was grown that might produce four or five grains for each one sown. This was usually given some of the best ground, since oats would grow on the poorer, but also because it was the "drink crop" used to brew ale. This was, of course, a vital consideration, and a quarter of the land might be used for barley, or *bear*, as they called it. Barley was much eaten in soups, but in bread or girdle cakes it was hard fare. Napoleon was supposed to have said, "*bon pour Nicol*," when offered black bread by an Austrian peasant. Maybe it was good for his horse, but if that is how pumpernickel came to be named, it must have been made with barley meal. The oats produced only about three grains for each one sown:

"...ane to graw, ane to gnaw,
and ane to pay the laird withaw."

Peas and *kail* would grow in the cold soil, and everyone tried to have a *kailyard* to produce what he could. *Kail*, or kale, provided greens that survived the winter cold. They knew it was good food, but could not know it provided the vitamins that saved them from scurvy. Flax was important, for linen could be woven at home or by a weaver, but only after a great deal of skilled work went into all the stages of preparation and thread making before the weaving could even start. Wild thistles were an important food plant for they contributed a mysterious something that gave the people strength in the spring. This they knew, but we, who know what that something was, don't even put thistles in soup, which they did, and they made this life-saver a national emblem. Old people and children were lucky to live through March, when a little greenery and sunshine would appear, bringing greens to eat, a touch of cheer, and vitamin D to go with the C.

CHAPTER XIII

RUN-RIG AGRICULTURE

The number of Cistercian monks at Melrose Abbey had diminished to around a dozen when the Depo man and his wife arrived, I believe, in early 1562. The Reformation, two years before, had cut all ties between the Abbey and Rome. In 1608 the Regality court of Melrose was presided over by the last surviving monk, Dene Jhone Watsone. Henry Depo is listed at that session (Vol. I, *Regality Records of Melrose*, p. 68). Presumably, a new and better educated clerk wrote Henry for the first time, instead of Hendre, which he apparently recognized as not being a real name. What he did not know was that the man's name was really André, as has been explained before. The 47 years between 1561 and 1608 were momentous for Scotland, but crucial to us. André and his wife had come to Scotland, married, raised their children and seen many grandchildren in those years.

We are accustomed to having events move faster now, but those people, whose mode of living barely inched along, and where innovation was frowned on, thought things changed too fast. Their patterns of thought, rooted in oral traditions going back to the stagnant Dark Ages, had no reference points but memory. Almost nothing that was to be found on a printed page came within their ken. Their counterparts exist by the million today, for television is no substitute for books. Lengthy sermons and paintings brought the Bible to people through the ages, but, as we might say, second hand, through the interpretation of the priest or minister.

Modern transportation, communication, and technology is not much over 100 years old, but perhaps the speed of change has overwhelmed our capacity to comprehend and control the forces we have set in motion. Something like the ancient story of Pandora's box has now been updated in our era of technology. Have machines now outdistanced the human psyche? For instance, technology now permits us to give our children money, powerful cars, liquor, drugs and the leisure to mix them as they choose. Newspapers chronicle what happens when benumbed juvenile minds are put in charge of these ingredients.

We live 4 1/4 centuries after the Reformation in Scotland, and that came 4 1/4 centuries after the founding of Melrose. The original *Maol ros* (bare moor) abbey was begun 3 centuries prior to that by the followers of St. Columba. Thus eleven and a half centuries separate us from that monastic endeavor of 839.

If one had an inclination to play with dates, and the length of the human life span, he might find that St. Columba, as a boy, could have heard the life and parables of Jesus from the lips of a succession of old men. Each might have listened carefully as a boy, and then repeated what he had heard. What had first been told by the apostle Peter, who had known Jesus, could have been carried by word of mouth. Fewer than twenty men could have been in the chain of transmission. Just this sort of a succession may very possibly be contained in the writings of the fathers of the church. A linguist who is a friend of mine, Dr. Robert T. Meyer, of Catholic University, Washington, D.C. has worked for many years translating the Greek Fathers, and other ancient documents of this kind. The continuity of Faith of the Church exceeds by far any of the frailties of the men who stumbled in these centuries. The Faith survived the dissolution of the Roman Empire, the Dark Ages, Feudalism, the degradation of the Church, and the Reformation. Quite a hardy Faith!

Since Dr. Meyer had never interrupted his ruminations long enough to learn to drive, I was driving him home from the grocery store about thirty years ago when I asked him to say something in old English. He asked how some Beowulf would do. I don't remember how it went, but it was an impressive, sonorous recitation. Many years later, my wife and I were staying at a bed-and-breakfast in Oxford, in May of 1976. In the hallway, Dr. Meyer came through a door, to our mutual astonishment. He always stayed at this place near the Bodleian Library, and couldn't believe that we hadn't learned about it from him. We talked the next day. He was translating Ancient Irish laws. When I asked him how many people could do that he told me that there might be six. Some old writing in Scots is scattered through my story. It is almost readable. It gives at least a slight indication of the way our written record has come down to us. Dr. Meyer, Emeritas Professor, worked for years at Edinburgh, Oxford, Michigan, and Dublin in Greek, Latin, and Sanscrit, but most recently on Ancient Irish laws. This astounding man, so unpretentious as to be almost invisible, quizzed me, in turn, about horticulture. To me, he is a prodigy of linguistics, almost utterly removed from the cutting edge of the contemporary world. Like a window on the ages, he provided me with a view that juxtaposes those essential times with the present. (Dr. Meyer died October 7, 1987 in Wales, following a conference at Oxford University.)

I wonder if time may be just one of man's inventions? It is said that man is another animal, the only one that reckons time. For instance, only he knows about yesterday, and talks about his ancestry and of millions of years' worth of yesterdays as if he could comprehend these concepts. Astrophysicists have calculated when the first yesterday began, just before the Big Bang occurred. They put a decimal point before several dozen zeros, and said that fraction of a second of time expressed the moment before which there was no universe, only God, which seems reasonable to me.

The master builder who knew how to build Melrose, and the monks who quarried, hauled and laid the cut stones, solved all the questions of time, past and present. These men knew that tomorrow was the day to improve on yesterday, that their handiwork was for the Glory of God, their reverent worship. Nothing else mattered to them.

The Depo family lived north of the River Tweed, about an hour's walk from the still magnificent ruins of Melrose. On Sundays they would have been required to walk to a parish church of some kind near the Abbey. It was in ruins then, for stones were being taken constantly. In 1618, ten years after Henry Depo was last recorded in the Regality Records, a parish kirk was constructed within a section of the nave using stone taken from other parts of the huge complex of buildings. A bell cast in Holland in 1608 was installed and still hangs in a small belfry above the south transept gable. The Depo family undoubtedly saw this bell hung late in their lives. This church within a church was dismantled in 1810, and a new one was built on a knoll near the weir where water for the Abbey had been diverted from the Tweed. Very likely children of the family attended this church and were recorded under variations of the name Depo. This is indicated in the family chart in Chapter XV. There must be people in that area today whose ancestry through matrilineal lines goes back to the Depos of Moshouses. The family chart shows a few instances, but there must have been many, of marriages into local families so that our name disappeared into the surname of husbands. I wonder if any of those families know the name of the first wife?

My hand-drawn map of Melrose (Figure 7), not to scale, was adapted from the *British Land Survey of 1924*. It has such detail that even windmills, houses, and paths are shown. The scale is 6 inches to the mile, and the contour interval is 100 feet. This survey shows an intricate maze of stone-walled fields which are now almost all gone in favor of big fields for tractor operations. The stone walls were a vast improvement gradually brought into the agricultural picture in the 18th century. In all the centuries before that, back to the Cistercian beginnings of tillage, there were almost no walls. This was the run-rig system of agriculture, and we will try to outline it here.

The contour lines, roads, and location of *farmtouns* (towns), the streams, *mosses* (boggy places), and the town of Melrose, the whole

Run-rig Agriculture

area, all are brought into a clear panorama. In fact, when I was fortunate enough to see it in September of 1985, none of it seemed strange to me. My maps had not prepared me, however, to quickly assimilate the scope and meaning of the Abbey. Its once-upon-a-time magnificence, and function, had to be restored, in my mind's eye, in far too little time.

The Tweed at Melrose is 300 feet above the North Sea level, and the Depo house was just below the 900 foot contour. This makes for a climb of 600 feet in about 3 1/2 miles. About five hundred feet of this climb is in a two-and-a-half mile hill beginning at the north bank of the Tweed. After that climb, the remaining 100 feet of elevation is rather gently rising valley land which the road avoided in favor of the drier ridge route. There were no large areas of *moss* along the way, but one can be certain that in 1562 a great many hillside swamps with scrub trees, brushy growth, reeds and sedges were scattered along this route. The very extensive moss above the 900 foot contour is now grazing land, but then it was a place where men and animals could easily get bogged down or lost. In escaping from reivers or invasions, local people had the advantage of intimate knowledge of their own *moss*. By the same token, reivers had their own hiding places where they could butcher or regroup. Innumerable springs and runs flowed in all directions out of the hilltop *moss* just above the ancient steadings at Moshouses. I did not have much time to spend in this vicinity where our ancestor knew every turn, but I did step just inside a bit of swamp (at 900 feet above sea level and on a slope). Mainly alders were there. They would have made firewood for André, but not fenceposts. I got my feet wet within ten steps. In a nearby meadow, they were wet again, and we got a car stuck in mud two feet off the hard road, but just for a minute, for our crew pushed it out while I drove; my only driving experience in Scotland, but it was on my ancestor's home ground.

This wetness, and dense scrubby growth, not fit for anything but rough grazing in the sixteenth century, extended uphill, and to the north. Cropland had been grubbed out of the area south of this road, and the house and barn were next to the road. The Depo farmstead, and a cluster of other cottages, would have had a view covering 180 degrees of arc, generally south, for several miles. The mill at Langshaw, and the three ancient peel towers, which are still there as ruins, would have been prominent in the view.

Langshaw mill, owned by the Abbey, was less than a mile away to the viewer's right. On beyond it the valley of Allan Water descended from the northwest. Moss Burn mingled its waters just above the road crossing, which I suppose had been a ford, and a foot log. The mill-stones were turned by this water-power. Of the three peel towers, one, just past the mill and a bit uphill, was the defendable tower of the Colmslie family. A couple hundred yards south was the Hillslop tower with a small burn running between. The Langshaw tower was on the near side of the streams, almost within the settlement with its mill, smithy, houses, and later-on a school. I cannot be certain, but there are records that make me feel certain that more than one son and daughter of our family, married within the scope of this view.

Such boggy land on pretty steep hillsides is rare over most of the earth's surface, I believe. Egypt with its sand is the opposite, but I have seen similar boggy sites in Alaska. The vast tundra regions of Siberia may be comparable, but much colder. The Scots were tough people to make this land as productive as they did so long ago.

In the Highlands, and the Lowlands too, this wetness means that draining land, not irrigating it is the problem. Crops, even most trees, won't grow with their feet in water. Grazing animals utilize these areas with little preparatory work, but they also require grain, and the people need grain for food and drink. For people to live in this difficult place, cropland had to be wrested out of the bogs and brush so that grain could be grown.

I don't mind admitting I have a pet peeve with the notion insistently expressed by some people, that no one should eat meat, only vegetable matter. This theory may work in a supermarket, but for eons of time over most of the earth only animals could utilize the rough vegetation, or do the work needed to raise vegetable foodstuffs for the human species. Animals need a little grain to piece-out their weeds, brush, brambles, and grass. Their flesh makes it possible for their masters to, in effect, eat the brambles, weeds and grass. By vicariously eating inedible lignin that even a cow can't digest without the help of bacteria, mankind has been nourished. It seems sophomoric to be completely ignorant of, or act superior to, this rationale. We would not be here if our ancestors, especially the women, had not understood this keystone of human sustenance which isn't too different from other omnivores.

Some may think that abstention from meat elevates one to a higher plane that regular humans cannot inhabit. By locking into a shell of exclusivity they can look down upon the masses of the unenlightened. There are countless millions who, in the aggregate, abjure a large portion of the food stuffs man has had to rely on from his beginning as an omnivore. They justify their brain quirks by stomach watching. This introspection with childhood and other fantasies can be rationalized into categorizing some food as good, and the rest bad. A boy who worked for me in a creamery store wouldn't eat eggs - I never asked why. In an emergency I once tried to give two Navajo headmen some fish with the potatoes and coffee I had to offer, but through my interpreter one abruptly informed me that it was all right for me to eat fish, but he would not. The other man was a revered elder, and he ate fish with me. There are powerful reasons, I suppose, for food exclusivity, but I take off my hat to those who view all food as God-given nourishment to be used so they can get on with the hard work of the world. Picky eaters are rarely found in the really tough front lines where brains and strength are smoothing the way for others. I feel sure that God never bats an eye if someone has to eat the cow, our go-between, so we may gain nourishment indirectly from brush and weeds. That goes for fish, too.

By using the maps, I have estimated that the Abbey lands may have totaled as much as 26,000 acres. In early history, immense grants were often given by rulers. In that context, this large acreage is not surprising, for one can recall that English and Spanish kings granted unbelievable acreage to individuals. Lord Fairfax received a Virginia so big that Melrose would seem like a mere dot. The monks could not handle this amount of work alone, but it was necessary to have the land produce as abundantly as possible. Wool became an export crop, besides providing the main sustenance for the people through its by-products: lambs, milk, meat and hides. When the new arrivals, the Depos, appeared on the scene, they found methods of husbandry that had scarcely changed for centuries. Neither had lived on a farm, but they learned to cope, for the records show that they and their descendants survived, and prospered.

In much later times, improved agricultural methods and seed varieties were more or less forced down the throats of tradition-bound tenants by lairds and supervisors. An enlightenment was creeping in and filtering down from the educated upper classes. The reason improvement came was that increasing population, coupled with better transport, demanded increased production and sales beyond the neighborhood. The husbandry in 1562 was rooted in feudal life. In fact, Depo and his neighbors were referred to in the old language of feudalism: pp. 67 - 68, Vol. I, *Regality Records of Melrose*:

> "...tenants and occupiers of the lands of Colmsliehill and Apiltrieleaves, James Moffat, John Moffet, and Robert Hall, feuars of the toun and lands of..., Henry Depo, John Notman called Little John..., Robert Mitchell, John Carter...feuars of the toun and lands of Moshouses."

A superior landholder was an *heritable feuar*, among other gradations of position.

Run-rig Agriculture

> "...Feuars, tenants and occupiers of the touns undermentioned which are thirled (bound), to the said mill (except teind, and seed corn, i.e., tithe, etc.), and pay the multure (fee), being a peck of multure for each threave."

On page 38, Hendre Depo and Jhone Notman are referred to as *portionaris* of Moshouses. Four medieval characterizations of our man are in these excerpts, and the word *vassal* is also used. It may be noted that James Moffat, and John Moffet, who were probably brothers, had their name spelled two ways by the court clerk. Sixteenth century Scottish spelling is almost a marvel to us who have so meticulously tried to standardize usage. We can read these old records, stumbling over or being baffled by the many words not to be found anywhere but in dictionaries of archaic Scots, and not always there. I think likely if one could sit in on a court session, or a conversation of the day, total bafflement would be all that could be gained from listening. The court clerk spelled one Moffat with an "a," the other brother got an "e." This means he either didn't give a hoot what he put down, or he was unable to put on paper the vowel-like rumble he heard emanating from some sort of a gutteralizing voice mixer that those Scots used in speaking. Our clerk, at least, did better than the Hebrews of old who wrote their books without any vowels. Each reader supplied his own, with mixed results. The Scots used any of the five, six, or seven vowels which the reader could pronounce as he chose.

Fifty years later, a James Moffat witnessed the baptism of James Depo, a baby. I don't remember meeting these people, but they seem to me to be inlaws. The relationship is obvious in my generational chart. I can easily believe that one of Hendre's granddaughters married a grandson of either James or John Moffat, of the quotation above. This couple had a son, James Moffat. James Depo had a baby named James, and asked his brother-in-law, James Moffat, to witness the baptism. It happens every day.

The Moffat house and the Depo house were probably visible from one to the other, so a marriage between these two families was not hampered by distance. Colmslie Tower, near which the Moffats lived, is still standing in ruins just west of where the Langshaw Mylne foundation stones still outline its location. The Depo farmstead 400 feet higher than the cluster of cottages and the tower near Allan Water, would have been conspicuous close under the brushy expanse of the Moshouses Moss, the highest point. All the neighbors in the area probably walked to that big moss to gather brushy firewood and gather up their grazing animals every day, and the boys and girls may have spoken to each other.

The medieval system of living clustered in farmtoun cottages and byres with common grazing land, arose partly from the need for protection against raiders of whatever sort. The three peel towers were within a few hundred yards of the Langshaw community, which was much more important than other places, for it had the all-important grist mill, undoubtedly a blacksmith shop, and a school of some sort. The generational chart shows that the other witness of the baptism discussed above was Adam Hislope. It could scarcely be questioned that Adam was also a brother-in-law. Courtships depended on foot travel, and these people all lived very near each other. The chart also shows a Blaikie, and a Mein. They did not live as near by, but still in the Melrose Parish. I believe these people were all related, not just strangers called in to witness the baptisms. These surnames are all prominent in the annals of Melrose, and they are linked to the Depo family by marriage. There may be records that amplify this linkage, but it has to be significant that the new family was so quickly privileged to join important families through marriage. Obviously, it seems, it was well known at Melrose that the new family had been sponsored by important personages.

The clusters of habitations and out-buildings, or farmtouns, were very numerous in the Melrose jurisdiction. They owed their origin very largely to the fact that plowing land had to be a joint or communal effort. Men working together, not always in perfect harmony we can be sure, pooled their animals, their helpers, and their one plough to raise their individual crops on an area called a *ploughgate* of land. Except for plowing, every other operation was done almost entirely by human labor. A farm toun was thus a *ploughgang* community.

Just a word about the term *portionar* referred to above. It is part of the mystery of run-rig farming to have many designations for the tenants, and it is part of the picture that ultimately everyone was a tenant of the monarch, even the commendator. Some of the designations may simply have been redundancies hanging on from feudal days. The plural, *portionaris* lumps Notman and Depo together, but why this new and different term for these long time tenants? Could they have been namesake sons of Hendre Depo and Jhone Notman, both about 25 at that time, and working portions of their father's ploughgate? Sons had to be helped to start somewhere, and the home farm was the most likely place. It was common for sons to work as ploughboys, called *half hinds* (skilled farm workers). They were paid with room and board plus the use of a *kailyard*, where they grew the vegetable we find among garden seeds under the name, Scotch kale. They would also expect to have grazing rights for a few sheep. We don't call the *kailyard* a garden spot, for there were no vegetables in Scotland then except *kail* and peas.

We know there were numerous Depo sons and daughters. The latter would marry, as we have said, into nearby families. The sons could not stay as young adults in their parents tenancy except by taking up a role as a hired man. There was a place for them as *bothy boys*. A farmer, variously called *husbandman* or *gudeman*, *feuar* or even *vassal*, needed workmen to help out. At the least one hired man, plus the *gudewife*, and the children as they grew, might suffice, but this would be a minimum operation. Numbers of men might work for him if he had become a higher status tenant with more land. The categories of tenants, of land tenure, *bonnet lairds*, etc., are far too complicated to study in this simple story about the queen's horses, her French stable-boys, and the one elusive Lady.

In those days, children worked hard from the time they could first herd the geese, some sheep or a single cow. I saw this in Egypt with quite a jolt, for many boys spent their days chasing birds out of bean fields. Child labor had to wait for the industrial revolution, two hundred years later, for the most horrible exploitation of children and women to occur in England and Scotland. Then the "higher-classes" reached their low point, as they exploited their helpless workers without mercy. They had made an arrangement with God that the lower classes did not have feelings nor hurt, at least not much. I have a child's primer, little older than I am, that has a picture of "better-off" children laughing at a ragged boy because "his father is poor." It's still too typical, not illustrated in children's books anymore, just practiced in the schools, especially by high-school children.

When boys outgrew the limited space in the family home and could work like men, they moved into a booth-like hut called a *bothy*, along with other single men. This accommodation is not unrelated to transient worker's quarters today. These were the *bothy boys*. They could have a little cooking fire, but ate very badly, for cooking was scarcely possible when fatigue, and drunkenness, so often intervened. In time of rain, wind, snow and cold these men suffered under a thin blanket on a board bunk. The number of people who helped in the farming could vary. One ploughman (or *hind*), might have a helper (a *half hind*), but larger places had other workers. There were herders, threshers, even landless indoor servants, and outdoors "taskers." Only the most menial worker was paid in money. The preferred wage was subsistence, a bit of land to cultivate and space for a very few animals.

We can only guess how the Depo family ranked and performed in this long-ago society, barely emerging from feudalism. We do know from records that the name spread widely in the eastern Borders, eventually into England, just across from the southeastern Scottish border. The name also spread out from Edinburgh, where we find there are more records than elsewhere. It appears that there was no mixing of the two branches. The chart shows that the siblings of the first family went their separate ways, which in time created two branches. The dramatic origin was forgotten through the many generations, except in the one line that went to Glasgow, remembering the original marriage merely as a family story.

There are a few exceptions, but it seems likely that not many descendants became farmers. There was an option that they apparently took in most cases. That was to acquire a skill or trade in the towns. The apprenticeship route to the recognized crafts and guilds was long and arduous, and some may have taken that path. In fact there are records of sons being apprenticed. There were many occupations that could be entered simply by going to work in a minor job and working up. Merchants and traders, for instance, often started on a shoestring, and sometimes became rich. Well-off merchants were increasingly accepted as leaders, and could even become full citizens or burgesses. For a number of reasons, I believe the Depo descendants favored non-agricultural occupations, down to the present. I don't believe there were any actual farmers among the Deppas in the United States.

It is interesting to me to speculate on the dispersal and occupations of the children of Hendre Depo and his wife, the very well educated, very experienced former lady in the queen's train. One of the daughters, and apparently two of the sons, were brought up in the Capital, and this city environment strongly corroborates the lady-in-waiting element of our legend. Such a mother could accept the farm-wife status for herself, and understand how lucky she was in a society where life was held so cheaply, and where opportunity to advance was so limited. She knew cities and apparently sent three of her children to acquire city benefits. Her other daughters, though, had no real choice but to marry local boys, and they were farmer's sons. We have written down the names we have found, all farmers. Descendants with those surnames may still be farmers, for they had the entre to tenancy, and local acceptance, without which there was little hope of moving onto the land.

By the same token the Depo sons had slight chance of gaining acreage in their own name. Even more important could have been the influence of the mother pointing out opportunities in town, a place that would frighten most bothy boys, and half hinds. The father, too, was accustomed to city life. Dieppe was an international port, full of tradesmen of all kinds, and André may have been totally lost when he found himself trying to run a farm. It is interesting to me, personally, to study details of life in those times, but there is no way we can know just how our family coped with the life they were so lucky to have handed to them. Maybe André had a particular skill that fit his neighbor's needs and helped carve a niche for his family. My mother's father was a farmer all his life in Steuben County, New York, and I have a picture of him with his horses and whole family in front of their nice home on Northrup Street. Not too long ago, I found a big old account book, and learned that Alfred Northrup bought oysters from Fulton Market in New York City. He had them shipped by train to the little town near his farm where he sold them to the local people. Moral: It is not safe to assume that farmers are just stuck-in-the-muds.

Farmtouns probably began before grain was grown except in occasional patches, perhaps before Scotland was ruled by a king in the 11th century. Herder's huts, with crude sheepfolds to protect against losses to wolves, may have merged to become the first communities. Such widely scattered sheep ranges would naturally develop into more distinct settlements where sheep were augmented by oats, barley and very little else for a long time. The first records of Melrose that I have studied refer by name to a large number of stable communities in 1608. They had been there for centuries. The early oats and barley were scarcely better than wild forms, but the addition of grain to the diet of man and beast had become the absolute basis of nutrition. Ale, and the inevitable torpor and drunkenness were severe detriments in the lives of men, women, and children. Only a poor fraction of energy was left when drink took precedence over all. Gross malnutrition can easily be mistaken as laziness and stupidity, a very common characterization of rural Scots in those times.

The Cistercians were a closed, primarily agricultural religious order. Thus they specialized in minding their own business and farming in the hours from before daylight until after dark. In addition, their religious duties were onerous and never neglected. One such duty was to provide a priest for the local people, though they would have preferred not even that much contact. This regimen of constant work had been applied to the lands of the Abbey through all the successive lifetimes of devoted monks and laymen. The fatal flaw in the plan grew from an imperceptible retreat from dedication and piety, perhaps because the building was finally completed, and they began to get rich. It took centuries of ecclesiastical degeneration before the Reformation all over Europe intervened to change everything. There were destroyers from outside which must not be overlooked in this picture, but they cannot be tabulated here.

By the time our first family settled in at Melrose, the ancient church had been dispossessed, and a commendator, in effect, owned the estate with rights to the income. The tenants may have noticed little change. After the Norman Conquest, the spread of monasteries and abbeys amounted to an invasion all over Britain. Finally the Lowlands of Scotland became well covered with "daughter" houses of "mother" abbeys in England. The Cistercians followed the rule of St. Benedict to the last letter, (*ap apicem litterae*), making this the most austere of orders. Melrose had been colonized from Rievaulx, in Yorkshire. In time, the severity of conformance was much lessened. Their architecture had approached flamboyance. Nevertheless, these monks, and lay brothers, were masters at reclaiming waste lands for cropping; *maol ros*, (bare moor) became the rich and productive Melrose. The name tells what pioneers they were. The emphasis was always on sheep, for cropping would not have been possible as a first step. Do not visualize the beautiful animals of today. Their sheep were tough, rangy, badly fed, and small, but they did yield wool, lambs, milk, meat, manure, and hides in that order of importance. Cistercians were adept at diverting and controlling watercourses, even the River Tweed, where they made a diversion and flume to take water to the abbey.

They built water-powered grist-mills where their tenants were required to take their grain to be ground. For emphasis, it will be noted here that Hendre Depo agreed to this requirement in 1586. This significant date is brought up in Chapter XI. The grist-mill was a very important source of income for the abbey, and led to constant evasion by the tenants. They went to private mills and their wives ground some grain in hand *querns*, even though they were "*thirled* to pay the multure."

The miller was a notorious short-changer in collecting the fees, and the miller's knave expected a tip besides. They all wholeheartedly hated each other, and culprits were endlessly haled into court and fined.

The colonizing monks from Yorkshire had been in intimate contact with English, even Norman, agriculture for centuries. Whatever the pattern of land use at Melrose it was not Scottish, but transplanted English. It was open-field-strip cultivation, a term that we will try to explain. Before that, the Celtic custom for 2000 years, or before the dawn of northern European history, had been to enclose small fields in which to raise their oats and barley. The newer method, so old that no one fully understands it now, involved cultivating land having virtually no interior walls or fences.

This chapter was titled "Run-rig Agriculture" more out of hope, than confidence that we could explain the term. This was certainly the form of agriculture our ancestor had to learn in his new role as a farmer. Archaeologists try to riddle out the old method by studying aerial photographs which still show the gentle corrugations across fields where the old ridges, or *rigs*, were plowed toward a middle so the crops could thrive up out of the water which could make the soil too wet for a crop. Historians comb old writings for hints about the method, but the lawyers, priests, and royal officials who did almost the only writing then paid no attention to what

Run-rig Agriculture

farmers were doing, unless they failed to go to church, and pay their taxes. The Scottish word for ridge is *rig*, with numerous connotations as Robbie Burns versified:

> "Corn rigs, an'barley rigs
> An corn rigs are bonie;
> I'll ne'er forget that happy night,
> Amang the rigs wi Annie."

When crops and animals are both raised without fences, the constant problem is to prevent the crops from being grazed, especially when the herbage is succulent grain which, after all, is a grass. Geese are voracious grazers, as I learned when I succumbed to folk lore and raised 30 goslings to Thanksgiving-dinner-size with inadequate fences. The solution in handling the several kinds of animals in the run-rig system was to have common grazing grounds outside the village, and use herders. An encircling wall was built with not much stone. By digging a ditch, and throwing the earth, stones, and brush so as to make a dike, or balk (*baulk*), a more or less animal proof barrier could be made. The general wetness probably kept the ditch full of water, an added deterrent. Boys were the usual herders to make this system work unless, like Little Boy Blue, they were under the haycock fast asleep. The first word we have of Hendre Depo, by name, is when he sued his neighbor for trespass damage and won.

Grazing on these commons outside the toun barrier was augmented by utilization of the stubble after the oats, and barley had been harvested. An animal eats just so much, and the herds could be mixed equitably so long as each man had equal numbers to graze. They could clean up the stubble and the rough weedy *baulks* at will. It was only the growing crop that created a problem. Grazing without fences presented difficulties for the herders that we can only guess at. Men were cheaper than fences, but it wasn't just the cost of herders. Fencing materials were not to be had at a local store.

A Navajo family often had from 200 to 400 sheep and goats, and they were open herded, but kept overnight in corrals, usually a fence of juniper branches. These fences were effective, and since no metal was used, a section of fence was taken down and rebuilt with each passage in or out. Indians had no domestic animals before the Spaniards came, nor did they have traditions from their Mongolian origins. A very practical difference between the Celtic traditions and the Navajo, was that there was unlimited pinyon and juniper for the Navajo to use. Across Europe and Scotland, sturdy brushy trees had been pretty well cut down before the tribes had climbed out of barbarism. This digression from the layout of run-rig is partly an attempt to look into the minds of the people of long-ago who used it. At least we should consider our shortcomings of competence to understand them. We have become so dependant on money and stores to supply every need, and have so expanded our concept of need, that one has to fight off the thought: why were they so stupid? Their system had its rationale, it's just that we imperfectly understand it. Human labor provided the power, and tradition the method. The Bible told how men had herded animals, so there was no need to change; nor were there any resources with which to make a change.

Each of the neighbors in a farmtoun had an enclosed farmyard with little separation of the human and animal occupants. Buildings to hold some animals overnight, to store fodder, grain, harness, and hand tools were there. At harvest time, the *corn*, as they called the oats, and the *bere*, or *bear*, as they called the barley, was cut and stacked, or *stooked*, to use their word. After two weeks of drying in the field, the sheaves were brought up to the barnyard. There they were expertly laid up in the specially selected stackyard to dry out in high thatched stacks ready for threshing. All animals had to be kept away from the precious crop as it dried. The threshing was a tremendous job that went on for weeks and used the labor of all the family, as well as special taskers and threshers. The bothy boys lived in their bothy, which was also in the barnyard enclosure. If this sounds a bit crude, then the picture is getting across, for we have not told the half of it, nor smelled it either.

Run-rig Agriculture

The biggest job of the year was plowing, and I will hazard some guesses, for not much is to be found in books. Run-rig may have been the only system that could have worked with the cumbersome plow they had, as will be shown. Oats had to be planted early; thus the plowing had to be done while the soil was heavy with the winter wetness. The oat land was the outfield, the land farthest from the barnyard. It often had lain fallow for one or two years while the beautiful but useless spiny shrub, variously called *gorse*, *whin*, or *furze*, used the interim to spread across the soil to make the plowing and even the grazing more difficult. Virtually all the fields sloped, but even so were usually wetter than they should be for grain. Thus an advantage in run-rig was to help the water drain away.

A cluster of neighbors each had to have access to his own strip of cropland radiating out from his farmyard. The ideal would be like spokes from a hub, but probably this ideal was rarely reached. It is quite likely that a few dominant tenants had this better arrangement, and others found access to their strip fields wherever they could, often some distance away on other roads, or lanes. To complicate this confused problem, there were great differences in quality of site, as well as convenience, so arbitration between the neighbors was a constant wrangle to alternate usage of the many strips, or run-rigs, for the system was communal to a degree. Year by year, the rotation of the good, bad, and indifferent rigs bred contention, for these people were not especially noted for placid and gentle relationships even within the family. With such matters all settled, the community plough would be gotten out.

Assuming the simplest situation, the plowing would proceed so as to skirt obstructions such as wet places or rock piles, and would aim at the farthest point at which the rig could not run farther. When this point had been reached, the furrow would cross to the other side to start back to the beginning. A good eye could determine pretty well how wide a piece could be laid off in any terrain. Since the rig may have been in place beyond memory of man, there was little reason for changes. However, if the outside furrows were not nearly parallel, or if they wavered in and out, there would be an unplowed piece left in the middle which could not be planted that year. Year after year the plowing would move earth from the outside toward the middle. The plowed strip would thus become a distinct ridge, or rig, and the edges would become drainage channels.

In laying out a new field, another plan could be to plow the first two furrows down the middle, back to back continuing until the width encountered obstructions at the edges. The rigs varied from about 15 to 40 feet in width, and a no-man's-land was left between the plowed strips. These rough *baulks* contained the area lost to cultivation, for you cannot come out even when rectangles are laid out on bulging or irregular topography. In modern contour farming, "point rows" which cultivators can't handle well, are avoided by having strips of meadow absorb the variable widths or balks. This seems to be exactly the same idea as in ancient run-rig. The rough *baulks* caught all the debris thrown out of the plowed part. The stones and brush became overgrown with weeds and bushes, more or less a jungle. It would be grazed along with the stubble in the winter.

The plowing we have so off-handedly spoken of was not done with a hydraulic-lift gang plow. The power was supplied by horses sometimes, but oxen were preferred for several reasons, the last one being that at the end of his useful days he could be eaten or sold for meat. He could live on much coarser feed than a horse, and the manure was more valuable. He was more placid, by far, and his harness was the durable wooden yoke and iron chains. He also demonstrated the Anglo-Saxon way of forming the plural with "-en." We still say oxen and children, but no longer do we speak of ashes as ashen, nor do we say *eyen*, or *eggen*. This plural ending, like the ox, has almost had its day. Most Americans have never seen an ox team. Recently I saw a T.V. movie of a pioneer with his oxen in horse harness. He was on the wagon seat, driving them with reins to their bridles and bits. What I hoped to see was the movie director with a horse bit in his mouth, for it certainly couldn't be put in the mouth of an ox. How many who were watching this historical film knew that anything was wrong, and how many had any idea how an ox is hooked up and driven?

I have walked on mats of brush in Yorkshire so dense and springy it scarcely seemed possible that soil could be found underneath. There wasn't much there, but there was a great plenty of rock for building endless walls and stone buildings. In fact, some of the building may have been done to gain the soil lying around between the rocks. The Scottish farmers faced similar dense growth and perhaps less stone. The plow they used to turn the brush and heavy soil had to be so strong that it was huge and ungainly, for it was of wood except for a bit of iron at the tip. Each tenant in the farm toun furnished an ox and a workman, or whatever was agreed on. Between eight and twelve oxen were hitched to the plow. This was a plough team.

Two men had to lead this incredible procession, so that the plough, far to the rear, might turn a correct furrow slice. Another man held the plough handles. One cleared brush off the share and one tried to keep it in line with the preceding furrow by a pole fastened to the front, near the coulter. In the Melrose area an eight ox team might plough 104 acres in a year and this was a ploughgate of land. Such a minuscule accomplishment for such a creaking, and grunting assemblage is almost beyond imagination. Very little can really be known of this kind of daily life, for no one wrote about ploughmen at the time. The term *ploughgate* is in the Domesday Book, but was obsolete before dictionaries were invented. In old English law, the work of one ploughteam was called a *ploughland*; in Scotland, a *ploughgate*. A *hide* also was a measure of land: the amount needed to support a *hind* and his family for a year. It varied from 80 to 100 acres, as best I know, that is. It was two hundred years after Hendre's time before a good iron plow was invented and for sale. The need had been there, but money and steel had to precede the invention.

It is a good thing that I finished grade school before starting to write this, for now I have become so British I find myself spelling plow, plough. That would have been marked wrong in Number 7 School in Jamestown, New York, in 1916. Other Briticisms may have crept in also, and I have made little effort to "correct" them. Perhaps a book about my Scottish ancestors should have its Americanisms "corrected"; but spelling plow, plough, may come naturally to me, for I had ancestors from both Yorkshire and Scotland.

The land nearest the buildings was called "infield," and the more distant was called "outfield." Oats would grow year after year on outfield if it were allowed to lie fallow occasionally to recover some fertility. Infields had manure carried to them, i.e., *muckit land*. Women cleaned out the barnyard muck and carried it, on their backs, in homemade panniers. Ponies were sometimes used. Flax, *kail*, and *pease* were very important, and shared this better land. The process of breaking down the flax-stems to get the fine fibers ready to spin was a long hard bit of women's work. Spinning the thread was done in the home, but weaving cloth was usually done by weavers. Homemade rope could be made by twirling straw with a crooked bit of branch or iron, but good rope was of linen. A recent T.V. program showed that women, carried away from Troy and Hellenic cities by the hundreds, became slaves working the flax. The process was identical to that in Scotland, a 4000-year period without a process update; a bad time for patent attorneys.

At harvest time, the Scots used a hand sickle that was very crude in design and far inferior in manufacture to my Northrup family harvest sickle which I treasure. Its long, slender curving blade doesn't fool me into thinking it couldn't ruin your back in a good 16-hour day of cutting and tying grain. A man or woman could cut and sheave an acre of grain in four days. This harvesting went on for weeks.

In much of Scotland too much water on the land is a problem. In 1976 on a trip around the Highlands before I had any idea I

Run-rig Agriculture 255

might solve my Grandmother's riddle, I saw reforestation projects like I had never seen before. In May, water was pouring off the western mountains, and planted conifer seedlings were visible everywhere. They were protected by high deer-proof fences, a tremendous achievement. The foresters know how completely deer and sheep grazing can eliminate tree seedlings and the better grass and browse species. Furrows had been plowed downhill where it didn't seem a goat could walk, much less the heavy equipment that must have been used. Drainage was the obvious necessity for those seedlings to get started on their ridges. I learned, too, that crops such as potatoes were planted up out of the water. So too, on the Melrose farms. They plowed downhill to get rid of water, just the opposite of the general practice in the U.S. where contour terraces and furrows are essential to save water and soil except on the flattest of the great plains.

Each family had one or more cows and horses in addition to sheep. The Hopi and Navajo Indians, at least those of fifty years ago, had horses and sheep. There were differences of course. The Hopi in their 800-year-old towns had much better dwellings than the Scots, and they had corn, squash, beans, wild nuts and game, but there were no fish. The Navajo, who were johnnie-come-latelies in the land, could steal crops, women and children from the Hopi, but I never heard them called reivers. It is hard to say who had the better deal in 1562. When I was very young in a Pennsylvania mountain town with a big tannery, my father had a store, and we had a black cow. It, and others, would be driven to the town cow pasture after the morning milking. I can still hear their bells clanging as they walked. They would be waiting at the gate of the mountainside pasture in the late afternoon for the boys to let them out. They were impatient to take their milk home where they could put their muzzles down to some grain in the manger. Our cow didn't give milk; you had to take it from her.

Farming continued as we have very roughly outlined until a new era commenced around the time of the American Revolution. The *gudemen* resisted change, but gradually the run rigs were cleaned out, and stone walled fields appeared. The iron plow revolutionized cultivation, and boys and girls could quit the herding, and go to school. A requirement even appeared that girls not go to sewing classes until they had gained certain reading, writing, and arithmetic skills.

From the earliest times, two roads went from Melrose north to Edinburgh, and south to the border with England. A road then was not much more than a horse trail, but in 1985 I found that these were both good roads. There was also a direct foot path from Moshouses to Melrose, and it is still there. Another road from the Abbey mill at Langshaw ran past the Depo house, continuing on east to Stitchill, where the queen lost one of the French workers who cared for her horses, as we have told.

"Liddesdale's robber hordes" rode out of their Borderland retreats which surrounded that "medieval nightmare called Hermitage, a gaunt, grey Border castle with a little river running by its walls." "It is not as big, but in its way it is more impressive than Caernarvon or Edinburgh, or even the Tower of London." It was the guard house of the bloodiest valley in Britain. It is no surprise to learn that one owner was boiled alive by his neighbors. This description is adapted from an exciting history of the Border Reivers, *The Steel Bonnets*.

James, the 4th Earl of Bothwell, like the rest of his Hepburn family, was master of this ancient fortress for only a tiny part of its history. He was very important in the history of our family, and insofar as he travelled between this castle and his Crichton, which was a more elegant castle on the way to Edinburgh, he could have ridden past the Depo house. Some horse feed or a bite for himself could be obtained there. However, his elaborate machinations caught up with him, and he was exiled from Scotland sometime in 1562. He came back, of course, to the destruction of Mary. It is pointless to follow his activities for this year and a half. His hand can be seen in the selection and placing of the men of Dieppe on the Dutch ships, and the placing of André at Melrose, as has been told. His exile in 1562 was the same year, I believe, that the queen provided a wedding for our pair. All of this would coincide with a move to Moshouses in the early spring, when palace festivities, such as weddings, were a most welcome diversion from the Scottish winter. The agricultural year began then, too. That is when we became Border-Scots, with a very unusual Scottish name offhandedly bestowed on three French stable-boys by the Lord Treasurer's payroll clerk.

CHAPTER XIV

EXCERPTS FROM SCOTTISH DOCUMENTS
SAMPLE OF LEGALESE

This charter of alienation (transfer of property ownership), is copied from the *Melrose Regality Records*, Volume III, page 288, (1579). Illiterate farmers faced legalistic documents such as this at every confrontation with lawyer, priest, or educated official. This excerpt would have been written in a script of those times. It shows, better than a description, how legalisms overpowered very simple matters. Perhaps this minute enumeration of each asset shows that all-inclusive terms had not developed at this early time. Nowadays there are brief ways of showing total ownership, and transfer.

> "...Having and holding all and whole my half of a husband land foresaid with pertinents occupied as above by the said Edward and lying as is aforesaid, to the foresaid Edward in liferent for all the days of his life, and to the said John and his heirs foresaid and assignees, heritably, of me and my heirs in fee and heritage and in free blench (A.S. free of deceit) farm for ever by all their right meaths ancient and divided as they lie in length and breadth in houses, buildings, yards, fields, ways, paths, standing and running waters, meadows, pastures and pasturages, mills, multures and their sequels, hawkings, huntings, fishings, peataries, turferies, coals, coalheughs, doves, dovecots, rabbits, rabbit warrens, smithies, brew-houses, brushwood, broom, woods, plantings, copses, firewood and thatch, quarries, stone and lime, with courts and their exits, herields, (A.S. herian, praise), bloodwites, (A.S. blood),

and markets of women, with common pasture, free ish and entry, and with all and sundry other liberties, commodities, profits, easements and their just pertinents whatsoever as well not named as named, under the earth and above, near and remote, pertaining or which may justly be held to belong to my foresaid half husband land with pertinents, in any manner of way in time coming, freely, quietly, fully, entirely, honourably well and in peach without any obstruction recal gainsaying or hindrance: Paying therefor yearly the said Edward Romanus during the whole period of his life, and the said John and his heirs foresaid, to me and my heirs one penny usual money of the realm of Scotland upon the ground of the said lands at Whitsunday in name of blenchfarm if asked, and to the abbot and convent (monk) of the monastery of Melrose and their successors the sum of 12 s. and 5 d. money foresaid at two terms in the year, viz. Whitsunday and Martinmas in winter by equal portions, with one and a half poultry and half a carriage, (an amount of burden carrying) and that for all other burden exaction demand or secular service which from the said half husband land with pertinents can justly by any whomsoever be anywise asked or required. And I forsooth John Romanus with express consent and assent of the said John my son and heir apparent, and my heirs foresaid, shall warrant acquit and forever defend all and whole my half husband land with houses, buildings, tofts, crofts and gardens foresaid and their whole pertinents, to the foresaid Edward Romanus during the whole period of his life and to the said John his son and apparent heir, and the heirs abovewritten, in all and by all against everything deadly. In witness of the which thing to this present charter subscribed with my hand my own proper seal is appended, with the subscription manual (signed by hand) of the said John my son and apparent heir in manner following in token of his consent and assent, at Blainslie the seventh day of May 1578, in presence of these witnesses, Thomas Scot in Hanein (?), William Chein in Blainslie, Gavin Carter there, William Haw, younger, there, and John Bryden, notary public, with divers others. Jhone Romanus, elder, with my hand touching the pen led by the notary underwritten; Jhone Romanus, younger, with my hand at the pen led by the notary public underwritten; That it is so John Brydein, notary public called to the premises, subscribing with his own hand, affirms. Which charter of alienation so made and by us carefully considered and examined as is aforesaid we ratify approve and for us and our successors for ever confirm in all its points, clauses and articles in form and effect as is abovewritten. In witness whereof to the premises subscribed with our hand and the subscriptions of our said coadjutor and the convent of our said monastery in manner following, the common seal of the chapter of our said monastery is appended, at our said monastery the ... day of August 1579, before these witnesses."

FIGURE 8

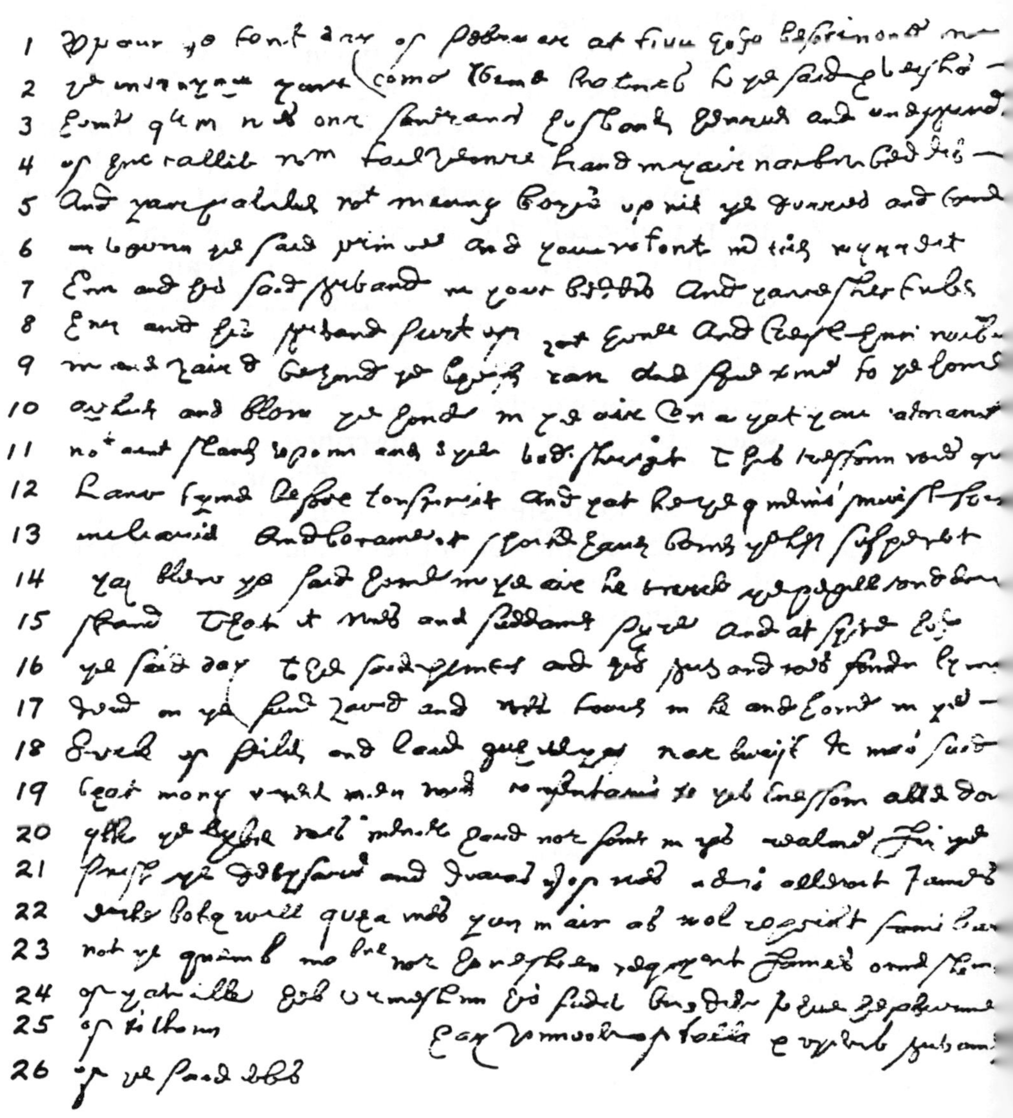

Pollock Manuscript Folio 38.

FIGURE 9: TRANSLITERATION OF FOLIO 38

1   Upon the tent day of Februar, at twa houris befoir none in
2   the mornyng thair come certane tratouris to the faid proveiftis
3   hous, quhairin wes our foueranis hufband Henrie, and ane feruand
4   of his, callit Williame Tailyeour, liand in thair naikit beddis;
5   and thair privilie, with wrang keyis opnit the durres, and come
6   in upoun the faid prince, and thair without mercie wyrreit
7   him and his faid feraund in thair beddis; and thairefter tuke
8   him and his feruand furth of that hous, and keift him naikit
9   in ane yaird beyond the theif raw, and fyne come to the hous
10 agane and blew the hous in the air, fwa that thair remanit
11 nocht ane ftane upoun ane uther undiftroyit. This treffoun wes of
12 lang tyme befoir conspirit, and that be the quenis maift fam
13 iliars; and becaus it fhould haue bene the lefs fufpectit,
14 thaj blew the faid hous in the air, to caus the pepill under
15 ftand that it wes ane fuddane fyre. And at fyve houris
16 the faid day, the faid prince and his feruand wes fundid lying
17 deid in the faid yaird, and was tane in to ane hous in the
18 Kirk of feild, and laid quhill thaj war burijt. It was faid
19 that mony greit men wes confentaris to this treffounable deid,
20 quhilk the lyke wes neuer hard nor fene in this realme. In the
21 firft the devyfaris and doaris thairof wes, as is allegit, James
22 erle Bothwill, quha wes than mair, as wes reportit, familiare
23 with the quenis majeftie nor honeftie requyrit; James Ormeftoun
24 of that ilk, Hob Ormeftoun his fader broder, Johne Hepburne
25 of Boltoun,   Hay younger of Talla, and vtheris fervandis
26 of the faid erlis.

(See commentary on next page.)

Commentary on the transliteration
(previous page)

This tangle is English, in Scottish handwriting. Many words are legible, unlikely as that may seem at first glance. Thair, that, the, than, and this demonstrate the letter "thorn" on almost every line. Line 10 quite clearly reads "...and blew the hous in the air..." The unclear words defy casual study, and half the letters range from difficult to impossible. I can't help but think that the weiter did not know how to spell "majestie" in line 23, a ruse that still works today.

Line 14 nearly repeats line 10, but the word translated as "caus" seems illegible to me, although this is a small matter, considering that the editor deciphered hundreds of pages like this one. The word "before" in line 12 is in very clear script, but the words following show that letters which should be clear become infested with squiggles. "James" in line 23 shows that the writer could make a plain "m", but his "e", as usual, is a tiny circle swallowed up in its flourish and the next letter, in this case an "s" with a big tail overhead. Another poser is "r" which is at its clearest in "Kirk", line 18. Some letters bear no resemblance to modern forms, and can be found with no help. "Fuddane fyre" in line 15 embarrasses me as an idiocy that even our American printer/scientist, Ben Franklin, used without protest, a man who didn't hesitate to handle lightning, but didn't try to stop fuddane fyre.

The locale is shown on the Plan of Edinburgh, in Figure 1.

GLOSSARY:
Line 2: provost's house.
Line 3: sovereign's; servant.
Line 6: wyrreit (This verb killed the said prince; dictionaries don't define it, but he was strangled.)
Line 9: fyne or syne means afterwards, ago, or since.
Line 18: until.
Line 21: devisers.

Excerpts from Scottish Documents

A DIURNAL (Journal) OF REMARKABLE OCCURRENTS THAT HAVE PASSED WITHIN THE COUNTRY OF SCOTLAND
since the death of King James the fourth till the year MDLXXV.

As edited and printed at Edinburgh MDCCCXXXIII. by The Maitland Club

This unknown diarist failed to mention the wedding of any of the ladies-in-waiting to the queen, nor did he mention the arrival of her precious horses, and their caretakers, from France. We had hoped to find a record of "our" wedding or even that of any of the ladies-in-waiting, for he did write about many much less important events. Most of what he told was at second hand, except for the queen's arrival and her processional, as can be judged by reading the portions we have excerpted. What went on inside the palace was apparently not seen by him. The Journal is interesting, however, for such archaic writing is not ordinarily available for study. Our excerpts cover either historical occasions or sidelights of the times. I don't know how to pronounce or accent the words, but do know it is necessary to pronounce most of the "fs" like "s" and to remember that -*is* signifies the plural.

"..Vpoun the xix day of Auguft lxj, Marie, quene of Scottis, oure fouerane ladie, arryvit in the raid (roadstead) of Leith, at fex houris in the mornyng, accumpanyit onlie with tua gallionis; and thair come with hir in cumpany monfieur Domell, the grand pryour, monfieur marques, (d'Elbeuf) the faid quenes grace moder broder, togidder with monfieur Danguill, (d'Amville) fecond fone to the conftable of France, with certane vther nobill gentilmen; and at ten houris the famen day, hir hienes landit vpoun the fchoir of Leith, and remanit in Andro Llambis hous be the fpace of ane hour, and thairefter wes convoyit vp to hir palice of Halyrudhous.

Vpoun the xxiiij day of Auguft, quhilk wes Sonday, the quenes grace caufit fay mes in hir hienes chappell within hir palace of Halyrudhous, quhairat the lordis of the congregation wes grittumlie annoyit."

This journal details page after page of the queen's activities from the day she set foot in Scotland. The *twa gaillionis* (galleys) *quhilk brocht the queenes grace* started *hame to France*, and a few days later elaborate welcoming ceremonies were staged. A great procession of her retinue and nobles went from the palace by a road along the north wall of the city to the castle high on its hill where *a yet* was made to her, an honor I cannot identify. After a noon repast, many staged events interrupted the mile-long return down High Street to the palace. By referring to Chapter Nine, it will be seen that saddles, bridles and foot mantles were being paid for on the same day as this celebration. The 30 horses were needed, but they and our two Frenchmen were stranded, and no one knew that they were in Tynemouth, England, waiting to be redeemed. The Lord Treasurer, by paying the many separate bills, shows that the harness and garments had been made and delivered. The diarist shows that the procession was staged immediately after the things had been made. By studying the two old books it is clear that the 15 ladies, including our ancestress, were in the procession with costumes and harness complementing the queen's outfit. Thus we find that researching the horses has uncovered several interesting details about Mary's personnel, equipment, and activities. This welcoming at the very beginning of Mary's reign was a high point, and she remained in favor with her people really as long as she deserved, although there are many opinions about that.

Most of the words of the following extract suggest their modern counterparts. Others I bracket with their probable meanings, but some have been left to the imagination or to those readers who are fluent in archaic Scots.

"...Upoun the fecund day of September lxj, the quenes grace maid hir entres in the burgh of Edinburgh on this maner. Hir hienes depairtit of Halyrudhous, and raid be the lang gait on the north fyid of the faid burgh, vnto the tyme fcho come to the caftell, quheir wes ane yet maid to hir, at the quhilk fcho, accumpanijt with the maift pairt of the nobilitie of Scotland except my lord duke and his fone, come in and raid vp the caftell bank to the caftell, and dynit thairin; and quhen fho had dynit at tuelf houris, hir hienes come furth of the faid caftell towart the faid burgh, at quhilk depairting the artailyerie fchot vehementlie. And thairefter, quhen fho was rydand down the caftellhill, thair met hir hienes ane convoy of the young mene of the faid burgh, to the nomber of fyftie, or thairby, thair bodeis and theis coverit with yeallow taffateis, thair armes and leggs fra the kne doun bair, cullorit with blak, in maner of Moris, (Moors), vpon thair heiddes blak hattis, and on thair faces blak vifouris, in thair mowthis rings, garnifit with intellable precious ftaneis, about thair neckkis, leggis and armes infynit of chenis of gold; togidder with faxtene of the maift honeft men of the toun, cled in veluot gownis and veluot bonettis, berand and gangand about the paill (bearing and carrying about the canopy) wnder which her hienes raid; quhilk paill wes of fyne purpour veluet lynit with reid taffateis, freinyiet with gold and filk; and efter thame wes ane cart with certane bairnes (children), togidder with ane coffer quhairin wes the copburd and propynek quhilk fuld be propynit to hir hienes; and quhen hir grace come fordwart to the butter trone (public scales) of the faid burgh, the nobilitie and convoy foirfaid precedand, at the quhilk butter trone thair was ane port (gateway) made of tymber, in maift honourable maner, cullorit with fyne cullouris, hungin with fyndrie (sundry) armes; vpon the quhilk port wes fingand (singing) certane barneis in the maift hevinlie wyis; vnder the quhilk port thair wes ane cloud opynnand (opened) with four levis (leaves), in the quhilk was put ane bony barne (pretty boy). And quhen the quenes hienes was cummand (coming) throw the faid port, the faid cloude opynnit, and the barne difcendit doun as it had bene ane angell, and deliuerit to hir hienes the keyis of the toun, togidder with ane bybill and ane pfalme buik, coverit with fyne purpourit veluot; and efter the faid barne had fpoken fome fmall fpeitches, he deliuerit alfua to hir hienis thre writtingis, the tennour thairof is vncertane. That being done, the barne afcendit in the cloud, and the faid clud ftekit (closed); and thairefter the quenis grace come doun to the tolbuith (city hall and jail), at the quhilk was ... vpoun two fkaffattis (?sconce-like shelters), ane abone and ane vnder that; vpone the vnder was fituat (sitting) ane fair wirgin, callit Fortoune, vnder the quhilk was thrie fair virgynnis, all cled in maift precious attyrement (attire), callit ... Juftice and Policie. And efter ane litell fpeitch maid thair, the quenis grace come to the croce (the market cross), quhair thair was ftandand four fair virgynnis, cled in the maift hevenlie clething, and fra the quhilk croce the wyne ran out at the fpouttis in greit abundance; thair wes the noyifs (noise) of pepill cafting the glaffis with wyne. This being done, our fouerane ladie come to the falt trone, quhair thair wes fum fpekaris; and efter ane litell fpeitche, thaj brunt (burnt) vpoun the fkaffet maid at the faid trone, the maner of ane facrifice; and fwa that being done, fho depairtit to the nether bow (lower gate in the city wall), quhair thair wes ane vther fkaffet maid, havand ane dragoun in the famyn, with fome fpeiches; and efter that the dragoun was brynt, and the quenis grace hard ane pfalme fong, hir hienes paft to hir abbay of Halyrudhous, etc., etc., etc."

Excerpts from Scottish Documents

During the next few days, the queen went to Linlithgow palace, her birthplace, then to Sterling castle, Kincardin, and Dundee. While she was away, Archibald Dowglas was elected provost of Edinburgh. He caused a proclamation to be posted on the city cross in High Street,

> "...with a trumpeter and maffer; commanding and chargeing all and fyndry monks, freris, prieftis and all vtheris papiftis and prophane perfonis, to pas furth of Edinburgh within xxiiij houris next efter following, vnder the payne of burnying of difobeyaris vpoun the cheik, and harling of thame throw the toun in ane cart; at the quhilk proclamatioun the quenis grace was verry commouit."

On the next day, "Mr. Thomas Makcalyean wes chofin proveft of Edinburgh, and Archibald Dowglas difchargit, for making of the proclamatioun foirfaid without the quenis awyife, togidder with all the bailyies."

This big book is full of action including many cases of men being "put to the horne." (Under Scots law, letters of horning ordered a person to pay or perform as ordered by a court.)

> "...Vpoun the xxij day of September, the yeir of God foirfaid, Matho fumtyme erle of Levinax, wes be oppin proclamatioun at the mercat croce of Edinburgh, relaxit fra the proces of our fouerane ladies horne, be fchir Robert Foirman of Luthrie, knycht lyoun king of armes...and deliuerit the wand of peax to Johne erle of Athole, quha reffavit (received) the famyn in the faid erlis name."

It is interesting to note how the Latin *pax*, (peace), was retained in the Scots *peax*. How did they pronounce *peax*?

Things were different then than now in other respects:

"...Upoun the firft day of September 1570, thair wer tua perfonis brint in the caftell hill of Edinburgh for the committing of the horrible finne of fodame; the ane thairof was callit Johne Swan, alias Reidpath, the uther of the fame, Johne Litftar blaksmyth. In no tyme heirtofoir wes it hard that any perfonis in this countrie wes fundin gyltie of this cryme."

Thieves attacked Bothwell outside his castle, and

"...gaif him thrie woundis, ane in the bodie, ane in the heid, and ane in the hand; and my lord gaif him twa ftraikis with ane quhingar at the paip, and the faid theif depairtit; and my lord lay in fwoun, quhill his feruantis come and carijt him to the Hermitage. At his cuming thairto, the faidis thevis, quhilk was in prefoune (prison) in the faid Hermitage, had gottin furth thairof, and wes maifteris (masters) of the faid place, and wald not let my lord Bothwell in the faid place, quhill ane callit Robert Ellot of the Schaw, (of the notorious reiver family, the Elliots), come and faid, that gif thaj wald let in my lord Bothwill, he wald faif all thair lyvis and let thame gang hame; and fua thaj leit my lord in; and gif he had not gottin in at that tyme, he and all his cumpany haid been flane. And the faid theif that hurt my lord Bothwill, deceissit within ane myle, vpone ane hill, of the woundis gottin fra my lord Bothwill of befoir.

"Vpoun the fyftene day of the said moneth of October, our fouerane ladie raid fra Jedburgh to the Hermitage, quairin my lord Bothwill was liand in mending of his woundis, and fpak with the faid erle, and returnit agane the famyne nycht to Jedburgh.

"Vpoun the twentie fyft day of the faid moneth, the quenis majeftie, throw hir great ryding befoir reherfit, (rehearsed or told) wes fa hevilie vexit with the het feveris, that thair was nane that belevit that fho fuld leive, and lay fra nyne houres to ane efternone as fho haid bein deid, bot thairefter convalefcit and become better, quhaifoir was maid publict prayaris in all pairtis. All the tyme of our fouerane ladies being in Jedburgh, the kingis grace wes nocht with the quene, bot was with his fader, halkand and huntand, the weft pairtis of this realme; fo fone as he wes adverteift of hir infirmitie, he come to Edinburgh vpon the twantie fevint day at evin, and raid to the quenis grace to Jedburgh vpoun the twantie aucht day in the mornyng. And efter his cuming to the faid burgh, he was not to weill intertynijt as neid fuld haue bene;...

"...Vpoun the nynt day of the faid moneth of Maij, our fouerane ladie and the faid erle Bothwill wes proclamit in the college kirk of Sanct Geill (St. Giles) to be marijt togidder.

"Vpoun the ellevint day of the faid moneth, our fouerane ladie and the faid erle Bothwill come furth of the caftell of Edinburgh, and wes lugeit (lodged) in the abbay.

"Vpoun the tuelf day thairof, betuix fevin and aucht houris at evin, James erle Bothwill wes maid duk of Orknay and Jetland, with greit magnificence, and four knychtis wes maid thair;...and thair wes few or nane of the nobilitie thairat.

"Vpoun the fyftene day of Maij 1567, Marie, be the grace of God quene of Scottis, wes marijt on James Duke of Orknay, erle Bothwill, lord Haillis, Crychtoun (one of his castles) and Liddifdail (his Hermitage fortress in Liddesdale), great Admirall of Scotland, in the palice of Halyrudhous, within the auld chappell, be Adame bifchope of Orknay, not with the mefs (mass) bot with preitching, at ten houris afoir none (4:00 A.M.). Thair wes not many of the nobilitie of this realme thairat,...with certane vtheris fmall gentillmene..."

Thus did the diarist record the wedding of Bothwell and Queen Mary, but not of our lady-in-waiting.

CHAPTER XV

EVOLUTION OF THE SURNAME, DEPO

The surname that began in the same year that Mary, Queen of Scots returned home from France evolved through twenty recorded spellings. In the end, two spellings survived that we know of: "Dippie" in Scotland, England, Australia, New Zealand, and "Deppa" which was brought to the United States by James Deppa, the last name on the list. (Also, in 1895 at least, the spelling "Dippie" was in Toronto, Canada, as I discovered in the book, *Michigan Birds*.)

The "Dippie" spelling is first seen in 1663 (Item 12). That is 99 years after the founding of the family. In this length of time a great proliferation of the foundation stock must have occurred. Sons and daughters spread out for three generations, but the records show very little of what must have happened. We found eight variant spellings within the first century of the family. Twelve more were added probably before 1800. There must have been a great many individuals involved. There is only one consistency in this orthographic frenzy. It went on in two localities: the Canongate/Edinburgh, and the Coldstream areas. The name was in the cities of Berwick and Kelso, but in between, within an 18 mile radius of Coldstream, were many villages where the surname was well known. In Scotland the towns were Coldstream, Duns, Chirnside, Swinton, Greenlaw, Ednam, Kelso, Berwick and others. In England the name was known in Wark, Ford, Etal, and a little more to the south, in Glanton, Whittingham and Wooler. These names are known through the Dippie/Dixon family. One need not get very deep into Scottish history to find that the disastrous battle of Flodden Field was near the town of Ford in 1513. Berwick and other places had been in Border contention for much of their long history. Village people could be farmers, but it is likely that this family was mostly engaged in trade or crafts.

Individual preferences, education, disinterest, all led to this long list of variants. Sometime in the 1700s the spelling "Dippie" almost seems to have been agreed on, for all other forms disappeared except the one that is found only in the United States. Deippa, (item 6) recorded in Canongate, may have left a trail leading directly to the man who went to Glasgow, then America, with that name virtually unchanged and appearing nowhere else. My original interest was to find the progenitor of my line, but in the end I spent more time studying Scotland and all its people. My immediate family line had to be left out on a limb, in a manner of speaking. The whole family tree is too big for one person to cut up in all its branches, and the story of Queen Mary's Scotland changed from a digression to a major objective. Our story had to include some background about her, and we found that her biographies lacked the many details which are recorded about her horses, her horse farm and her three stable-boys. This part of her story has probably never been told before. What I have added in Chapter Nine about her eleven ladies-in-waiting and their riding gear may also be a new insight. In reading a very prominent biography of my favorite queen I also discovered that it had her French home, the castle Ste. Germain-en-Laye, mislocated a whole watershed away from the Seine where my son, Bruce, visited it recently. It is possible that I have also made some mistakes, but if so they can rest in peace alongside the "Dippie" entry in *Surnames of Scotland*, discussed at length in Chapter Five.

The people of our line have walked in five centuries, and we know the actual day they started out. Before long, we can say that six centuries have seen them. One of those centuries belongs to me, or even one and a half, for neither my parents nor my grandparents seem far away in time, nor mysterious to me in memory. Beyond that, I have to depend on reading books, and seeing landscapes. When blended by experience, these ingredients can re-create my people in my mind's eye. Scotland, Melrose, the Canongate,

Holyroodhouse, the castle, and all the rest, had to be seen. Then my predecessors could be visualized in their daily affairs. The many dates and the interactions of all the people are no longer a blurred, amorphous haze. Many have become definite individuals to me; nor are they necessarily all glamorous. I learned better than to expect that long ago.

There may be more spellings than those listed, but I don't believe the pronunciation would change much, no matter what the spelling. My guess is that the combination of accent and enunciation of these Border people produced a sound hovering around the phonetics of Deppo, Dippie, Deppie, no matter what marks were put on paper. Long ago Scottish spelling was a sort of pictograph. Certain curlicues were memorized as meaning certain words in about the same way that a child recognizes his mother by her general look, and not her exact specifications. The fact that twenty variants of a short name could be contrived proves this. This must be some sort of a record. Due entirely to lack of precedent, these people had to head out into the unknown when they tried to write their name. In those days, too, different spellings were sometimes deliberate efforts to keep the various uncles and cousins separated.

A great many more birth, baptism, and death records exist than I have found, I am sure, but most will be in the 17th and 18th centuries. Many of the earliest have succumbed to time and neglect. Most events were never recorded, or were soon lost in little parish churches. Burials, except in towns, were often in family plots, I suspect. They would soon be overgrown by the bracken and whin, and reclaimed by nature's inexorable process that cultivation can hold back only temporarily, even today. A family burial plot can soon be lost.

Entries on our chart have an asterisk (*) when they come from written records. The pages of comments have item numbers that refer to the chart. The first parents are shown as having nine children, but that would be only a medium sized family. Eight of these are derived from recorded descendants shown by the doubled or tripled capital letter headings. Hypothetical dates for some births and marriages were needed to make the chart's construction possible but in every case support for the assumption can be traced to a recorded fact as shown by the starred entries. Parents, grandparents, and children may validly be linked without individual statistics. The starred dates had to be matched with reasonable assumptions about the parents, and grandparents. A basic presumption was that a baptized baby had a father, and that he had a father with the same surname (we hoped). One of the disappointments has been the absence of mothers' names. Even there we found obvious connections as in items 9, 10, and 11.

Just as the earth would soon be covered with aphids if they multiplied in uninterrupted geometric progression, so with this family through 425 years. By about 1650 we have listed only about 20 individuals. If the first siblings had expanded to the present without hindrance, we would be inundated with relatives, but there are not too many of us now. The daughters and their daughters in this line are unknowns, but the number of families that have intermarried must be enormous indeed. It is at least interesting to consider that invisible network of families behind and all around us.

When I think of the many people who don't know the name of their grandfather, I am pleased, but not smug, that I know that the name of my great, great, great, great, great, great, great, great, great, great, great, great grandfather was André Depo.

THE CHILDREN
GRANDCHILDREN and GREAT-GRANDCHILDREN
of
OUR PROGENITORS

A Lady-in-Waiting ——— married in 1562 ——— Hendre Depo (#3)

A	B	C	D	E	F	G	H	I
Daut.	Daut.	Son	Son	Son	Daut.(#4)	Son	Son	Son
b.1564	b.1566	---Dippo	---Dippo	---Dippo	Katherine	---Deippe	---Deippa	---Depo
	mar.'84	b.1570	b.1572	b.1574	Dippo *	b.1578	b.1579	b.1580
		mar.1595	mar.1592		b.1576	mar.1603	mar.1603	mar.1604
					mar. Alex.			
					Moresome *			
					Edinburgh *			
					1595 *			

BB	CC	DD(#5)	EE		GG	HH	II
Daut.	Son	Son	Son		Son	Son	Son(#11)
b.1600	Jas.Deipo*	Wm.Dikpo*	---Dippo		---Deippe	John Deippa*	James Depo *
mar.'18	b.1610	(sic)	b.1615		b.1605	b.1605 (No.6)	b.1620
	mar.1635	b.1593			mar.1625	mar.I.Walker*	mar.1644
	No. 9	tenant @				Holyroodhouse	
		Ednam.				1626*	
		1614 *					

BBB	CCC		EEE (#15)		GGG		III
Daut.(#10)	Son		Son		Daut.(#7&8)		Son
b. & bapt.*	Wm.Deipo		John Dippo *		Euphemia		James Depo
1655.Jas.	b.* & bapt.*		b.1650		Deippe *		bapt. Apr.12
Deipo witn.*	1646 *		Fined.		b.1628		1656 *
his sister's	witn: Jon*		1682 *		mar. Robert		Witnesses:
(Mrs.Andrew	Deipo,John				Moresone *		James Moffat, *
Mein) daut.	Blaikie*				1647 *		Adam Hislope *
No. 9 *					Buried in		
					Holyrood		
					Chapel cem.		

* Data taken from Scottish Records.
  Unmarked entries by calculation.
  Numbers in parentheses refer to items on the
  Surname Table and in the Commentary.

Figure 10: The Depo Family Chart

THE DEPO FAMILY CHART

The chart starts with the lady-in-waiting and the stable-boy, and shows their children, grandchildren, and great-grandchildren. If we knew the full roster, there would be over 100 names instead of the 21 shown. Every slot that is covered by a Scottish record has an asterisk (*). The references are keyed together by the item numbers on the listing.

The name of only one child, Katherine, item 4, has been found in the records, and none of her children. She would normally have had children, and a record of them may be in the vital statistics of Edinburgh under the name of Morrison, or variant. A search might uncover the surname of Katherine's grandparents. Nothing could please me more than to know the family name of the lady-in-waiting who married the stable-boy of our legend.

Katherine's brothers are spaced out datewise on the top line. This has to be hypothetical, but their sons and grandsons have been found in records. Under the generally accepted theory that children have fathers we were able to link the three generations together. Six sons were needed on the top line to account for the younger progeny. Actually, I can scarcely believe that all of the records have been found that lead back to the first generation sons. As for daughters, I found only Katherine, but very likely she had several sisters. I added one as the first child simply to reconcile the many dates that had to be fitted together. This big task required that the birth and marriage dates of parents and their children had to be estimated to fit the actual dates we had in hand from records.

The girls of the family will be known by names and dates only by finding a record somewhere. By lucky chance, a birth, marriage, or death record might be found. Since the women's husbands' names are not known except in the few cases on the chart, baptismal and other records of their children cannot be looked for. Burial records of women were under their maiden name at that time in Scotland. Many burials, I feel sure, were in isolated grave sites that were forgotten through the years.

Stooping nearly double, I scrambled up cleated boards laid on the steep passageway in the Great Pyramid. My wife made the climb too, though many younger women turned back. Energetic Egyptian helpers pulled and encouraged. It was a great dream come true for me. As a freshman in 1928 I had written my long-term-thesis on this ancient wonder of the world. When we got to the burial chamber at the top there was the huge, empty, uncovered stone sarcophagus into which our tour clown promptly lay down. Of course my mind was racing with this evidence of mortality, futility, antiquity, etc., etc. An immediate distraction though, was the engineering whereby the immense weight above the empty chamber had been supported. Massive stone lintels could be seen high overhead and I learned that criss-cross above them other tiers bridged from wall to wall until the peak was reached. The pharaoh is gone, but he saw to it that he was not to be forgotten.

At the Tower of London I learned that in a clean-up effort, in a basement, a great number of bodies, some in arrow boxes, were jumbled together, all unmarked and in complete disarray. In my indian-country work in the southwest I encountered several situations where burials had been uncovered, and one where nothing had been done to take care of the horse or its owner who had taken a hard route out of a refused marriage proposal. One time I moved a dam rather than a burial, and in another case a Smithsonian man was called in. Ancestors' graves are not so impersonal, yet when and for how long, can they be intimately cherished? Very, very old graves are mostly lost and memories of people buried not only grow dim but disappear as the span of time stretches beyond one generation.

FIGURE 11: EVOLUTION OF OUR SURNAME
Hendre Depo and his descendants, as found in Scottish records.

Item number	Date	Name, as found in the reference cited	Spelling number	Citation or event from the records
1	1561	Dieppe, Dieppois	1	Identification on arrival
2	1564	Depo, Alexander	2	First recorded name.
3	1586	Depo, Hendre		Recorded at Melrose.
4	1595	Dippo, Katherine	3	Married Alexander Moresome.
5	1614	Dikpo, William		A misread Dippo.
6	1626	Deippa, John	4	Mar. I.Walker in Holyrood/Canong.
7	1647	Deippe, Eupham	5	Mar. Rob't Moresone, burgess "
8	1665	" , Euphemia		Relict of Moresone, buried/Holyrood
9	1646	Deipo, James	6	His son,Wm., baptised in Williamlaw.
10	1655	" , James		Wit'd. bapt. of A. Mein's Daughter.
11	1656	Depo, James		Son James bapt. Witnesses named.
12	1663	Dippe, Robert	7	All three spellings below were used
		Deippe, "		by Robert D. Item 13 the same.
		Dippie, "	8	Made marr.contract Oct.7, 1663.
13	1676	Deippe, "		Burial in Greyfriars Churchyard.
14	1671	Deppo, Robert	9	Different spelling, same man.
15	1682	Dippo, John		Fined 50 pounds for contumacy.
16	1694	Deeppie, William	10	Burgess in Canongate; a brewer.
17	1695	Dipo, James	11	Tombstone in Earlstoun.
18	1703	Deipie, James	12	Apprenticed by his father.
19	1715	Depic, Jean	13	Married James Thomson.
20	1720	Deepie, William	14	Married Margaret Clapham.
21	1732	Deepie, Dorothea		Married William Clarke.
22		Diepe, John	15	S.Leith gives no detail.
23	1761	Diepy, Thomas	16	Married Agnes Turner.
24	1790	Diepie, Mary	17	Married Isaac Grey.
25	1881	Deppa, James	18	Died 1881 in N.Y.State.

Commentary in the following pages is identified by Item Number in col. #1 above.

COMMENTARY ON THE NAME LIST
AND FAMILY CHART

1.   Dieppe, Dieppois 1561.

Several people fluent in French helped me to correspond with the Mayor of Dieppe and Archives De La Seine-Maritime at Roen, France. I had hoped that the manifests of the two horse-ships might have been preserved inasmuch as the departure of Mary, the widowed French Queen was no small event. France does not maintain national archives, and my efforts yielded no names or useful data. Correspondence with Dutch officials, while cordial, also failed to provide data.

2.   Depo, Alexander 1564

This man was recorded in the *Accounts of the Lord High Treasurer of Scotland*, Vol. XI, p. 354. Dr. Michael Lynch, in the Department of Scottish History, University of Edinburgh, provided this crucial citation on the earliest record of our name.

3.   Depo Hendre 1561 - 1586 - 1606 - 1607 - 1608

Ref: *Records of the Regality of Melrose*, copied from the original manuscript and edited by the Scottish History Society, Vol. I, 1914.

This man, who was a native of Dieppe, France, married one of the eleven ladies-in-waiting to the queen, who are still anonymous. Virtually nothing is known about them, but in Chapter Nine some records of the Lord High Treasurer are reproduced verbatim. They repeatedly show that there were eleven, in addition to the four famous Maries. The story of this Melrose family lacks the mother's touch, but it must have been entirely unique among the rough country people who seldom left their own homes for more than a few hours and almost never got out of sight of the smoke of their own chimney. Depo, himself, was obviously French, and different in the eyes of the native Scots. As we have suggested before, he may have resembled the Scots, even to having blue eyes, for the natives of Dieppe had come from the north, Vikings. There were perhaps thirty farmtouns, and scores of men, women, and children, in the bailiwick that they could have known. The family was different, but it was accepted, for they lived there more than forty years. For his part in this success story, André was accepted into the closely cooperative work teams and plough-gangs of Moshouses. He went there in his early twenties, and may have brought useful skills learned in the seaport city of Dieppe. These two were the founders of our family, and it was their wedding that was remembered as a tradition in my family in the United States.

The wife and mother can be given much credit. We don't know much about her beyond the fact that she must have been of an old Scottish family. Having been in the queen's service, she was adaptable, widely experienced, and, in her own way, diplomatic. Otherwise she would have been sent back to her parents from France. She was not disagreeable, nor ill-favored, and these traits helped in Melrose. These two were the founders of the Dippie/Deppa family.

The queen sponsored their marriage, and imagination has to be depended on to fill in the story. Three years to the day after Queen Mary landed, she gave orders to keep records. This was two years too late to note the wedding we are looking for, that between André and his lady. Numerous weddings in the close circle of her domestic staff are featured in biographies of the queen, but that brief hiatus was a crucial gap for us. Throughout those months there were many festive celebrations, but no one had the duty of recording these events. 1562, the probable date of "our" wedding, could have been a midpoint in such festivities. The queen's reign deteriorated so rapidly that the gaiety phase must have climaxed rather early. Certainly the greatest spate of jolly celebrations must have been before, not after, Riccio, and Kirk O'Field.

The Register of Marriages is in the *Buik Of The Canagait*, 1564-1567, edited by A. Calderwood. There is also a Register of Baptisms beginning in 1564. Canongate, which is mentioned so often, has nothing to do with a cannon. The word involves ecclesiastical, or canon, law, in many ancient and church-related meanings.

My unfailing well of Scottish documentation, Dr. Lynch, helped me through another thorny thicket. It was the Reverend John Craig, colleague of the Reverend John Knox, who, in 1567, married the queen and Bothwell in the great hall in Holyroodhouse. It seemed probable that he had officiated at all the many weddings sponsored by the queen, and that he had kept a private log which would record the people in the wedding we seek. That was a futile hope, for the details are much more complicated. Dr. Lynch wrote a detailed letter quoting from *Fasti Ecclesiae Scoticanae*, which looks to me to be Scottish Ecclesiastical Register. Craig may have officiated if Depo married before April 1562, but after that date he had become minister of the parish of Edinburgh. Even then, he may have officiated as a visiting minister, as seems to have been true for Bothwell and the queen. He probably married our ancestors. Almost certainly he married their daughter, Katherine, in Edinburgh five years before he died as the records tell.

At some point, these matters have to be passed over, but it is hard to decide which stone to leave unturned. The historical documents are endless, but then the useful ones have been found in obscure hiding places, although not in this minister's private record book.

4. Dippo, Katherine.

Katherine Dippo married Alexander Moresome November 19, 1595. Ref: *Register of Edinburgh Marriages*, by Scottish Record Society. The only record about her that we have found is the marriage. Very likely other entries exist if there is a Moresome family history. Her name is on our chart as a child of our couple, for her 1595 marriage presumes an approximate 1576 birth date. No children are known, but might be found in birth, baptism, or marriage records. Her siblings' approximate birth dates can be estimated through the dates when their children and grandchildren-to-be were born, baptized, or married, but her birth date is fitted into the appropriate gap. The diversity of spellings facilitates tracing these people. If they had all been named Smith, the job would have been impossible.

Although I had read Black's *Surnames* in Edinburgh in 1969, his paragraph on "Dippie" was not enough. My first lead toward finding the meaning of the legend repeated by my Grandmother and my Aunt Lizzie came from a grand lady, Sheila Macbeth Mitchell, a genealogist of Edinburgh. In October 1977, the Washington, D.C. Star newspaper carried a story about her, and on November 22, she appeared on T.V. with Jacques Cousteau in a Greek harbor. Going down in his diving bell, she saw the sunken Brittanic, a hospital ship on which she had been a nurse when it sank in 1916. This story also stated that she and her 91-year-old husband had recorded 50,000 gravestone inscriptions in Scotland. I wrote to her, and received four handwritten pages of the first hard evidence on my Scottish ancestors including the record of Katherine's marriage. She also referred me to the Regality Records of Melrose, especially Volumes I and III, and numerous other record books, as well as the Border Magazine article which had led to all the misinformation. Her friendly and competent response to a stranger's letter has been a high point in my work. In December of 1986 she responded to a letter from me writing in a bold hand that although she could scarcely see the letters as she wrote, she remembered our exchange nine years previously and hoped to have my work read to her on her 97th birthday, June 12, 1987.

If we could know all that Katherine knew about her family, we would have the whole picture. We can tell by her marriage date that she was not one of the earliest Depo children. The chart shows that she had older brothers and sisters, as evidenced by dates of children and grandchildren. These second and third generations actually dictate the construction of the chart.

The reasonable and natural explanation for the marriage to an Edinburgh man is that she grew up in that city with her mother's parents. Her grandparents asked that she live with them for a good reason I believe. When their five or six year old child had been given up to be a companion to the child queen, they might well have insisted that this granddaughter should live with them in their old-age. Back at Moshouses apparently there were two or three boys, and maybe a young sister of no help in caring for the new baby. Also, the mother could let the child go, for not too many miles separated the two homes. By the old Scotch formula she would have been named after a grandmother or after her mother, in the set sequence: mother's mother, father's mother, mother. If she were the third daughter, she would have been named after her mother whose surname we wish we knew.

5.   Dikpo, William   1614

This name is obviously an understandable error in reading a clerk's "Dippo." He was recorded in the Calendar of Laing Charters, edited by J. Anderson (Edinburgh, 1899) No. 1714. This was an instrument of sasine dated July 21, 1614. This legal proceeding adjudicated disposition of land rights. William Dippo (Dikpo) was one of 58 tenants of Ednam on the Eden Water. This extensive land area had been a Benedictine Priory. The life-rent was being given to a daughter and future son-in-law of Sir Archibald Sterling of Keir.

Dr. Michael Lynch sent this excerpt to me with the comment that this parish was immediately adjacent to Stichel. He said there was a clear connection between William Dippo and Alexander Depo who "dwelt in Stichel." Very likely, William was a nephew of Katherine who had to leave the crowded Melrose home when he was a young man, and go to the agricultural areas near Kelso to find his own tenancy.

6.   Deippa, John   1626

This entry and number 7 are from the Register of Marriages for the parish of Holyroodhouse or Canongate as quoted in Chapter ten, ."..marriage of John Deippa and Isobell Walker 24 December 1626..." A study of the chart and all the circumstances creates a strong case for believing that this grandson was the founder of my Deppa line. At some time in the future the mislocated "i" was dropped, and the name became "Deppa." John Deippa was a member of the palace parish which meant that he lived in that suburb. His father lived there, too, and also his father's sister Katherine, John's aunt. She married in the Edinburgh parish as did her great-niece, Euphemia. Both married Morrisons. As clearly as though it were written it can be seen that these people of the Depo line were brought up in the grandparent's home. Perhaps the house was kept in the family through inheritance; at any rate they were all Canongate residents. It had to be the father and mother of John Deippa who first impressed the original story on a son's mind so thoroughly that it never failed to be repeated through four centuries. The Border uncles and aunts were certainly known to exist in the early decades, but were perhaps never seen nor communicated with and, of course, this lack of contact worked both ways. In the crucial early years of virtual chaos in the Borderlands, travel and communication was nonexistent for most people. The members in the south probably maintained some semblance of a relationship for they clustered, often within walking distance of each other, in small towns not far from Berwick in both Scotland and England.

When Glasgow burst into seething industrial ferment, a man named Deppa left the Canongate in the late 1700s or early 1800s and either walked or rode the stage forty miles to the west to find work in the shops.

It requires conscious effort to keep the elapsed time of these events in perspective. The sequence we have just run through in a few sentences stretched out through nearly a hundred years as may be seen in the family chart. Through this period most people were neither prepared nor able to read and write or send letters. There were professional writers, but one didn't hire them to dash off chit-chat to relatives. The extracts we have included show that there was no sophistication in the script or the spelling. Not until the 1700s did the upper classes discover they were being viewed as countrified and even boorish, often by commoners who labored at their letters more diligently than did the sons of lords.

It is very likely that the many spellings of our surname were pronounced more or less alike. Starting off with a "D" followed by a rumble in the throat flavored with a "p" sound the name ended with the inevitable diminutive "ie" at the end. It is interesting that the valid "ie" of Dieppe, where both vowels are pronounced, was never used, except contrariwise as "ei," except twice in the late 1700s. The list of 20 spellings shows what I think is a growing awareness as education progressed through the many generations. When Dieppois was phonetically written Depo, no one was in a position to question it. Katherine, and others, chose to use the "i" instead of the "e." It took 70 years for the "i" and the "e" to both be used again, but backwards. The French city, Dieppe, was the main port connecting France and Scotland, so that was a familiar name in the commerce of the time. These people knew that Dieppe was their town, and they were not about to leave out any of the letters even though they could not be pronounced in Scots. As time wore on, the double "p" gained strength and the many spellings boiled down to only two. I have read that languages begin with complex words and compound words. As in Chinese, simplification carves off letters and polysyllables and conciseness sets in, as in our name.

7.   Deippe, Eupham or Euphemia   1647

Married Robert Morisone (*Register of Edinburgh Marriages*). Also see items 4 and 8, and the Family Chart. As in Katherine's case, the daughter and granddaughter of a foreign farmer marries into an important capital city family. This would be an improbable scenario, except that Eupham's great-grandmother was not a farmer's wife. She had sent her little girl off to be a lady-in-waiting to Mary, the Queen of Scotland, and Crown Princess of France.

When this young lady came back from France and married, she lived with her French husband at Melrose. She sent at least one daughter and apparently two sons to live in the Parish of Holyrood/-Canongate. Eupham's father was evidently the son of one of these sons. This was a small city when Queen Mary's child companions were chosen. The parents of the one we are interested in must have been rated among the "old families." The city was clustered tightly around the fortress castle and the residential palace, about a mile apart. When Eupham married, she entered the same family as her Aunt Katherine. The Morison family, with many variant spellings through the XVth Century and later, had many members who were burgesses, in the law, notary, and military occupations. One had been a priest. Eupham Deippe married Robert Moresone, Burgess of Holyrood/Canongate. If she had children, they are lost somewhere among the Morrisons of this world.

8.   Deippe, Euphemia 1665

As "relict of Robert Moreson, Burgess of Canongate, she was buried in the Abbey of Holyrood on 17th May 1665" (reference *Protestant Exiles from France*, Agnew, Vol. I, p. 259). Robert predeceased Euphemia (she was a widow - see number 7). Was he buried at Holyrood, or did she have an exceptional prerogative going back to the time when her great-grandmother had been married there? Such a burial connotes unusual circumstances in her antecedents. They might be summarized: the great-granddaughter of a tenant farmer, or vassal, with an unheard-of French-sounding name marries a Burgess of Canongate-Holyroodhouse, and is buried in the Palace Cemetery. Scottish records tell us these facts, but our legend gives the simple explanation.

9.   Deipo, James 1646

Evolution of the Surname, Depo

Items 9, 10, and 11 are from the *Register of Baptisms* for Melrose compiled and printed by the Scottish Record Society in 1913. Mr. R. M. Strathdee of the Scottish Genealogy Society generously furnished these extracts. They appear in the family chart under tripled capital letters. The three babies fit the great-grandchild slot in my chart.

James Deipo, the grandson of Hendre, had his son William baptized in Williamlaw on September 9, 1646. Witnesses were Jon Deipo and John Blaikie. Jon, we can believe, was brother to James, and a good reminder that if our chart were complete, every name on it would be surrounded with countless brothers and sisters. All of them, when married, could touch an equal number of neighboring families - a vast interlocking relationship. Very likely Hendre's children and grandchildren did not ordinarily marry outside of the Melrose communities. Jon Blaikie, witness, was probably the husband of a sister of James Deipo. At least that's more reasonable than thinking he was a bystander off the street called in to witness a baptism.

10.   Deipo, James 1655

This is the same James as Number 9, but this time he served as a witness at the baptism of Andrew Mein's daughter. It seems to me that Andrew Mein's wife was very likely James' sister. In 1606, about the time Andrew was born, the court in Melrose was petitioned to recognize William Mein as heir to the estate of David Mein of Newsteid. He was entitled to "sax acres of townland, and sax acres of coit yard land." Newsteid is just east of the town of Melrose. William Mein, the heir, could well have been father-in-law of James Deipo's sister. A move of six miles to town into a land-holding family seems to be indicated here for one of the Depo women. They would have attended the same church. This seems to have been a town family, not farmers. The other witness at this baptism was Adam Hislope, who was witness again the next year at the baptism of James Depo, *q.v.* Was he husband of a sister of the baby's father? The Hislope name identified a settlement about 2 miles west of Moshouses, the Depo home place. A "peel tower" there marks this as an old and important family.

11.   Depo, James   1656

Except for Hendre and Alexander Depo, this James Depo, and son of the same name, are the only instances we have found of Depo. Logic is the last thing one looks for in a name, but Depo meant Dieppois, and applied properly only to the two men (and the boy, Alexander, who was killed) who got off the boat. The fact that only James Depo used that form could mean that he was either loyal to his parents' family name or that Hendre's wife knew that Dieppois (Depo) was not correct for her children, and was able in most cases to steer them away from using it.

This woman is invisible in the records, but she must have been remarkable, to say the least. As a companion of the child queen, she was undoubtedly educated with all the Scottish and French court children who, we have read, were all educated together. Although she was a Scot, she was almost certainly more fluent in French than in her native Scots. However, one wonders if she had any reading or writing materials once she adopted the role of a farmer's wife, with its constant toil. If she did, it would have been great if she had written up her family history and saved it for me.

When baby James Depo was baptized in a Presbyterian service in Melrose, the witnesses were James Moffat and Adam Hislope. The name Moffat occurs repeatedly in the *Regality Records* as residents of Threipwode, or Threipwoid, which roughly may be translated as "no man's wood." Maybe James Moffat married a sister of one of the Depo boys. At any rate, they lived only about a mile and a half apart - say a 25-minute walk. Both Adam Hislope and James Moffat figure in many actions in the court records. Moffat was apparently a bondsman involved in many cases.

12.   Dippe, or Deippe, or Dippie, or Depo, Robert   1663

Agnew (see full reference in item 8) provided the information that Robert, who couldn't settle on how his name should be spelled, "..was an upholsterer and trunk maker in 'Caldtoune', Edinburgh." Perhaps the spelling "Dippie" originated with him; at least I have not found it previously recorded. Agnew also said that Robert "made a marriage contract there 7th October 1663."

Agnew didn't suggest that our family began in Scotland as Huguenot refugees, yet this sentence and one other were seized on, embellished with much irrelevant refugee history, and published. This is the sole and completely erroneous documentation for the widespread idea that we arrived in the tide of refugees. This observation is made with a wry personal knowledge of the many years of work and expenditures that were required for me to search out this four-century history of our name. After Agnew's prestigious two volumes were published in 1886, and the Dippie name was found in it, what followed was perfectly understandable. Nothing had ever before been seen about the family, in a book. Many people in the Berwick area, named Dippie, were much interested in the family origin. They had family charts going back into the last quarter of the 18th century, and could see no argument against assuming their ancestors had arrived as Huguenot refugees. More than likely a minister showed them the book, written by a minister, that had the words, Dippie, and refugee, in its pages. Neither the record books nor the twentieth century scholarship that has been available to me were in existence in the days when word went out that the Dippies were Huguenot refugees. It may be, too, that I have been extremely fortunate to have had the leisure in my seventh decade and beyond, to work almost full time on this job with the new invention, the computer. Almost as an afterthought, I would comment that the man from Dieppe was almost certainly a Huguenot, which is fine with me. The girl who went off to France to be a lady-in-waiting was almost certainly a Catholic until she turned Presbyterian in August of 1561, by edict.

Only by lucky accident was an occasional official record made and not lost, in the long ago times of our family's beginnings. Now some of them have been found and fitted into a sequence, all because I could not forget a story I often heard and thought about as a boy. Without benefit of some conjecture, all of these apparently discrete and isolated snippets of data would remain fodder for bookworms in archives. There is a surprising amount of solid documentation undergirding our legend, and undoubtedly much remains unfound.

Robert, of the quadruple name (Depo, Number 12), may have been brother to Eupham, or Euphemia, Deippe. Only 11 years separated their deaths, and both were unusually well-recorded in Edinburgh.

As I work with these names, I realize that I haven't the slightest idea how they were pronounced. The best guide I have is a tale about a famous "southern" name, "Taliafero." It is said that the family called themselves "Darby"! Anyhow, there are now plenty of Darbys. I think likely that after "Depo," all the spellings came out sounding like "Deppy" or "Dippy."

13.   Deippe, Robert (of item 12. Also, see Robert Deppo of item 14).

"His will was proved (probated) in 1676," just 13 years after his marriage (item 12) in 1663. "He was buried in Greyfriar's Churchyard." (map p.67) (R.F. Black, *The Surnames of Scotland* 1974).

Our present information doesn't shed any light on the special status enjoyed by Robert Deippe and Euphemia Deippe Moreson, a status which provided burial for him at Greyfriar's (perhaps his family's parish), and at the palace cemetery for her, which further strengthen belief that the Canongate was the family home. The marriages and burials of these two obviously close relatives in the capital city, and of Katherine Dippo, are incongruous with the supposition that their parents and grandparents were nothing more than Huguenot refugees, refugees who had supposedly crossed more than 600 miles of the violent North Sea to an inhospitable land, when escape to England or Belgium was possible by foot or by rowboat. Hendre Depo had to scurry to the baille court to be threatened with ancient thirlage edicts, while others were married and buried at the palace. It's an unusual story, but the story line scans, our legend explains it, and the logic holds up. We have only the outline of events spanning the first century, but if one could only account for each of the 36,000 days during which the story progressed, there would be no skepticism, for each step in the story is so normal that the participants probably complained about the monotony.

14.   Deppo, Robert   1672

Ninety-nine years after Agnew wrote his version, I received an update on Robert's marriage. Helen Dingwall, research student of Dr. Michael Lynch, University of Edinburgh, provided the following: "Robert Deppo, a trunk maker in Calton, became a burgess in 1671 by right of his wife, Elizabeth Serjiand, daughter of an upholsterer." This seems to be the same man, using a fourth spelling of the name, eight years later. Still in the same business, but now a burgess, or fully-qualified voting citizen. (Ref: Canongate Burgess Roll.)

Miss Dingwall also found it recorded that a testament (will) is listed for Robert Deppo on April 23, 1671. The date of this will, and the one in the next entry (item 15), point to the likelihood that this Robert Deppo was the father of the trunk maker.

15.   Dippo, John   1682

Selections from the *Records of the Regality of Melrose*, Vol. III, February 1, 1917, Scottish History Society.

John Dippo of Craigsfuird, was fined 50 pounds for contumacy on March 11, 1682, by the Baillie of the Regality. His servitor, William Purves, was fined the same (Vol. III, pl 24). The fines, as well as most trade at that time, were in pounds Scots money, worth about 1/4 the sterling pound.

Dippo and Purves were among 132 fined in one court session in Melrose. All Lowland jurisdictions saw similar action. The defendants were *covenanters*. The courts called them "irregular persons, and delinquents." They were defying royal edicts that the Episcopal Church of England was to be the "established" and supreme church of Scotland. A century before, the Presbyterian reformers had done much the same thing to the Catholics, but they did not have as great power and violence as the king's forces.

The reign of English Charles II saw persecutions of the covenanters that are beyond comprehension. A large share of the Lowland Scots, including ministers, refused the mandated Episcopal service, and held house and field conventicles even though preaching was punishable by death. Shortly, mere attendance or the giving of a wrong answer to a test question that had no right answer, could mean being shot on the spot. There are pitiful stories of this happening in the midst of a man's family.

Enormous totals were exacted in fines often diverted to such officials as the infamous Lauderdale. Another such, Bishop Sharp, who was murdered, was avenged in the rout of 5000 covenanters. Prisoners were tortured, mutilated, and hanged; 250 were battened down in a ship's hold to be "transported" as virtual slaves in the Barbados. The ship sank. In one campaign to break the Scots, 9000 soldiers were quartered in private homes in southwest Scotland.

Just to keep the relationship of these events in mind, note that King Charles II died three years after John Dippo was fined. The King never visited Scotland, but he had "Bluidy Clavers" (Claverhouse) and "Bluidy MacKenzie" and all the rest to carry out the horrible routine for him in the 1680's. This was the "killing time" in Scottish history, but, ironically, it coincided with a period of scientific and cultural advance in the rest of Europe, and in America.

The story of our family requires at least this much reference to the covenanters, and to the killing time. There can be no question that John Dippo of Melrose, and his relatives, were Presbyterians. This sect represented freedom of the common people against the excesses of the aristocracy, the Crown, and the Church of England. The religious intolerance of the wilder covenanters, however, were a degrading aspect of this history. Who can fathom the atrocious things that have been done in the name of religion? Some of this threat certainly touched the lives at Melrose, but except for John Dippo and Purves we have no details. (I think that Purvis was a Depo in-law. I have not traced it out either for that instance or another in 1916.) The Deppa family that went to America were Free Church Presbyterians

16.   Deepie, William 1694

Ref: *Canongate Burgess Roll* in Scotland Record Office.

He became Burgess in the Canongate in 1694 by right of his father, Robert Deppo, a trunk maker. He is listed in the poll tax as a brewer worth 2000 *merks* (approximately 1,300 pounds), with a wife, 3 children and 2 servants. (Ref: Miss Dingwall and Dr. Lynch.)

The wildly variable spelling of our surname had evolved for about two centuries before settling down, apparently to only two forms, one of which was then carried to the United States. In this turbulent time when spelling meant little there was the utter novelty of the name, there was no precedent, no arbiter, no writing to refer to that was acceptable or accessible. Each made up his own spelling, but used about the same pronunciation. The Smiths, Browns, Hunters, Halls, had no such problem. Our people were on their own in a place where many names were 10 centuries old.

17.   Dipo, James 1695

Ref: D. C. Cargill, *Tombstone Inscriptions*, Vol. I, Edinburgh Scottish Genealogical Society.

The inscriptions -

on top: "Hear lys James Dipo in Earlstoun who did"

on the front: "the 8 day of Feb. 1695 26 years"

This young man lived about 4 miles northeast of Melrose, leaving not a shred of evidence about himself except for the unique way of spelling the name.

Earlston is a good example of how spelling can corrupt a meaningful place name. This place has nothing to do with any earl. It was an ancient earthworks to help protect the Border Marches. The name *arcioldun*, meaning "prospect fort," was mercifully corrupted for our special convenience to "earlstoun" so it could be pronounced. In America a name is a name, but it is almost axiomatic that place names in old countries arose from some very good reason long forgotten, as in *arcioldun*.

18.   Deipie, James   1703

Ref: *Register of Edinburgh Apprentices*. "Son to William Deipie, wright in South Leith prenticed to John Denholme - wright. Dec. 1, 1703."

This item, as well as items 19 through 21, were furnished by Mrs. Mitchell.

Items 19, 20 and 21 are from *Irregular Marriages in South Leith*, Kirk Sessions Records, 1697-1818. An irregular marriage was one performed outside the established church.

Evolution of the Surname, Depo

19. Depie, Jean 1715

29th December 1715 - James Thomson and Jean Depie married by Mr. John Shand.

20. Deepie, William 1720

William Deepie, wright in Leith, and Margaret Clapham married by Mr. James Humter at Edinburgh, 5th July 1720. Witnesses: Hugh Patterson, writer, and Robert Clapham, wright in Edinburgh.

21. Deepie, Dorothea 1732

9th November 1732 - William Clarke, sailor, and Dorothea Deepie married by Mr. Patrick Middleton at Canongate. Witnesses: John Brown, cork cutter in Leith, and Mary Donaldson, his spouse.

22. Diepe, John

The poll tax for South Leith gives no detail except that he was a wright. (Note: South Leith is at the north edge of Edinburgh and part of the seaport city of Leith.)

23 - 26:

Data for items 23 through 26 is from family history in possession of ship captain David M. Dixon, Australia.

27. Deppa, James 1806-1881

My great-grandfather died in Briscoe, Sullivan County, New York. This is about 100 miles from New York harbor, where he, his wife and two sons and two daughters landed in 1850. They had lived in the Camlachie district of Glasgow. Two baptismal records of their children in that city have been found in Glasgow's great

Mitchell Library, but grandma often said that nine had been buried in Scotland. I have no doubt that the terrible killer, cholera, put them in one of the mass graves required by the epidemic horror. One daughter married Henry Dunlavy and remained in Glasgow. Although two boys and two girls were brought from Glasgow, only my grandfather, Robert, married a Scots woman. Only she had the ancient obligation to pass on family history. Grandma was a Highland Campbell. Completely unpretentious, but strongly committed to her own kin, she could tell about everyone in the family. She was born in 1850, and lived for 89 years.

She knew, and told me, who her parents, grandparents, and great-grandparents were. She learned our story from her husband's father, and mother. She was fifteen and a half when Robert came home from Virginia, was discharged from the Union Army and they married. Her mother-in-law, too, was a Highlander, Marian MacKenzie, with the same obligation to perpetuate the family story. The husband's name took precedence over that of the mother's line for that was the name to be preserved. Grandma would have been amazed to know how unusual her storytelling would become, how rare, in her own children's generation. My father never mentioned it, but he, and I, my two brothers and my mother all heard it together, and I suppose my father, and his brothers had heard it often. Only his sister, my Aunt Lizzie, ever repeated it, I am sure.
Reminiscing practically died when cars, outside entertainment and activities supplanted family life. History was turned over to scholars. Almost no one wrote about his family.

I cannot prove it, but I believe my line has been a succession of town and city dwellers. Beginning in Canongate/Edinburgh, then Glasgow, then the woods towns of New York and Pennsylvania, these people were city-wise to a degree not known in the Borders where the legend was never known. During the many generations in the environs of Canongate the very beginnings were next door. The people involved were well known, as intermarriages began to weave a network of relatives. The romantic beginnings were told and retold until the meaning of the tale disappeared into the mists of time and only eleven words were left:

"A lady-in-waiting to the queen married a stable-boy."

PART OF THE INTERMARRIAGE NETWORK

Men and women descended from Andre Depo have been joining other families through marriage for about twelve generations. It would be futile to guess the number of surnames involved, but the list would be long. A few Deppa intermarriages are listed below, from memory. Two people of the line named "Dippie" provided names linked with their family. Many other surnames certainly belong in the genealogy.

Deppa, J.W	Dippie, J.G.	Dixon, Capt. D.
Campbell	Wight	Hay
Munro	Wilson	Nelson
Craig	Allan	Steedman
Northrup	Purves	Melrose
Wadsworth	McCubbin	Taylor
Lange	Tait	Johnston
Swanson	Riddell	Henderson
Cox	Morgan	Greenlaw
Townsend	Mackie	Renton
Davis	Roberts	Whitelaw
Ellis	Linn	Donald
Mayes	Falconer	David
Miller	Sutherland	Hunter
Jones	Rae	Connel
Loftus	Bell	Duncan
Schultz	Anderson	Fleming
Hosley	Woodhead	Porter
Starley		Rintoul
Hanchett		Sommerville
McDonald		Henry
		Luke

Marriage connections from 17th-century Scottish records:

Morrison	Walker	Hall
Clarke	Clapham	Gagie
Hislope	Thomson	Palmer
Moffat	Blaikie (p228)	Wardel
Mein		Lowry
		Paxton
		Webster
		Grey

Figure 12

BIBLIOGRAPHY, GROUPED BY SUBJECT *

Accounts/Records

Accounts of the Lord High Treasurer of Scotland, Volume XI (1559-66), edited by Sir James B. Paul, Edinburgh, 1916. First published 1877.

Accounts of the Master of Works for Building and Repairing Royal Palaces and Castles. Edited 1957.

Accounts of the Treasurer of Scotland, Volume XII (1566-74). Edited by Charles T. McInnes. Her Majesty's Stationery Office, 1970.

Barony Parish Registers. Camlachie in East Glasgow.

Buik of the Kirk of the Canagait, The, edited by A. Calderwood. General Register House, Edinburgh, 1564-67. Also Register of Baptisms, from the Old Parish Register series.

Calendar of State Papers, Reign of Elizabeth, edited by Joseph Stevenson. London, 1866.

Canongate Burgess Roll, 1671. Poll tax records, Scotland Record Office.

Census for Camlachie - unindexed. Mitchell Library, 1841.

Commissariat records (wills) throughout Scotland.

Department de la Seine. Archives. A letter.

*This list of references does not follow strict bibliographic form, for many of the sources are quite informal: maps, records, indexes, registers, letters, etc.

Diurnal of Remarkable Occurrents That Have Passed Within The Country of Scotland Since The Death Of King James The Fourth Till The Year MDLXXV. Maitland Club, Edinburgh, 1833.

Edinburgh Hearthtax Rolls, 1694.

Fasti Ecclesiae Scoticanae, edited by H. Scott. Edinburgh, 1915.

Glasgow Post Office Directories to 1850.

Glasgow Voters Roll of 1840.

Irregular Marriages in South Leith.

Kirk Sessions Records - 1697-1818.

Maps of British Land Survey of 1924. Library of Congress.

Maps of Central Glasgow and Camlachie, by Chamber of Commerce of Glasgow.

Plan of Edenburgh (sic) Exactly Done From Original Map. Dewit,1947. Reproduction of a 20" x 43" city plan by Trustees of the National Library of Scotland.

Maps. Camlachie, 1860 & 1980. Mitchell Library.

Microfilm of Crematoria. (Eastern Necropolis.) Glasgow.

Records (unprinted) of the 17th Century. Minister's Examination Rolls for the Canongate - 1661 and on. *Lists of Householders. Poll and Hearth Taxes. Burials for Edinburgh. Canongate and Holyrood Chapel Burying Ground.* 1567 to 1854. Mother's names not recorded until 1615.

Records of the Baron Court of Stitchill, [1655-1807], edited by C. B. Gunn. Scotland History Society, 1905.

Bibliography, Grouped by Subject

Records of the Regality of Melrose, Volume I, transcribed by Charles S. Romanes, 1914.

Register of Apprentices of the City of Edinburgh, [1582-1666], edited by F. I. Grant. Scotland Record Society, 1906.

Register of Edinburgh Apprentices, edited by F. Grant. Scotland Record Society, 1583-1666.

Telephone and other directories throughout Scotland.

References

I. Architectural

Medieval Religious Houses: Scotland, by Easson and Cowan.

Palace of Holyroodhouse. Reference to marriage records of the Abbey of Holyroodhouse, 1561-64 (letter), and Scottish Record Office of H. M. General Register House, Edinburgh, 1984. Alphabetical index of Register of Marriages for parish of Holyroodhouse, or Canongate, commenced 20 August, 1564. Published by Scotland Record Society, 1915. Edited by Francis J. Grant. New Register House, Edinburgh.

Scotland's Ruined Abbeys, by H. C. Butler. MacMillan & Co., London, 1900.

II. Libraries

Borders Regional. Hawick, Scotland. Provided *The Border Magazine*, and Tombstone references.

Catholic University. Has a complete set of the *Regality Records of Melrose*. Dr. Meyer told me that these books were donated by a Cistercian brother which addles my sense of time, for Melrose was a Cistercian Abbey founded nearly a thousand years ago. *Scots in Poland* also here.

Harvard College. Provided references not available at the Library of Congress.

III. Language

Anglo Saxon Dictionary, Toller, Oxford University Press.

Concise Scots Dictionary. By 33 Contributors. Aberdeen University Press, 1985.

Dictionary of Obsolete, and Provincial English. Wight, London, 1857.

Encyclopedia Brittanica, 1939.

Jamieson Etymological Dictionary of the Scottish Language.

Oxford Dictionary of English Christian Names. Withycombe, 1950.

Oxford English Dictionary. Oxford University Press, 1961.

Treasure of Our Tongue, The, by Lincoln Barnett. Alfred A.Knopf, 1964.

Webster's International Dictionary, by Noah Webster, 1864. Revised 1893.

Recent standard dictionaries

Scotland

Border Antiquities of England and Scotland, by Sir Walter Scott. 1814.

Highland Clearances, The, by John Prebble. Penguin Books, 1963.

History of Scotland, A, by J. D. Mackie, Penguin Books, Ltd., 1964.

History of the Scottish People - 1530 - 1830, by T. C. Smout. Charles Scribners Sons, New York, 1969.

Irish and Scotch Irish Ancestral Research, by Margaret D. Falley, two volumes. Privately printed. Volume I Repositories and Records L. D. S. Library, Glenmont, Maryland.

Scot and His Oats, The, by G. W. Lockhart. Luath Press, 1983.

Scotch, The, by John Kenneth Galbraith. Houghton Mifflin Co., 1964.

Scottish Rural Society in the Sixteenth Century, by Margaret H.B.Sanderson. John Donald Publishers, Ltd. Edinburgh,1982

Scotland, the Place of Visions, by Jan Morris & Paul Wakefield. Pub. Clarkson N. Potter,Inc. New York, 1986

Scotland of Queen Mary, The, by Agnes Mure Mackenzie. MacMillan, 1936.

Scots In Poland - 1576-1793, by Francis Stewart, Advocate. Edinburgh University Press, 1915.

The Crofter and the Laird, by John McPhee. Farrer, Straus. N.Y. 1969

Ireland

Discovering Britain and Ireland, National Geographic Society, Washington, D.C., 1985.

Great Hunger, The, [Ireland] by Cecil W. Smith. New English Library, 1979.

Red Hand - The Ulster Colony, [Irish], by Constantine Fitzgibbons.

Scotch Irish in Northern Ireland and the American Colonies, by Maude Glasgow. Putnams Sons, New York, 1936.

Genealogy

Genealogical and Bibliographical Society, New York and Huguenot Society of America, 122 E. 58th Street, New York, NY 10022.

International Genealogical Index, 1855-75.

Place Names of Scotland, by James B. Johnston. London, 1934.

Scottish Roots, by Alwyn James. Macdonald Publ, Loanhead, Scotland.1981.

Surnames of Scotland, by Robert Fraser Black. The New York PublicLibrary, 1974 [1946].

Tombstone Inscriptions in Berwickshire, edited by D. C. Cargill. Scotland Genealogy Society, Volume 3, Edinburgh.

Bibliography, Grouped by Subject

History

American Heritage Book of Indians, The, by William Brandon, American Heritage Publishing Company, N.Y., N.Y., 1961

Border Magazine, The Volume XIV, 1909,(also 1908) by A. Walker, Galashields, p. 117.

Catalogues of the Jewels Etc. Mary, Queen of Scots, edited by Jos. Robertson. Bannatyne Club, 1863.

Celts, The, by Frank Delaney. Little, Brown, and Co., Boston, 1986.

Dark Ages, The, by W. P. Ker. Thomas Nelson, Ltd., Edinburgh, 1958.

Dictionary Catalog of Local History, Genealogy Division, by G. K. Hall & Co., Boston, 1974.

Directory of Historical Societies, U.S. & Canada. Nashville, Tennessee, 10th Edition.

First American, The, by C.W.Ceram. Harcourt,Brace, Jovanovich, NYC. 1971.

History of Epidemics in Britain, A, by C. Creighton. London, 1965.

History of Greece, A, by J. B. Bury. Random House, 1900.

History of Mathematics, by David E. Smith, Volume 1. Ginn and Co., 1923.

History of the Western World, by L. G. Cheney. Mentor Books, New York, 1959.

Horizon Book of the Renaissance, by J. H. Plumb and others. American Heritage, Doubleday.

In Search of the Trojan War, by Michael Wood. Public Facts on File, 1985.

Medieval Cities, by Henri Pirenne. Translated from the French by Halsey. Princeton University Press, 1956.

Norman Heritage, The, by Trevor Rowley. Routledge & Kegan Paul. London, 1985.

Outline of History, by H. G. Wells. Garden City, New York Publishing Co., 1931.

Political and Social History of Modern Europe, A, by C. Hayes. MacMillan Co., 1926.

Protestant Exiles From France - The Huguenot Refugees and Their Descendants, by Rev. David Agnew. Third Edition, Volume I, private circulation, University of Edinburgh. At Harvard College Library - rare.

Rash Adventurer, The, [Charles Edward Stuart], by Margaret Forster. Chaucer Press, Ltd., 1973.

Uses of the Past, The, by Herbert J. Muller. Oxford University Press, Mentor Press, 1954.

General

In My End is My Beginning, [Mary], by Maurice Baring. Heinmann, Ltd., London, 1931.

A Taste of Scotland, by Theodora Fitzgibbon. Avenel Books, New York, 1970.

Foxfire Books, The, 8 volumes. Doubleday, 1972-1984.

Golden Bough, The, by Sir James Fraser. MacMillan & Co. London.

Mary, Queen of Scots, by Antonia Fraser. Delacorte Press N.Y. 1971.

Mary, Queen of Scots, by Brysson Morrison. Vanguard Press, N.Y. 1960

Precipitous City, by Trevor Royle. Mainstream Publishing, Edinburgh, and Taplinger Publishing Inc., New York.

Saddles of Queens, [The story of the side saddle], by Lida F. Bloodgood. J. A. Allen & Co., Aldine Press, 1957.

Steel Bonnets, The, by George M. Fraser. Cox and Wyman, Ltd. Reading, England, 1971.

INDEX

1556 199
1561 31, 38, 57, 81, 93, 122, 135
1564 31, 83, 122, 135
1586 199
Abacus 85
Abbey 34
Abbott 52
Absent Vassals 197
Abstention from meat 239
Adam and Eve 27
Agnew 68
Ale 230, 246
Alexander 31, 60, 101, 122, 136
Alnwick 115
Ancient Irish 235
Angle 179
André 17, 60, 102, 103, 105, 122, 123, 136
Andrew 123
Apostrophe 136
Appalachia 4, 20, 132, 208, 225
Apples 192
Apprenticeship 245
Arabic numerals 84
Archaic Scots 241
Atomic bomb 25
Austin, Pennsylvania 64
Australia 273, 299
Bannock 42, 226
Baptisms 11, 242, 246
Barley 188, 250
Beheaded 38, 65
Beltane 42
Ben (see "but") 35
Beowulf 234
Big Bang 235
Bird-lime 228
Black death 12

Black, Robert F. 2, 11, 63, 68
Blackmail 45
Border 120, 130
Border Magazine, The 66
Border people 26, 43
Borders 30, 130
Bothwell 5, 18, 42, 58, 105, 128, 130, 172
Bothy 35, 244
Bothy boys 244
Britannica 216
Brogue 33
Broken-man 206
Brose 224
But (see "ben") 35, 223
Calendar 70
Camlachie 12
Campbell 9, 107
Campbell, Charles 38, 64
Cannon 129
Canongate 7, 32, 33, 42, 72, 78, 91, 159
Capsize 110
Catherine de'Medicis 17, 54, 55, 146
Catholic University 16
Celtic 248
Chains, gold ("chenis") 21, 114
Chapbooks 37
Chapman 37, 230
Chaucer 144
Chisholm, James 156, 195
Cholera 12
Cistercian 161, 247
Clearances 206
Commendator 34, 171, 186, 210
Contumacy 30
Corn/Oats 250

Costello, Pennsylvania 9, 12, 65, 218
Cousteau, Jacques 15
Craig, John 22, 179
Cro-Magnon 83
Crounis of the sone 111, 14
Crown'de soleil 111
Cute 40
Cutting (family name) 11
Dare (Latin) 171, 185
Darnley 5, 18, 19, 130
Dauphin 52
Deippa, John 178, 217, 288
Depo 1, 8, 15, 17, 52, 58, 78, 120, 131, 139, 183, 191, 206, 211, 244
Deppa 1, 12, 17
Deppa, Ervin 66, 70
Deppa, Sarah Elizabeth (Lizzie) 10, 71, 72
Deppie 67
Dialect, Scottish 20, 123
Dieppe 2, 11, 37, 58, 78, 90, 112, 118, 246
Dieppe, France 15
Dieppois 120, 139, 177
Diphthongs 218
Dippie 1, 17, 38, 49, 69
Dippo, Katherine 74, 88, 176, 179, 216, 279
Douglas, James 186
Drink silver 111
Dutch 101, 116
Edinburgh 33, 39, 62, 78, 105, 109, 112
El paso del norte 256
Elizabeth I 18, 53, 55, 61, 86, 94, 99, 140
-en, as a plural suffix 252
Equestrian team 56
Errors 54, 68, 118, 215, 274
Eupham Deippe 41, 69, 71, 72, 88, 107, 217
Fasti Ecclesiae Scoticanae 285

Feudal 196
Feudalism 240
Florida 59
Folklore 179
Fools ("fules") 20, 99, 107
Foot mantle 144
Foxfire Books 225
Francis II, King 52, 54, 56
French 5, 17, 31, 39, 78, 93, 104
French language 7, 17, 21, 53, 58
Gaelic 121
Galileo 135
Gallows 49
Gardener 86
Gardy loo 39, 40
Glasgow 9, 12, 63, 88, 245, 288, 300
Golgotha 40
Gorse 251
Gowrie conspiracy 40
Grandma vii, 9, 10, 16, 43, 64, 66, 300
Grant, Dr. Ian 178
Grants (land) 240
Griddle 224
Grist-mills 248
Grit (grith) 116
Gudeman 35, 243, 255
Haggis 228
Half hind 243, 244
Harvard College 16, 70
Hendre 120
Henri II, King 7, 54
Hepburn, Francis 186
Hepburn, James 18, 55, 256
Hermitage 146, 256
Hertford, Earl of 162
Hide (def.) 253
Highlanders 26
Highlands 38, 51
Hind 244
Hodden grey 177
Holyroodhouse 7, 19, 33, 39, 174

317

Hopi 26, 255
Horses 3, 16, 31, 55, 57, 95, 102, 109, 113, 128, 140, 159, 215
Horses, Clydesdale 130
Huguenot 32, 51, 55, 58, 70, 71, 78
Indians 174
Infield (see outfield) 188, 254
James V, King 7, 47, 92, 170
James VI, King 47
Jamestown, New York 195, 254
Jamieson 142
Jesus 234
Jewels 56, 105, 106
Kailyard 230, 243
Kelso 127, 181, 287
Killing time 15, 30, 49, 192, 296
King of Denmark 181
Kirk O'Field 284
Knaveship 205
Knox, James 122, 136, 216
Knox, John 21, 51, 103, 127, 136, 216
La Manche 58, 95
Lady Day 85, 122
Lady-in-waiting 10, 16, 31, 37, 65, 94, 108, 160, 272
Langshaw 238
Latin 81, 121, 123, 142, 152
Legend 30, 32, 65, 95, 100, 216
Legend, The Deppa ix, 10, 63, 108, 301
Leith 93, 172
Libraries
  Bodleian Library 235
  Catholic University Library 16, 308
  Harvard College Library 16, 68
  Library of Congress 16
  Mitchell Library 11, 300
Liddesdale 180, 256
Lifting day 230
Livres 93, 106

Logarithms 85
Lord High Treasurer 21, 5, 99, 101, 119
Los Alamos 25
Lowlanders 63, 296
Lowlands 35, 36, 38, 67, 179
Lynch, Dr. Michael vii, 22, 134, 135, 283, 285, 287, 295, 297
Malthus 13
Manhattan Project 25
Maol ros 234, 247
Maries 6, 16, 18, 142, 157, 283
Market cross 89, 102
Marriage that did succeed 181, 187
Mary Stewart 52, 90
Mary, Queen of Scots 1, 6, 21, 31, 53, 88, 90, 93, 104, 110, 129, 141
Massacre of Saint Bartholomew's Eve 18, 55, 59, 68, 70, 79, 122
McKenzie 11, 38
Melrose 15, 17, 32, 34, 52, 77, 101, 128, 135, 223, 237
Melting pot 62
Merse 128
Meyer, Dr. Robert T. 235
Michelangelo 135
Michigan State College 24
Minnesota 134
Mitchell Library 11
Mitchell, Sheila 15, 286
Moresome, Alexander 88, 279
Morpeth 115
Morrisone, Johnne 86
Moshouses 172, 220, 284
Moss 47, 209, 223, 237
Mother Goose 6, 214
Mourning 155
Muckit land 254
Multure 171, 199, 206
Munro, Isabella and William 65
Murder 105
Murray, Sir Jedeane 199

Navajo 24, 85, 176, 225, 250, 255
Nolt 229
Northrup 11, 217
Numerals
  Arabic 84, 85
  Roman 85, 141
Oats 175, 187, 228, 230, 248
Oral history 17, 233
Orangeman 38, 65
Outfield (see infield) 254
Oxen 252
Oxford 235
Palace 154, 290
Pandora's box 234
Papal Medals 70
Past tense 198
Peel towers 196, 238, 242
Peterson, Roger T. 227
Phonetic 193
Picts 179, 203
Ploughgate 243, 253
Poland 133
Pope 70
Presbyterian 22, 41, 49, 297
Pringle 188, 192
Protestant 51, 57, 59, 71
Pumpernickel 230
Pyramid, Great 280
Queen 4, 7, 21, 119
Quern 205, 248
Rebault, Jean 59
Register of Marriages 285
Reforestation 255
Reformation 171
Regality (def.) 171, 186
Regent 32
Reivers 30, 44
Riccio 102, 154, 284
Roen, France 112, 283
Roman numerals 85, 141
Romans 39, 40
Rotterdam 117
Rough wooing 110
Royal Mile 33, 39

Run-rig 182, 236, 248
Saddle 103, 104, 143
Sandy 120
Scotch 2, 9, 120
Scotland 19, 29, 35, 38, 90, 132, 274
Scots Pine 229
Scots, archaic 241
Scottish Genealogy Society 291
Scottish Record Office 178, 285
Scottish spelling 193, 218, 275
Selkirk 195
Shakespeare 46, 121, 135, 229
Sheep 229, 247
Sickle 254
Slaughter 90, 122, 132, 133, 135
Smout, Dr. T.C. 35, 219
Sone (son) 101, 103, 111, 122, 136, 137
Soul-bell 106
Sowans 224
St. Bartholomew's Eve Massacre 18, 55, 59, 68, 70, 79, 122
St. Benedict 247
Stable-boy 16, 31, 38, 54, 71, 72, 82, 90, 95, 100, 102, 108, 109, 117, 159, 185, 257
Stallion 109, 117
Starvation 227
Ste. Germain-en-Laye 6, 54, 100, 274
Steuben County, New York 246
Stewart, James 172
Stichell 68, 90, 101, 128, 130
Stirling Castle 111
Sullivan County, New York 9, 218, 299
Thirlage 205
Thistles 231
Thorn (letter) 116
Tradition 8, 43, 91, 216
Trojan War 214
Tweed, River 223, 236
Tynemouth 95, 111, passim

Ulster 9, 65
Universities
  Catholic University 16
  Harvard College 16, 68
  Oxford University 235
  University of Edinburgh 22
Vassal 34, 241
Vikings 11, 38, 58, 284
Wadsworth 11
Watsone, Dean 187, 233
Wedding 5, 23, 82, 106, 107, 257, 284
Whin 251
White Sands 25
Wickes, D.J.C. 178
Witches 41
Yet 270
Yorkshire 11, 19, 137, 161, 184, 247, 254

The marriage that did succeed for Mary,
B MAR   31814850095503
Deppa, James Walter.
PORTAGE PUBLIC LIB   04118

B   AUG 7 - 1991   Por.
Mar
    Deppa, James Walter
        The marriage that did succeed for
    Mary Queen of Scots

Portage Public Library